CHICAGO PUBLIC LIBRARY

R00787 21484

DISCARD

HD
9743
.S672
A44
1990

Almquist, Peter.

Red forge.

$35.00

DATE			

BUSINESS/SCIENCE/TECHNOLOGY
DIVISION

© THE BAKER & TAYLOR CO.

RED FORGE

PETER ALMQUIST

RED FORGE

SOVIET MILITARY INDUSTRY SINCE 1965

 COLUMBIA UNIVERSITY PRESS   NEW YORK

Columbia University Press
New York   Oxford
Copyright © 1990 Columbia University Press
All rights reserved

Library of Congress Cataloging-in-Publication Data

Almquist, Peter.
  Red Forge : Soviet military industry since 1965 / Peter Almquist.
  p. cm.
  "Revised version of the author's doctoral dissertation . . .
Massachusetts Institute of Technology"—Introd.
Includes bibliographical references.
ISBN 0-231-07066-7
1. Munitions—Soviet Union.
2. Soviet Union—Military policy.
I. Title.
HD9743.S672A44   1990
338.4'76234'0947—dc20

Casebound editions off Columbia University Press books are Smyth-sewn
and printed on permanent and durable acid-free paper

Printed in the United States of America

c 10 9 8 7 6 5 4 3 2 1

To my family

CONTENTS

INTRODUCTION

In October 1987, Communist Party General Secretary Mikhail Gorbachev toured the Soviet Navy's base at Murmansk. While in Murmansk, he delivered a speech in which he indicated that, while Soviet industry in general was plagued by low quality, "Lots of things are done well in the country: take defense. Here we are not lagging behind in anything. This means we know how to work."[1]

Since coming to power in 1985, Gorbachev has attempted to take the knowledge and experience developed in defense industries and transfer them to the moribund Soviet economy as a whole, through imitation (for example, establishing civilian versions of the military's quality control system) and through the wholesale transfer of personnel from the defense industries into key national economic positions. As Gorbachev's chief economic adviser, Abel Aganbegian, said on Budapest television, not only will the achievements of the defense industries be applied to Soviet industry, but "some of the specialists will be redeployed from the defense industry to other branches."[2]

The purpose of this book is to examine the Soviet defense industry since 1965, especially the views of certain "specialists": the industrial managers, the weapons designers and scientists, and the ministry officials. What management experience is Gorbachev calling upon when he promotes the former chief of the Ministry of Defense Industry's Main Technical Administration to Gosplan chairman or places the former Minister of Aviation Industry in charge of civilian quality control? Soviet defense industrialists are clearly having an impact beyond military production, and the title *Red Forge* refers not only to the traditional "metal-bending" role of the Soviet defense industries, but also to their role as a wellspring of many of the reforms being implemented by Gorbachev. To understand where the Soviet Union is going, it is useful to consider where many of those people leading it spent the last twenty-five years.

This book is a revised version of the author's doctoral dissertation for the political science department of the Massachusetts Institute of Technology. The members of my dissertation committee (Steven Meyer, Donald Blackmer, and Joseph Berliner) were invariably supportive and constructive. Steve Meyer is, in numerous ways, responsible for my interest in Soviet military affairs. Don Blackmer first introduced me to the pleasures of serious Soviet studies and to Soviet industrial management in particular. And Joseph Berliner volunteered his time and expertise to a student he had never met. It has been a pleasure working with these people, and I am grateful for their support and contributions. While each has contributed to this book, the author is responsible for how their counsel has been used.

Several fellow students also provided comments and support in one form or another. All are members of the Center for International Studies Soviet Security Studies Working Group (SSSWG). In particular, I have benefited from the help of Jeff Checkel, John Lepingwell, Matt Partan, Eugene Rumer, Dan Shephard, and Jeff Starr.

My research relied on a wide range of sources, from Soviet regional newspapers to declassified intelligence material brought to light under the Freedom of Information Act. It would have been impossible without the resources of Harvard's Widener Library, the unflagging help (and good cheer) of Tom Kiley and Patrick McMahon of MIT's Inter-Library Borrowing Service, and Susan Gardos of Harvard's Russian Research Center. Kira Caiafa of Viktor Kamkin's Bookstore regularly went out of her way to keep me up-to-date with invaluable material. I am also grateful to Herwig Kraus of Radio Liberty's Red Archive for access to the archive's biographical treasure trove, and to Steve Hayes of the American Center for International Leadership for making my trip to Munich and to the Soviet Union possible.

Intellectual support alone, however, does not a dissertation make, and MIT, the Defense and Arms Control Program (under Jack Ruina), the SSSWG, and the Ford Foundation provided necessary funding through almost all of my work. I was fortunate to have been a Ford Foundation Dual Competence Fellow for two years, which made it possible to devote time to improving my knowledge of both the Soviet Union and the Russian language.

Finally, I would like to thank my parents (who have encouraged me all along) and my wife Marty (who both encouraged and tolerated me all along). This book is dedicated to them and to Matthew Thomas Almquist.

CHAPTER ONE

A FRAMEWORK FOR ANALYSIS

It has been suggested that the Soviet Union does not *have* a "military industrial complex," but that it *is* a military industrial complex. In contrast, Soviet authors argue that a "military-industrial complex" is a product of capitalist states, reaching its zenith in the United States, where a union of military industries, the Department of Defense, and other related organizations use official and unofficial means to encourage U.S. aggression for their own gains. The Soviet Union, in the Soviet view, is immune from the curse of a military-industrial complex.[1] Yet the director of a Moscow factory found himself excoriated during the 1989 elections by a successful opponent as a representative of just such a military industrial complex.[2]

While such disagreement and inconsistency is not surprising, it serves to highlight a number of intriguing and potentially important questions: what is the impact, if any, of the military industries on policy making in the Soviet Union? Do they fit common western assumptions about the "merchants of death" arguing for more assertive and militarist policies in the hopes of profiting from it? Or is Soviet policy making and implementation so centralized that these industries are excluded from the policy-making process altogether, leaving them simply to implement policy made elsewhere?

In order to answer these and related questions, this study tests the hypothesis that the military industries of the Soviet Union have interests that parallel those of the military, that they benefit from the demands of the military, and that, as a result, these industries work with the military to influence policy making at a variety of levels. It will concentrate on three key components of the defense industries: the managers of the military plants, the designers and scientists involved in weapons research and production, and the defense industrial ministry apparatus.[3]

To facilitate the testing of this hypothesis, a general framework of decision making in the Soviet Union will be advanced, as will be a suitable definition of a "military-industrial complex."

For many years, western analysts have examined the way decisions are made in the Soviet Union in the hope of better understanding the process through which decisions are made, with the objective of making Soviet behavior more understandable, if not more predictable. This has been especially true in the last twenty years, as the focus of Soviet scholars has moved away from the "totalitarian model,"[4] which focuses on how the State and Party maintain control over society (an "output" of policy making), to increased research on the various "inputs" to Soviet policy. While it cannot be claimed that the totalitarian model has been completely supplanted in either the academic or policy making communities, it has been criticized from several sides, challenging the assumption that the Soviet Union is a monolithic power ruled by a dictator with virtually absolute authority.

The totalitarian model was criticized for at least two key reasons. First, it did not help the observer to understand *how* policy was made. The "black box" of Soviet decision making remained just as black, as the model's emphasis was on how the government related to (or controlled) and mobilized its people. By focusing on the outputs (i.e., policy decisions), the model minimized the importance of those factors (the inputs) that shaped the decision.

Second, it was becoming increasingly apparent that one of the principal assumptions of the model—that the leadership agreed on and followed the prescriptions of a clear "totalist" ideology—was becoming untenable. Evidence of fissures in the leadership began to be seen as systemic, rather than as aberrations. "Kremlinologists," carefully sifting through the protocol evidence reported in the Soviet press or by western observers, were able to glean evidence of the changing status (and, by inference, the changing impact) of members of the Soviet leadership. The analytic model adopted by many of these Kremlinologists became known as the "conflict school," after the basic argument that policy was frequently the product of conflict within the élite over personal power, rather than a result of ideological guidance.[5] Unlike the totalitarian model, the conflict school attempted to explain policy outcomes in a systematic, although sometimes obscure, way.

A natural outgrowth of the conflict school was the view that policy may be the process not merely of jockeying for personal power between individual members of the élite, but of jockeying between representatives of various competing factions, each with a different set of interests. Soviet decision making was increasingly seen not as an orderly process by which ideology was interpreted and imposed on a populace but as a competition for authority to implement programs and to protect the interests of each group's membership. Various individuals or groups, it was suggested, had or sought influence on decisions, and the decisions were seen increasingly as the result of compromises between competing interests.[6]

The nature of that influence is a central focus of this study, and I have adopted the definition of influence used by Peter Solomon: changing the probability of a given outcome.[7] This definition has a number of advantages: it is neutral as to direction, allowing both for pushing a decision (for example, through open advocacy in the press or in behind the scenes lobbying) a well as retarding one (for example, through active opposition while a new policy is being formulated or through foot-dragging during implementation); it does not require that a decision maker's mind be changed, only that the probability of a given outcome be affected; and, perhaps the most important, it can be applied across a political spectrum of decision makers, from the Politburo to the plant manager, and along a sequential spectrum, from an initial idea through the decision process and implementation.[8]

With this definition of influence in mind, it is next useful to consider Soviet decision making along three different dimensions: the decision *process*, that is, the pattern of behavior common to all decisions; the *nature* of the decision, that is, whether it is relatively narrow or will have broad impact on society; and the *openness* of the decision, that is, who is able to participate in it at each stage of the process and to whom the decision is relevant.

Brzezinski and Huntington have proposed four basic stages in the decision-making process: initiation, persuasion, decision, and execution. As they put it,

> *Initiation* embodies the first response to a new need or problem and the first formulation of a proposal to deal with it. *Persuasion* involves efforts to build up support for the proposal among a larger number of groups. In this phase, opposition develops, alternatives and amendments are suggested, and the original proposal is modified so as to win broader support. In the *decision* phase the modified proposal is either approved or vetoed by those who have the effective and legitimate authority to do so within the political system. The number of people who must approve the proposal so that it becomes "policy" or who can prevent it from becoming policy varies greatly from one political system to another and within any system often from one issue to another. Finally, in the *execution* phase, the policy which has now been blessed with legitimacy is presumably carried out. In actual fact, however, the policy-making process continues, and those groups which execute policy are able to remake it. In some instances, they have to change it significantly to achieve the principal goals of the policy deciders. In other instances, they may change it significantly to frustrate those goals. This phase hence is often characterized by adaptation and distortion.[9]

The Brzezinski and Huntington typology is a useful place to start, clearly laying out the stages through which any policy must pass to move from issue or idea to outcome. For purposes of this study, the importance of each set of actors at each stage will be addressed to indicate who is participating in the process at which stage, and what influence they may or may not have.

In addition to the process, it is useful to categorize decisions by type or by their nature. In this study, decisions are divided into three broad types, with the terminology and concepts derived from Soviet military thinking: doctrinal, strategic, and technical.[10] These might be just as easily labeled policy, tasks, and technical, but Soviet military discussions draw such a clear distinction between the concepts of doctrine and strategy that it is hoped that their broader application will clarify the nature of these decisions.

Doctrinal (or policy) decisions are those that set out the broad social objectives and expectations of society. In military thinking, these include expectations about the nature of a future war and the likely adversaries.[11] In broader social policy, this would include decisions about Soviet society as a whole, as well as specific societal issues such as whether or not to allow increased openness in the press, for example, or increased emphasis on environmental affairs. In addition, questions about the interpretation of the "outside world" would fall under the doctrinal rubric. Two important Soviet doctrinal issues, frequently discussed in the western press, revolve around the question of increasing or decreasing the reliance on centralized planning and those of how to balance resource allocation between heavy and light industries. These decisions are made at the highest levels: the Politburo and the Secretariat of the Communist Party.

Strategy[12] (tasks) lays out the plans for achieving the objectives established by doctrine and, more important, is based on the doctrinal views espoused by the higher authorities; strategy implements doctrine. For example, doctrine identifies the types of targets that are expected to be particularly important to the defeat of the enemy, and strategy determines how to neutralize these targets most effectively and efficiently. In social policy, strategy provides plans for achieving the goals set out by doctrine. If a doctrinal decision had been made to provide greater emphasis to the production of consumer goods, then the strategic decisions might revolve around which consumer goods should be increased, who should produce them, and from where the resources should come to finance the increase. Strategic decisions are made by the various ministries, closely monitored by the Central Committee's specialized departments.

Finally, there is the *technical* decision. These decisions are not questions of social objectives, or questions of how to accomplish such objectives, but are essentially problem-solving or choices between technical alternatives. Which engine has the best specifications and performed most effectively in tests? Where to site a dam? Which is the best region for a particular crop? Technical decisions are made, for example, at the level of factories.

The distinction between decisions is seldom clearly defined, and the areas are interrelated. The technically possible helps to shape the strategy adopted. The possible strategies certainly have an impact on doctrinal decisions, to ensure that there is a link between reality and doctrine. At the same time, the doctrinal objectives of the state (and Party) shape strategies chosen and the resultant technical decisions. In addition, decisions can be bumped "upstairs." But it is also necessary to recognize the distinction between these three levels of decisions to understand the route through which decisions pass, and the influences on decisions from above and below, and to help distinguish between actors in each of these areas.

Finally, the degree of an actor's influence will vary at different stages in a decision-making process depending on the *openness* of the decision: a plant manager will be unlikely to have direct influence of decision making at the highest level, but may well have an impact on how the decision is implemented, just as the Politburo may take a general interest in plant-level implementation but is unlikely to intervene except in special circumstances. A the same time, it might be expected that the specialist is called upon only at specific times, such as when there is disagreement between more senior leaders. Of clear importance is the nature of the issue and the question of whether a new policy is being formed or whether the policy is simply a marginal change from one already existing.

Similarly, there are clear levels of decision making, traditionally delimiting the degree of openness in general areas. Some decisions will always be made at the Politburo level because of their scope and importance (the areas of defense and foreign affairs are the most obvious cases), while others will most frequently be made at lower levels by ministers or staffs, by designers, even by plant managers.[13]

A good example highlighting the process, nature, and openness of a particular decision is the education reform debate of the late 1950s and early 1960s.[14]

In 1958, Khrushchev strongly attacked the Soviet educational system and proposed major reforms, which would combine work with study by requiring all students to enter the labor force upon completing seven or eight years of education; schooling at the higher secondary grades, and for the first two or three years at institutes of higher education, would be undertaken part-time or through correspondence.

The reform proposal, however, did not succeed. The actual reform legislation differed substantially in content and direction from Khrushchev's proposal, apparently as a result of pressure brought to bear by the members of various groups involved in the question. A public debate took place in a number of journals and speeches involving members of what have been variously referred to as "social groups"[15] and "technically-specialized issue-relevant interest groups":[16] educators, the educational bureaucracy, the Party élite, and the managers and workers who would have to accommodate the new laborers.[17]

The educational reform debate can be used to highlight the utility of applying the proposed decision-making typology. The *initiation* of the process, that is, the raising of the issue, had been under way for some time prior to Khrushchev's proposal, in public discussion, in internal studies, and in Khrushchev's own thinking.[18] The broader discussion and the process of *persuasion* began with the circulation of a memo detailing Khrushchev's views, in July 1958, to the Central Committee and reported to meetings of leading educational workers.[19] It was published only in late September of that year.

As noted above, Khrushchev's efforts at persuasion met with little success; his reform was, in many key aspects, gutted. The *decision*, codified in December as the Educational Reform Act of 1958, represented a victory for existing institutional interests rather than for Khrushchev, the proposal's originator.

Execution of the reforms, now more in line with the objectives of the educational ministries, schools, and industrial and party officials, also dissatisfied Khrushchev, as he pushed for more rapid implementation of the changes that had been approved. Rather than moving students out of school and into production, production-education was to be moved into the schools over the next five years, a period he felt was too short but could do nothing to change. Instead, he reduced the total years of schooling from eleven to ten. It appears that Khrushchev attempted to compensate for flaws he saw in the final decision by influencing how it was implemented.

The education decision is also useful for considering the *types* of decisions: doctrinal, strategic, and technical. While there are certainly a number of reasons for Khrushchev's reform proposal, it clearly would have represented a significant doctrinal shift away from "academic" education towards vocational or production-oriented education, reflecting a new (or renewed) social objective.[20]

Khrushchev's proprosals, and the counter-proposals of his opponents, were of a strategic nature, however. In order to implement his doctrinal vision, Khrushchev proposed a specific set of educational reforms to be administered by existing organizations. Much of the actual debate appears to have taken place at this level; nobody appears to have opposed the idea of increasing the links between youth and production. What was successfully challenged, however, was Khrushchev's view of how this should be realized.

Technical decisions in the education debate revolved around how to change the curriculum and the nature of the classes to be offered.

The degree of *openness* of the educational reform discussion reflect Khrushchev's personal style and the political constraints under which he was operating: he could not simply make a decision and impose it.

Khrushchev's proposals led to broad discussion and debate, both in open press and among specialists in the various relevant organizations.

By examining the decision along these various dimensions, we are able to consider clearly the most important questions about any decision: who shaped it, at which points did which people have influence, why was the decision open to their influence, and how was this influence wielded. In so doing, we should be able to compare this decision with others, to create a more comprehensive picture of decision making as a whole in the Soviet Union, and to address a much broader issue: which decisions are likely to involve broad participation, and which are likely to involve only a small group.

If the typology is presented as a matrix (see table 1.1), several terms might be presented in a graphic form using simplified and "ideal" forms of government for comparative purposes. The ideal pluralist democratic system would have a wide range of actors appearing in the initiation and controversy stages and a "legitimate" body making actual decisions. An ideal dictatorship, in contrast, would show the control of each stage by an individual or small group. In addition, the decision makers of a dictatorship are "illegitimate," that is, their rule is based on coercive power rather than authority. A subset of the dictatorship ideal is the military dictatorship, in which the military leadership is the controling group. The question of influence and participation in decision making, whether by groups or individuals, specialists, or bureaucrats, can then be approached in a systematic way.

One of the benefits of using Solomon's definition of influence is that it can be applied at any stage of the process and is independent of the hierarchical position of the actors. The participants and their relative impact may vary at each stage of the process. Solomon's work demonstrated that Soviet criminologists were able to exert considerable influence on the formulation of laws in the Soviet Union as a result of their contributions at each stage of the process: raising issues, debating the merits of various proposals, providing professional analysis, attempting to persuade decision makers (the Central Committee and the Politburo, in particular), and overseeing the implementation of decisions once made.[21] Gustafson makes a similar point in his study of environmental and water policy under Brezhnev.[22]

In the education reform discussed earlier, Khrushchev was clearly the initiator of the proposed reform. The Central Committee and the educational professionals were initial participants in the debate, until it became a more open subject of discussion when published in September, widening the circle of participants and, perhaps as important, their arena for participation. The law itself was the product of Khrushchev's initial proposal and the modifications of the Party Central Committee and Council of Ministers. And its implementation, as is so often the case in the Soviet Union, was left to those whose behavior was supposed to be changed.

The efforts to protect Lake Baikal from further pollution provide another example.[23] Lake Baikal became a rallying point for Soviet citizens concerned about environmental pollution, and the objections and concerns raised led to increased concern for the environment at the

TABLE 1.1. Hypothetical Decision Matrices

Decision Type	DECISION STAGE			
	Initiation	Pursuasion	Decision	Implementation
Doctrinal	many sources	many sources	legitimate bodies	many sources
Strategic	many sources	many sources	legitimate bodies	many sources
Technical	experts	many sources	legitimate bodies	experts

(a) Pluralist Democracy

Decision Type	DECISION STAGE			
	Initiation	Pursuasion	Decision	Implementation
Doctrinal	elite only	elite only	illegitimate bodies	many agents
Strategic	elite only	elite only	illegitimate bodies	many agents
Technical	experts & elite	experts & elite	illegitimate bodies	experts

(b) Dictatorship

Decision Type	DECISION STAGE			
	Initiation	Pursuasion	Decision	Implementation
Doctrinal	military elite	military elite	illegitimate bodies	many agents
Strategic	military elite	military elite	illegitimate bodies	many agents
Technical	experts & elite	experts & elite	illegitimate bodies	experts

(c) Military Dictatorship

doctrinal level. The participants at this level, both initiating the discussion and engaging in efforts to persuade the responsible Party and government officials, were scientists, artists, journalists, and other concerned individuals. The result was legislation to protect the Lake, to be implemented in part by the very ministries that had been actually polluting or threatening to pollute it. While there appears to have been a decline in pollution, implementation has proven a continuing obstacle, for there appears to be a lack of coordination between environmental monitors and polluters, as well as little agreement on either the state standards for discharge or the actual effluents produced at the plants.

As might be expected, as issues become more technical, the role of specialists may increase. And in the last several years, the role of specialist influence has become increasingly important in the Soviet Union.[24] In fact, one of Brezhnev's promises upon replacing Khrushchev was to restrict or to end intervention by political figures in specialized realms such as the sciences.[25] The specialists, those who make professional careers in a field, are involved directly or indirectly at each stage of the decision process: they may be the ones responsible for initiating a proposal; they are certainly involved in analyzing proposals for the political leadership (the Politburo, the Central Committee, and the Council of Ministers); through the process they are indirectly involved in high-level decisions,[26] while they probably retain some independent authority to make strategic or technical decisions subject to the approval of superiors; and they are often either in charge of implementation or are involved in its monitoring. What appears to have increased under Brezhnev is the scope and influence of specialist participation in general.[27]

By definition, specialists have a relatively narrow scope of interests and expertise. Their work must be integrated with that of other specialists, and, in turn, either integrated with existing doctrinal and strategic policies or it must stimulate the modification or replacement of such policies. This is the function of the "collective" decision-making bodies, in particular, the Politburo, the Party's Central Committee, and the Council of Ministers.

While the implementation of decisions is left (indeed, assigned) to the various ministries and state committees of the executive branch, integration of decisions takes place before this task is meted out. Most decisions come with a price tag or other inconvenience that must somehow be accommodated—for example, ensuring that a series of contradictory decisions have not been made or finding whatever resources are necessary as a result of a new policy. The Central Committee staff and the Council of Ministers, with the support of Gosplan and the other relevant state and Party agencies, have to integrate these decisions into legislation and regulations. In the educational reform example, the Central Committee appears to have been the most important integrator, the focus of the efforts of the specialists to shape the proposed reforms away from Khrushchev's original proposal to a modified version, having a considerable impact on the final policy.

But the Secretariat and the Politburo are dependent on information from others—in particular, from the Central Committee apparatus. As the eyes and ears of the Central Committee, the apparatus shapes the information received by the Secretariat and the Politburo and, thus, their interpretations. It is as a result of this dependence on the departments that the specialists have their greatest impact. The Central Committee apparatus is not large, perhaps fewer than 1000 people, and these individuals are closer to being political appointees literate in a subject than actual specialists in the field. But they have the authority to make use of the thousands of specialists throughout society.

At the same time, these specialists can use the Central Committee staff, the Supreme Soviet, the Council of Ministers, and the press to float ideas and proposals; the decision of which to use, is most likely to depend on the nature of the subject and the nature of the specialist's access. P. D. Grushin, for example, is a missile specialist who was a full member of the Communist Party's Central Committee. Such membership provides a forum for articulating views that is closer to the "heart" of Soviet decision making than would be membership in the Supreme Soviet. It is also more likely that an official such as Grushin will raise security issues at the closed Central Committee meetings than in the open press.

There are several points of access for outsiders wishing to influence the decision process, some formalized and institutionalized and others informal. The most obvious and direct, of course, is direct participation in one or more of the bodies most closely involved in the decision process as a member of the Politburo, Secretariat, Central Committee, the Supreme Soviet or the Council of Ministers. A closely related position is to serve on the staff of one of these bodies or to serve as an aide to a member. Working in a ministry provides some access, either through the minister himself or through participation in the analysis of various proposals. It should also be noted that participation takes place not only at the national level, but at the Republic and local levels as well.

Informal ties also provide another important access point. Soviet leaders frequently bring a number of clients with them into important positions. These clients are typically individuals known to the leader before promotion, such as Brezhnev's Dnepropetrovsk group or Gorbachev's apparent Stavropol' circle.[28] While they frequently do not work for their patron, they are often beholden to him and, in turn, they can call on the patron at times for support. Other informal ties might be expected to develop between individuals who have worked together in the past, and thus developed a cooperative relationship. For example, a designer in the defense sector might have developed close ties with Brezhnev while the latter was Secretary for Defense Industry, and this relationship might facilitate access to Brezhnev.

Between the formal and informal ties lie relationships based on individuals vested with state importance. The personal stature of a Sergei Korolev (designer of the first ICBM) or Andre Sakharov (frequently characterized as the "father of the Soviet fusion bomb") as the preeminent thinkers in their fields, rather than a specific post, provided access to Khrushchev and Brezhnev.[29] In many ways, the careers of such leading scientists and designers are the most dramatic and visible examples of specialist influence, for they have direct access (formal and informal) to the most important decision makers, but are not members of the leading Party organizations.

But does this access give the individuals, whether serving military officers or those working in the support sciences and industries, considerable impact on the policies of the state (and, of necessity, the Party)? Do they have the ability to prevent the making and implementation of decisions which they oppose, or to force through policies that are contrary to the interests of others? In other words, is the Soviet Union a "military-industrial complex," or, at least, does it have a powerful one driving policy?[30]

WHAT MAKES A MILITARY INDUSTRIAL COMPLEX

For a military industrial complex to exist in a meaningful way, the military and its supporting industries must have, first, complementary interests. By this is meant that one of the "partners" generally benefits from the self-interested actions of the other. In the United States, for example, when the services see a need to improve the quantity or quality of their arsenal, the military industries benefit from the contracts. At the same time, the services may benefit from the political influence that these industries have in Congress because the industries are, for example, major employers in a district.

Second, and equally important, both the military and the industry must have a means of influencing the political decision makers. In a military-industrial complex, a "silent partner" is an irrelevant partner. Similarly, partners with identical points of access and tools of influencing the decision maker add only volume, rather than necessarily adding impact. In an ideal military-industrial complex, the military and the industries would have different points of access and tools, creating a multisided approach to the political decision makers.

Again, in the case of the United States, the military is not allowed to use the traditional "political" tools of the democratic process. It cannot spend public funds to support sympathetic candidates, it cannot hold rallies, nor can it lobby for votes in Congress.[31] On the other hand, it controls much of the data and analysis used in making most defense-related decision[32] and, by tradition, is given considerable deference and respect in most military matters by the public and many members of Congress. The case of the defense industries is almost the reverse: in particular, they *can* spend money to lobby Congress and to influence elections, possibly leading to the effective "control" of a member of Congress.

Finally, the military must be seen as an important part in defending the sovereignty of a country. While this is, of course, one of the arguments that a military-industrial complex may try to "prove," it may *not* be the case when the government has decided to rely heavily on diplomacy in place of military capabilities or in a case where the threat is considered so insignificant (for historical, cultural, or geopolitical reasons) as to minimize the perceived role of the military. A European country, located at the heart of the last two World Wars, for example, may place greater emphasis on military preparedness than a relatively isolated country such as Australia or New Zealand. A state in which the military and industry have complementary interests and access to the decision makers, but in which there is little perceived need for the military, is unlikely to have an influential military-industrial complex.

By using the four proposed stages in a decision process (initiation, persuasion, decision, and implementation) and the three decision types proposed (doctrinal, strategic, and technical), it is possible to create a hypothetical template against which to gauge reality. By using such a representation, it should be possible not only to represent a military-industrial complex, but also to suggest at which points its members are most influential.

This book attempts to determine which of these "boxes" the military industries, in particular, fill.

CHAPTER TWO

THE ORGANIZATIONAL CONTEXT

Military production in the Soviet Union is the result of a complex of party and state organizations. It is shaped at different points by Central Committee secretaries and party departments, as well as state ministries and their associated research institutes, design bureaus, and production plants.

THE POLITBURO

The Politburo, of course, is the apex of decision making in the Soviet Union. Officially responsible for directing Party work between Central Committee Plena, the Politburo is the highest decision-making organization in the Soviet Union.

During Brezhnev's tenure as General Secretary (1964–1982), the membership of the Politburo has ranged from 10 to 16 full members and 6 to 9 candidate (nonvoting) members. Typically meeting once per week, the Politburo is ostensibly a collegial organization, and it is reported that decisions are generally made without an actual vote, but by consensus. Many of the questions revolve around economic and foreign policy questions,[1] with the latter taking precedence over all other subjects.[2] During the SALT negotiations, for example, the Politburo reportedly met frequently to discuss United States proposals and Soviet responses.[3]

The Politburo has a wide-ranging agenda, and each of the officials has a small staff to provide specialized support. For example, Brezhnev's foreign policy aides frequently suggested foreign policy ideas to Brezhnev without consulting with the Ministry of Foreign Affairs. Brezhnev also relied upon an old friend, K. S. Grushevoy of the Moscow Main Political Administration, for advice on military matters.[4] Ustinov's aides were I. V. Illarionov and S. S. Turunov. It is unfortunate that so little is actually known about these potentially influential individuals, whose role may be as important as that of the U.S. president's national security adviser.

The Politburo is typically the final arbiter in policy discussions, although it seems likely that many of the decisions are made de facto at the Secretariat level or in various Politburo subgroups, and then ratified by the Politburo. (Several Politburo members and candidate members are also secretaries.) The Politburo can become involved at any stage in the decision-making process, although it is often the object of persuasion, as its members or the Secretariat raise issues. In addition, it can become involved in any type of decision, whether doctrinal, strategic, or technical, although its primary role is clearly to shape broad policy and to resolve specific controversies.[5]

THE DEFENSE COUNCIL

The broad shape of Soviet defense policy and key doctrinal decisions are made by what may be the most select body in Soviet politics: the Defense Council (Sovet Oborony SSSR). The existence of this body was only publicly acknowledged in the early 1970s, and it was formally included in the 1977 Soviet Constitution as a state (rather than Party) organ, although it has apparently existed in other forms since the revolution. Brezhnev assumed the chairmanship in 1964,[6] and was followed in this post by Andropov, Chernenko, and the current General Secretary, Mikhail Gorbachev. It has been reported that the General Secretary, by regulation, is the head of the Defense Council.[7]

While the Soviets are reluctant to discuss their own Defense Council in great detail, they have been willing to discuss the defense councils of their Warsaw Pact allies. These discussions emphasize that the Council serves as the senior state body for decision making in preparing the country's defense, strengthening of its military readiness, determining the principles of organization of the armed forces, coordinating defense administrative needs with the economy, and making the most important appointments in the Ministry of Defense and General Staff.[8]

Under the 1977 Constitution, the Defense Council is formed, and its membership confirmed, by the Presidium of the Supreme Soviet (article 121, paragraph 14). Its membership other than its chairman is not known, but U.S. intelligence sources report that the Defense Council in 1978 consisted of Brezhnev, Kosygin, Ustinov, "and possibly four or five others."[9] Jan Sejna, Secretary for the Czech Defense Council from the late 1950s to 1968, states that the Czech Defense Council was closely modeled after that of the Soviet Union, and that the membership of both consisted of the General Secretary, his deputy, the prime minister, the minister of defense, the minister of the interior, and the chief of the State Planning Commission (Gosplan). Its secretary is generally the chief of the general staff, and the secretariat is a part of the general staff.[10]

The most detailed *Soviet* discussion of a defense council's membership concerns the Rumanian Defense Council, which is made up of the General Secretary (chairman and commander in chief of the armed forces), the prime minister, the minister of defense, the minister of internal affairs, the chairman of the State Planning Committee, the minister of foreign affairs, the secretary of the Supreme Political Council, the chief of the general staff, and "others appointed by the Central Committee and approved by decree of the State Council."[11]

It might be tempting to consider the Defense Council, dominated by civilians, a nucleus for "objective" (or, at least, alternative) analysis to that of the Ministry of Defense. This might be true if the Council maintained an independent staff, but, apparently, it does not. The military thus serves a number of key roles for the Defense Council: it can probably raise issues for consideration by the Council; it provides analysis of both its own proposals and those of others; and it serves as the Council's executive arm, implementing Defense Council decisions.[12]

It is thus apparent that while there is senior Party oversight of the Ministry of Defense and national security issues in general, the Ministry of Defense and its General Staff have considerable potential influence over policy at each stage: initiation, persuasion, decision, and implementation. Without an independent staff, it is difficult to imagine how the Defense Council might undertake critical or detailed analyses of MoD proposals and positions, even if it wished to.

Just as this suggests that the Defense Council is dependent on its subordinate Ministry of Defense and General Staff, the Politburo as a whole is probably dependent on the analysis and conclusions of the Defense Council. The Defense Council probably works out security problems and issues before they are brought before the entire Politburo, making it possible to present an initial consensus that might be altered "on the margins."[13] Of course, as the number of likely Defense Council members on the Politburo increased with the promotion of the minister of foreign affairs, the minister of defense,[14] and the chairman of Gosplan,[15] there may have been an increasing willingness to deal with defense issues in the larger group.

THE CENTRAL COMMITTEE

While the Central Committee includes a smattering of laborers, it is made up predominantly of leading figures in the regional and local Communist Party organizations, various social groups,[16] or organizations such as ministries or state committees. It is officially responsible for Party activities between Party Congresses, which occur about every five years. With the Central Committee meeting at best two or three times per year,[17] much of the day-to-day party work—from decision making to monitoring—falls upon the Politburo, the Secretariat, and the Central Committee's apparatus.

What little evidence is available suggests that the discussions of topics in the Central Committee can be quite intense: as one Central Committee member described it, "There is some hot discussion. . . . it is a bargaining process from beginning to end."[18] This is not to suggest that the actual Central Committee meetings are fraught with the open dissent one finds in, for example, the British Parliament. Presumably, most of this bargaining takes place in small groups outside the actual committee meetings. There have been, however, cases in which a Central Committee member's criticism of policy during the meeting cost him his position.[19]

The relationship between the Politburo and the Central Committee is a complex one, with considerable authority vested in the General Secretary, but the authority monitored by the Central Committee. While Khrushchev was able to use the Central Committee to save his career in mid-1957 when the so-called "anti-Party group" in the Politburo (then called the Presidium) attempted to oust him, the Central Committee of 1964 turned on him, with a majority reportedly favoring his ouster.[20]

The point here is that the Central Committee is not a mere rubber-stamp organization, but one with considerable potential impact—positive and negative—on policy.[21] It is an audience to which the Politburo's decisions must be at least acceptable. Not only are the members of the Committee the élite of the CPSU,[22] they are also among the best informed individuals about Party policies and state capabilities, and they are expected to ensure the correct implementation of Party decisions within their professional communities and geographic regions.

The Central Committee is certainly the most important integrative body in the Soviet Union, and other organizations that serve an integrative function such as the Council of Ministers and its presidium, the press, and the Supreme Soviet[23] are led by individuals typically sitting on the Central Committee and monitored by the Committee's apparatus. While the Central Committee is possibly the most important organization attempting to place proposed policy changes within a broader context, it is not necessarily the source for all or even most of these. Solomon, for example, found that the Central Committee and its staff played a smaller role than the ministries and the Supreme Soviet Presidium in initiating changes in the Soviet criminal code. The Central Committee apparatchiki played a consultative role, rather than initiating the policies or even performing the support work, both of which were left to the relevant ministries and state organizations.[24]

While virtually all doctrinal decisions pass through the Central Committee in one form or another for approval, it is unlikely actually to initiate many of them, given its infrequent meetings, diverse membership, and size (about 300 full and another 150 candidate members). The key doctrinal decisions are clearly made at the Politburo and Secretariat level, two smaller bodies with day-to-day responsibility for the Soviet Union.

THE SECRETARY FOR DEFENSE
INDUSTRIAL MATTERS

While the Defense Council apparently relies on the General Staff as its secretariat, the Politburo and Central Committee have the Communist Party Secretariat. Roughly comparable to a government cabinet in western democracies, the Secretariat is typically made up of about a dozen individuals with specialized responsibilities overseeing virtually every sphere of activity on behalf of the Party.

Secretaries are responsible for the development and oversight of broad areas such as agriculture, ideology, or heavy industry, and each exercises his authority through one or more departments in the Central Committee *apparat*. The Secretariat as a whole provides analysis and recommendations for the Politburo.[25] The two bodies, typically fewer than thirty people, provide both the general direction of policy and some specifics for its implementation; their function is to make all the doctrinal decisions, which provide guidance for the strategic decisions made by themselves and others.[26]

Little is known about the internal functioning of the Secretariat and its associated departments. It reportedly meets about once a week, on Wednesdays.[27] (This allows it to prepare questions for discussion at Thursday's Politburo meetings.) Each Central Committee Secretary reportedly has a small secretariat of his own, with those Secretaries who are also Politburo members (so-called "senior Secretaries") having two assistants and two secretaries, and the other Secretaries have one assistant and two secretaries.[28] In addition, it is estimated that the Central Committee staff numbers from about 1000 to 1500 "responsible officials."[29]

There is apparently no Secretary holding a general "defense" portfolio. Broad defense issues probably fall within the domain of the Defense Council. There is, however, a Secretary responsible for defense industrial matters, and he would seem to be the most logical source for information about, and analysis of, defense issues outside the Defense Council but within the Party organization.[30]

The specific role and duties of the Secretary for Defense Industrial Matters has not been described in the Soviet press. It is known that he oversees the military, defense industry, police, and space programs.[31] This means he is responsible for about twenty state organizations (half of which are defense-related) and a number of Party bodies, including the Department of Administrative Organs (which, in turn, oversees security, police, and justice ministries), the Main Political Administration (which ostensibly oversees the military, but focuses on the political education of the military rather than military *policy*), and the Department of Defense Industry (which oversees defense industrial ministries).[32]

While specific activities are difficult to trace, they are suggested by the description of Ustinov's responsibilities while in the post. According to his biography in the *Soviet Military Encyclopedia*, while a secretary, Ustinov

> coordinated and led the work of institutions, design bureaus, [and] industrial enterprises with the goal of the most complete fulfillment of the tasks of the party and the government on the long-range strengthening of the economic and defense potential of the nation, [and he] took up active participation in organizational work in the area of the development of technology [*tekhnika*] used for the research and mastery of space.[33]

THE DEPARTMENT OF DEFENSE INDUSTRY

Serving the Secretariat is the Central Committee's network of departments. A department, of which there were more than twenty until 1988, has a more specific area of authority and responsibility than does a secretary, and engages in the support work for the Secretariat, monitoring areas from culture to heavy industry, approving personal selections, and providing analysis for the Secretariat.

In 1988, the administrative structure of the CPSU was reorganized, and the 20 existing departments were collapsed into nine (Ideology, Social-Economic, Agriculture, International, etc.). The Department of Defense Industry was renamed the Defense Department, perhaps signifying more general responsibilities. O. S. Belyakov continued to be its chief, and N. M. Luzhin its first deputy chief.

In the Soviet hierarchy, a Central Committee department head is the superior of a minister, and each department monitors the ministries, state committees, and the departments in Gosplan which fall in its domain. A department is typically made up of 100 to 150 staff people.[34] Each Department has a head [*zaveduyushchii*],[35] a first deputy head, and one to five deputy heads. The latter supervise several sections (there are three to fifteen sections per department), usually organized along branch lines and corresponding to almost every ministry or major type of nonministerial institution. Staff members of such sections are called "instructors" *[instruktory]*, and there are often fewer than six instructors in a section.[36]

The Central Committees of the Soviet republics and the committees of the regions and cities also have departments, although they are not as large as those of the CPSU Central Committee, nor as specific. These departments play the same role as do the "national" departments, but on a local level, i.e., monitoring the implementation of Party decisions and personnel.[37] Details of the Defense Industry Department at the Republic and local levels are scarce, but Soviet sources have occasionally identified the chief of the Department of Defense Industry for various republics.[38]

The role and functions of a department have seldom been described in detail. Besides approving appointments to posts within their state responsibilities, departments are responsible for the information flow to and from the Secretariat, uncovering problem areas, preparing reports and studies, and recommending specific actions, either in response to a specific request or as a result of their own monitoring function.[39] A description by Valentin Falin, Deputy Head of the International Information Department, provides a rare firsthand description of the process. Noting first that "all foreign policy and national security questions must be discussed and decided in the Politburo," he goes on to state that

> the process is about as follows: the Ministry of Foreign Affairs prepares a paper that deals with the issue in question on the basis of concrete facts. If the issue includes national security aspects, then the Ministry of Defense and possibly other Ministries are drawn into the preparation of the paper, and a summary of views is drawn up. This summary is then handed to the relevant Department of the Central Committee, which employs its own experts and consulting staff, who check the facts before it is submitted to the Politburo.[40]

Note that Falin does not indicate the origin of "the issue in question," only that the Ministry and then the Central Committee departments undertake a study of it. Thus, the initiative might have come from the Ministry itself or from elsewhere.

The responsibility of the Department for "checking" the work of the Ministries creates an interesting potential dilemma. It is generally thought that a natural tension must exist between monitor and subject, because the monitor is rewarded for discovering errors and flaws and the subordinate agencies are rewarded if they hide such problems.[41]

The Soviet case, however, is somewhat different, as the work of these departments is almost certainly judged in much the same way that their charges are: by output, by development of a productive plan, and by that plan's successful completion. The Central Committee department staffs function as both monitors on behalf of the Party leadership and as advisers to the Ministries in their preparation of plans and proposals. We might thus expect the departments periodically to act as advocates on behalf of "their" Ministries and agencies before the senior Party officials.[42]

THE MILITARY INDUSTRIAL COMMISSION (VPK)

The Council of Ministers, the executive branch of the Soviet government, is made up of the ministers of each of the All-Union and Union-Republic ministries (that is, the ministries operating at a national, rather than solely republic, level), chairmen of state committees, and a number of other leading government officials. It is by decree of the Council that the annual and five-year plans become law, and the Council serves to coordinate their implementation. Virtually all the country's economic activity is managed from the Council of Ministers. Unfortunately, much of its work, like that of the Central Committee, takes place behind closed doors.[43] This may change with the creation in 1989 of a Supreme Soviet Committee on Questions of Defense and State Security, headed by V. L. Lapygin, a specialist in missile guidance systems.

As is the case with the Central Committee, there is a Presidium which meets weekly to manage Council affairs between sessions.[44] The Presidium is made up of the Prime Minister (or Chairman of the Council of Ministers), and several First Deputy and Deputy Chairmen. Included among the Deputy Chairmen are the Chairman of Gosplan, of the State Committee for Science and Technology, Gossnab (the State Committee for Material and Technical Supply), and the chairman of the Military Industrial Commission. Each deputy is responsible for a sector of the economy or of state activity, overseeing and coordinating the work of the ministries and committees involved.[45]

The senior state organization responsible for overseeing the defense industries is the Military Industrial Commission, or VPK, headed by a deputy chairman of the council.[46] The commission itself includes representatives of twelve ministries, nine of which are have a major role in defense activities.[47] In addition to these twelve ministries, it seems probable that the First Deputy Chairman of Gosplan responsible for defense industrial matters is a member (he is discussed in greater detail below).[48]

The VPK brings together (if only for once-a-year meetings) the key leaders of the Soviet military economy, working to ensure that the defense industrial plans are coordinated and fulfilled. It is also responsible for coordinating requests for foreign technology and farming these requests out to various collection agencies such as the KGB or the Ministry of Foreign Trade.[49] Presumably, much of the day-to-day work falls upon a small staff, although little is known about it, and thus this organization may well be the most knowledgeable about the Soviet military's technical level and how it compares to that of potential adversaries.

Acting like a "superministry," the VPK also issues orders to its subordinate ministries in the form of "operational decisions," which serve as the basis for ministry decrees. It is interesting to note that one of Gorbachev's first major decisions upon becoming General Secretary was the establishment of a similar structure for agriculture.[50]

The importance of the VPK is reflected in the fact that its chairman at the time, L. V. Smirnov, played a key role at the conclusion of the SALT 1 talks, where Kissinger characterized him as "one of the ablest and most intelligent Soviet leaders with whom I dealt."[51] Smirnov, to a greater degree than even Minister of Foreign Affairs Andrei Gromyko, handled the final negotiations in Moscow, resolving a number of outstanding issues. More important, at the final meetings between the United States and Soviet negotiators, there were no representatives of the military in the delegation; Smirnov was the delegate with the closest ties to the military community. And it was Smirnov who was apparently given the authority to make a number of strategic and technical decisions, virtually on the spot (albeit subject to subsequent Politburo approval).[52]

GOSPLAN

In addition to supervising the ministries, a Central Committee department is also responsible for the relevant sections of the State Planning Committee (Gosplan). Gosplan is responsible for determining how resources and responsibilities are to be distributed throughout the

Soviet economy, attempting to balance resources, requirements, and output.

While Gosplan is, on the whole, supervised by the Central Committee's Department of Planning and Finance Organs, the other Central Committee departments take an active role in Gosplan's work. For example, the Department of Defense also oversees the defense section(s) of Gosplan. Specifically, without the approval of the proper Central Committee department, serious planning decisions cannot be made.[53] According to one former Soviet economist, from the beginning of the annual planning process the political (i.e., Party) leadership fixes the control figures (the initial plan proposed by Gosplan to ministries for review and adjustment) so that each department is well aware of the resources at its disposal when it helps the ministries with its planning.

Within Gosplan, there are typically three to five First Deputy Chairmen and a great number of Deputy Chairmen, each with a specific area of responsibility such as agriculture or defense industry. The First Deputy Chairman responsible for Defense Industry, however, has a special position, for, during the Brezhnev era, he was usually the only Gosplan deputy also to have a seat on the Central Committee.[54] Whether this is because of a lack of confidence in the chairman or simply an acknowledgment of the importance of having another senior official competent in the defense industry *as a whole* participating in the Central Committee is not clear.[55]

Under the Deputy Chairman, Gosplan has three types of departments: summary functional (responsible for broad areas such as machine-building or agriculture), summary resource, and branch (responsible for individual industries).[56] A summary department overseas a number of branch departments, which are organized to parallel the ministries. Within Gosplan, there is reportedly a Summary Department for National Economic Planning for Defense Industry,[57] which probably oversees about ten branch departments responsible for the defense industrial ministries.

One interesting facet of Gosplan's role in defense planning is the reported presence of former and serving military officers working within the planning committee.[58] For many years, the military press had discussed the benefits of greater study of military economics, and a group of "economist-warriors" would be an asset both *in* Gosplan and in dealing *with* Gosplan.[59] The military press frequently contains articles by officers with advanced degrees in economics. These individuals may work for Gosplan or, perhaps equally possible, in the General Staff as economic experts or at various academies. (It is intriguing to imagine the General Staff developing its own cadre of economists to engage in struggles over procurement with a civilian Gosplan.)[60]

THE MINISTRY

If the Party structure is the nervous system for Soviet administration, then the skeleton upon which it rests is the system of ministries and state committees. Presently consisting of some sixty-four All-Union and Union-Republic ministries and twenty-two state committees,[61] the system provides an administrative bureaucracy for almost every imaginable branch of society in general and the economy in particular, from industrial construction to foreign tourism and culture.

There are three types of ministries: the All-Union, the Union-Republic, and the Republic ministries. The All-Union (A-U) ministries are those with particular *national* significance and functions. The Union-Republic ministries are those with both national and republic-level responsibilities, and which exercise the same functions on both a national and republic level. Finally, the Republic Ministries are those that exist to serve the special needs of a republic. The ministries responsible for military production are, as might be expected, All-Union ministries.

A ministry is responsible for the development of its branch of the economy, execution of the state plan, and the introduction of new scientific-technical and administrative developments, regulating the activities of its subordinate scientific, design and production organizations.[62]

This is a broad mandate, and in operation it means that the ministry is responsible for developing (with Gosplan) a plan for its branch and ensuring that plan's fulfillment. The ministry is responsible for its own administration, as well as the plan's success or failure at the enterprises and institutes under its control; the ministry is ultimately held responsible for the shortcomings of its subordinate organizations.

In practice, this means that the ministry tends to have the same incentives that the enterprises have to seek attainable goals—goals that can be exceeded (in order to ensure bonuses) without bringing too much pressure for greater work in the next year. This has led to an incrementalism in the planning of output, as each year's targets are only marginally higher than those of the previous year.

Because the final plan is a legal document carrying the force of law, it is important to consider briefly the course of its development. It is likely that much of the politicking that takes place in the Soviet Union takes place in the course of plan preparation, as laying the proper groundwork to balance supply and demand is clearly a key to a successful plan.

The Five Year Plan begins with a series of doctrinal decisions: the objectives set by the Central Committee and the Politburo.[63] (See figures 2.1, 2.2 and table 2.1). These "Draft Guidelines" set general objectives, and are developed with considerable input from the Central Committee departments, the Secretariat, and, of course, Gosplan. Based on the CPSU guidelines, the Council of Ministers issues a similar set of basic guidelines (for the Eleventh FYP, these were issued in early March 1981). These general guidelines are "operationalized" by Gosplan and the Council of Ministers, and broken into annual and quarterly plans.

The annual plans, of course, are much more specific than the Five Year Plans, detailing inputs and outputs expected of various ministries and committees. In May of the preceding year, the Council of Ministers issues "control figures" to the ministries, that is, objectives for the ministries to fulfill. These control figures are intended to integrate the ministry's capabilities with the objectives of the FYP, and are produced by Gosplan in close coordination with the responsible Central Committee departments.[64] Estimates of capabilities are generally based on the actual output of the preceding year—the most reliable indicator of potential performance.

Over the next several months, the planning and other functional

FIGURE 2.1. General Procedure for Annual Planning

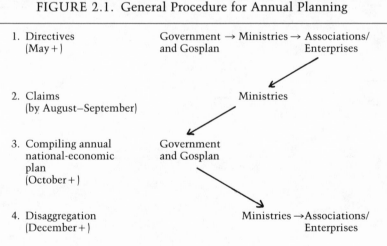

1. Directives (May +)   Government and Gosplan → Ministries → Associations/ Enterprises

2. Claims (by August–September)   Ministries

3. Compiling annual national-economic plan (October +)   Government and Gosplan

4. Disaggregation (December +)   Ministries → Associations/ Enterprises

Source: P. W. Davies, "Economic Planning in the USSR."

FIGURE 2.2. Soviet Planning Within the Ministry

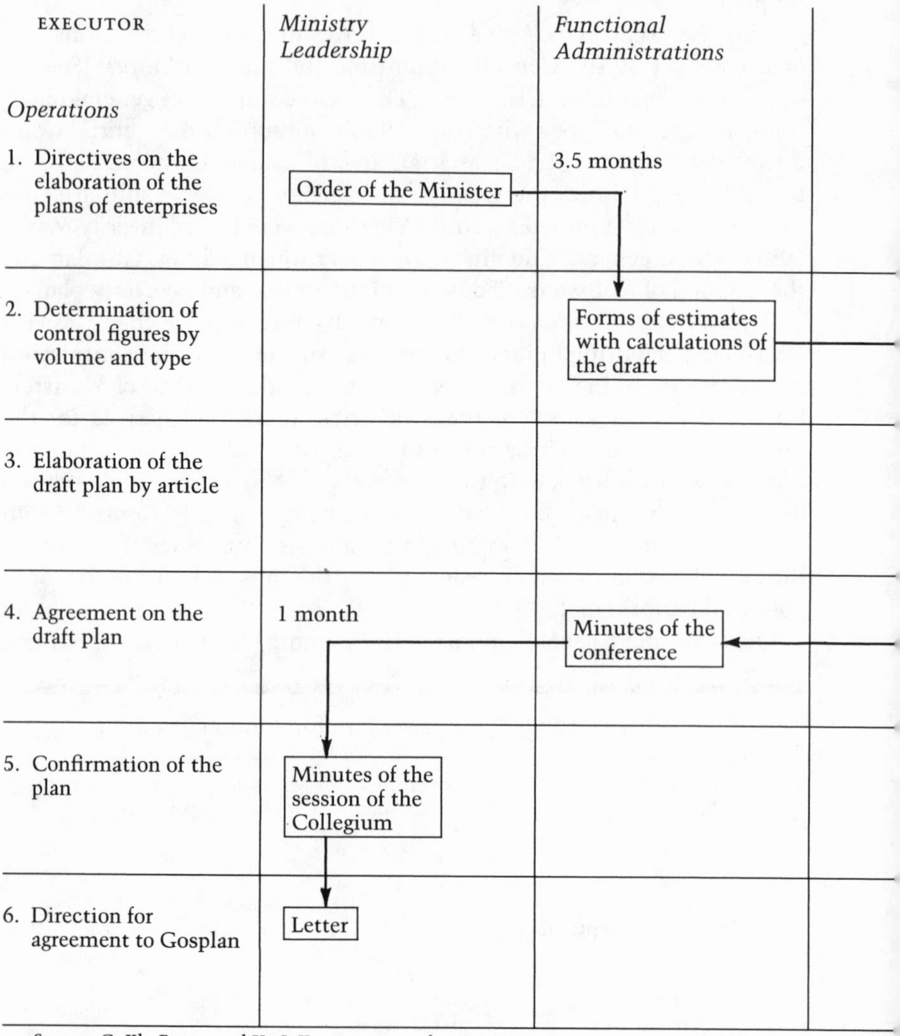

EXECUTOR	*Ministry Leadership*	*Functional Administrations*	
Operations			
1. Directives on the elaboration of the plans of enterprises	Order of the Minister	3.5 months	
2. Determination of control figures by volume and type		Forms of estimates with calculations of the draft	
3. Elaboration of the draft plan by article			
4. Agreement on the draft plan	1 month	Minutes of the conference	
5. Confirmation of the plan	Minutes of the session of the Collegium		
6. Direction for agreement to Gosplan	Letter		

Source: G. Kh. Popov and Yu.I. Krasnopoyas, eds., *Organizatsiya upravieniya obshchestven-nym proizvodstvom*, p. 153.

FIGURE 2.2 (cont.)

Associations & Enterprises	Initial Information	Prepared material
	Decrees of the USSR Council of Ministers	Order with indicators of period of preparation of draft plan
1.5 months	Initial figures of Gosplan	Forms 1-3,4, accompanying materials
List of the most important articles	Long-term plan of development of the branch	Form 7, information in substantiation
5 days	Information in substantiation (material for discussion)	Minutes
Conclusion of the functional Administrations		Decision of the Collegium
	Decision of the Collegium	Draft Plan, substantiation

TABLE 2.1. Elaboration of the Plans and Forecasts of Economic and Social Development of the USSR

Type of Plan	Organs Responsible	To Whom Plan Submitted	Period of Development
1. Complex program of scientific-technical progress for 20 years with the elaboration and extension for new Five Year Plan every five years.	USSR Academy of Sciences, State Committee on Science and Technology, State Committee on Construction [VPK?:-PA]	USSR Council of Ministers	Two years prior to beginning of new Five Year Plan
2. Draft of the basic direction of economic and social development for 10 years. Attached to this are indicators of the first Five Year Plan laid out by year and indicators of the second Five Year Plan established for the last year of the Five Year Plan (investment on the whole for the FYP). Each 5 year document is defined more precisely and extended to the new FYP.	Gosplan, together with the USSR ministries and the Union Republic Councils of Ministers	USSR Council of Ministers	One and a half years prior to beginning of new Five Year Plan
3. Control figures on the basis of indicators and economic norms on the forthcoming FYP with assignments by year.	USSR Gosplan	USSR ministries and departments and the Union Republic Councils of Ministers	One year prior to the beginning of the new Five Year Plan

4. Control figures, which are worked through in the ministries and departments and in the Union Republic Councils of Ministers.	USSR ministries and departments and the Union Republic Councils of Ministers	Production associations (enterprises) and organizations	In the course of the month after receiving the control figures from Gosplan
5. Draft FYP of economic and social development of the associations (enterprise) with preliminary agreement on list [nomenklatura] with suppliers and consumers (with allocation by year).	Associations (enterprises) and organizations	USSR ministries and departments and Union Republic Councils of Ministers	
6. Draft national FYP, balanced by all indicators (with allocation of tasks by year).	Gosplan USSR	USSR Council of Ministers	Five months prior to beginning of FYP
7. List of complex goals of the program, order, and time of their elaboration (amounting to the Five Year Plan).	Gosplan USSR with the participants of ministries and departments	Confirmed by Gosplan USSR	One and a half years prior to beginning of FYP
8. Draft annual national plan (on the basis of the FYP and the counter-plans of associations and enterprises, which are generalized in the branches and union republics.	Gosplan USSR	USSR Council of Ministers	Four months prior to beginning of FYP

Source: G. Kh. Popov and Yu. I. Krasnopoyas, eds., *Organizatsiya upravleniya obshchestvennym proizvodstvom* (Moscow: Moskovskyy Universitet, 1984), pp. 41–42.

administrations of the ministries develop plans for the enterprises and associations, based on the ministry's objectives and assignments. These directives are passed down the hierarchy to the production units, which analyze the plan requirements in their own planning organs and develop a draft plan laying out their contributions and requirements (figure 2.3). This is returned up the hierarchy to the planning adminis-

FIGURE 2.3. Soviet Outline of Administrative Levels (1984)

```
                    ┌─────────────────────────────┐
                    │  USSR Council of Ministers  │
                    └─────────────────────────────┘
                                  │
              ┌───────────────────────────────────┐
              │  Interbranch Central Organs of    │
              │  Economic Administration (VPK?)   │
              └───────────────────────────────────┘
                                  │
                    ┌─────────────────────┐    ┌──────────────────────┐
                    │  Branch Ministry     │╲   │ Scientific-Technical │
                    └─────────────────────┘ ╲  │      Council         │
                                  │            └──────────────────────┘
              ┌───────────────────────────────────┐
              │  Main Administration [Glavki]     │
              │     or Industrial Association     │
              │  [Promyshlennoye ob"edineniye]    │
              └───────────────────────────────────┘
                                  │
              ┌───────────────────────────────────┐
              │  Industrial Complex, Trust,       │
              │    or Production Association       │
              │  [Proizvodstvennoye ob"edineniye] │
              └───────────────────────────────────┘
                                  │
                    ┌─────────────────────┐
                    │ Enterprise Director  │
                    └─────────────────────┘
                        │             │
          ┌──────────────────┐   ┌──────────────────┐
          │  Chief Engineer   │   │ Deputy Directors │
          └──────────────────┘   └──────────────────┘
                        │      │
                    ┌─────────────────────┐
                    │     Shop Chief       │
                    └─────────────────────┘
                                  │
                    ┌─────────────────────┐
                    │    Section Chief     │
                    └─────────────────────┘
                                  │
                    ┌─────────────────────┐
                    │       Master         │
                    └─────────────────────┘
                                  │
                    ┌─────────────────────┐
                    │      Brigade         │
                    └─────────────────────┘
```

Source: Adapted from O. A. Deyneko, *Sovremenniy organizator proizvodstva* (Moscow: Ekonomika, 1984), p. 50.

trations and other functional administrations within the ministry, which, in theory, then take about a month to develop a ministry-wide plan which is submitted to the collegium of the ministry, comprised of the minister, his deputies, and the heads of the key administrations. Clearly, much discussion and negotiations must occur at each of these levels.

After the collegium's approval of the ministry plan, it is submitted in August or September to the Council of Ministers and Gosplan, and through October these two bodies attempt to reconcile planned production with claims on resources. By December, the "final" plan is sent by the Council of Ministers to the ministries.

As a result of this process, there is a natural pressure from the ministries for resources for their projects and from production units to exaggerate the materials they require, providing a margin of safety against the expected cutbacks. Enterprises try to reduce target levels and increase resources, while Gosplan strives for the opposite.[65] Because the ministries are responsible for the output of the enterprises, they tend to support their subsidiaries: from the plant manager to the minister, the objective is to develop a plan that can be met, to produce just enough to obtain the bonuses without incurring too much responsibility (and consequential future commitments). Aware of this, Gosplan relies heavily on norms of production in its estimates of requirements and output, but Gosplan is constrained as well, for the planners at Gosplan are aware that the ministry's proposals were developed under the watchful eye of the staff of the responsible CPSU Central Committee Department. Gosplan will be cautious in challenging the ministry, despite its mandate to increase the economic efficiency (increase production with fixed resources or keep production the same with reduced resources) of the ministries in an effort to stimulate economic growth.

The process by which the plans are formed, an institutional process by which doctrinal objectives become strategic plans, goes to the heart of ministerial management and allows us to consider the organization of the ministry. Its "central apparatus" consists of the minister, his deputies, the main branches and functional administrations, and departments,[66] overseeing a ministry that typically has a staff of a minimum of 700 to 1,000 officials.[67] At the apex of this structure sits the minister, responsible for the ministry as a whole. His deputy ministers coordinate the activities of the separate organs of the ministry's central apparatus, as well as supervising the work of various industrial organizations.[68]

Below the deputy ministers, the structure of the ministry rapidly broadens. It is at this level that we find the heads of administrations or main administrations (*upravleniye*, sometimes translated as "directorate").

In general, these administrations are of two types, one overseeing the actual administration of the ministry (functional administrations) and the other overseeing the enterprises and institutes in the ministry's control (production administrations, or, increasingly over the last decade, industrial associations).[69] The *functional* administrations, common to all ministries, are responsible for maintenance of the ministry and coordination of the subordinate organizations (rather than having actual production responsibilities). The production administrations have direct control of the ministries' enterprise.

Since the early 1960s, the Soviet administrative apparatus has encouraged the merging of various related enterprises into production associations (*proizvodstvennoye ob"edineniye*), typically placing four or five enterprises under the administration of its leading enterprise. These production associations are, in turn, responsible to the industrial associations which are replacing the administrations (frequently referred to as *qlavki*, or "main administration").

The minister, his deputies, and several leaders of various main administrations make up the ministry's collegium, the body responsible for collective decision making. The collegium, typically fewer than fifteen people, is a consultative body whose main impact is through its development and approval of the ministry-wide plan.[70] The recording secretary of the collegium collects proposals from the ministry's "subdivisions" (the administrations and departments), which are approved by the deputy ministers in charge of these subdivisions. The secretary generalizes and integrates the proposals and issues, and this circulates among collegium members. A second draft is prepared, incorporating any changes (the process by which changes are made is not discussed). This second draft is submitted to the minister, who adds his comments. A third draft is then prepared, indicating each subject's priority and who will discuss each subject at a collegium meeting. After discussion of this draft and the issues raised, a fourth version is circulated, after approval by the minister, throughout the ministry.[71]

Differences between the subunits of a ministry are resolved at the collegium, which frequently calls on representatives from the lower organizations to defend their position before the collegium.[72] In addition, there are occasional "enlarged" meetings of the collegium, in which outside officials and experts involved with the ministry's work participate in an effort to solve problems. These other officials might include the secretary responsible for the ministry, representatives from the Central Committee department charged with overseeing the ministry, Gosplan personnel, and others. Reports of such meetings make them appear to be actually collegial in nature: problems are discussed in an effort to solve them, and ministers are criticized, if not at the meeting itself, then in the press reports of the meeting.[73] Finally, decisions of the collegium are implemented by order of the minister.[74]

Paralleling the predominantly administrative collegium is a second body, the Scientific-Technical Council (*nauchno-tekhnicheskii sovet*, or NTS). The NTS consists of the leading scientists and technical specialists with the ministry's specialization, and is responsible for both advising the minister and his staff on scientific issues and for guiding the ministry's scientific development.[75] It reviews drafts of annual and long-range plans of scientific, design, and experimental work, and evaluates Soviet and foreign technology and considers how it might be used to increase the technical level of Soviet science and industry. It also makes general and specific recommendations about the technical policy of the branch, tries to measure the effectiveness of Soviet technical and scientific policies, and makes recommendations on the awarding of the Lenin and other prizes.[76]

The Scientific-Technical Council apparently has close ties with the ministry's scientific and design organizations. The two basic types of research organizations are the *nauchno-issledovatelskiye instituty* (scientific research institutes, or NIIs) and the *konstruktorskoye byuro* (design bureau, or KB).

Soviet theorists have argued that it is necessary to have scientific research organizations separate from the day-to-day concerns of the production enterprise, emphasizing that "the task of the production enterprise is production and the output of products in coordination with the plan, and not scientific-research work. NII and [KB] . . . must be independent of the current needs of production."[77]

While both the NII and the KB have been separated from production enterprises, the essential difference between the NII and the KB is that the NII is engaged primarily in basic research, rather than engineering. The focus in the NII is on theoretical development, rather than production of a final product. "In general, in the NII it is customary to have theoretical-experimental work and design-testing work, including the production and elaboration of a prototype, but the leading work is theoretical-experimental, and design-testing has subordinate significance."[78]

The KBs, on the other hand, emphasize conversion of new principles developed by the NIIs into new designs or applications of technology.

Work in the KBs focuses on "draft-design work and work on the manu-facture and finishing of prototypes, while experimental-theoretical [work] has secondary significance and relatively less weight than in an NII, and is carried out in so far as it is needed for decisions on this or that draft proposal in the case of the design and manufacture of new equip-ment."[79]

The Soviets emphasize the relationship between the two types of organizations. The KB serves as the bridge between general theoretical research and its application, and for that reason, most of the attention in development work is given to the KBs.[80] In addition, Soviet scientific planning indicates that basic science takes up a much smaller fraction of a ministry's resources than does the design work associated with KBs.[81]

The NIIs, because of the nebulous mandate of theoretical research, may not have as much direct influence on doctrinal and strategic deci-sions as the designers (if, of course, the designers have influence). The design bureaus also have much closer ties with production, perhaps creating a "bloc" capable of swaying decisions. In addition, the design-ers appear to be the focus of leadership attention when changes are sought: it seems easier to expect better and more creative use of exist-ing theoretical work than it is to press for better basic research. Cer-tainly the results are more immediately apparent. On the other hand, the designers are dependent on the basic research and technical hand-books prepared by the NIIs, and the staff of the NIIs actively participate on the commissions reviewing new design proposals and prototypes.

The structure, however, clearly gives a special place in Soviet sci-ence and society to the designers, who are required to integrate theory with Soviet production capabilities. This places a burden of responsibil-ity on the designer, but as a result of his prominence, may also offer unusual personal contact with the political leadership. Perhaps most importantly, he is well aware of the limitations and requirements of the Soviet production base (at least in his area of work). (This will be discussed in greater detail in chapter 4.)

PRODUCTION ORGANIZATIONS

Production associations have been formed in the Soviet Union since the early 1960s, made up of existing production organizations (for ex-ample, enterprises, existing associations of enterprises, or research organizations). These associations became one of the "basic units of production," in Soviet parlance.

In 1970, there were 608 such production associations, and in 1980, 4,083.[82] By 1984, it was reported that the number had reached more than 4,500, and that these included 18,000 production units and enterprises and more than 575 scientific research and draft-design organizations. Two hundred and fifty of these associations were scientific production associations[83] (*nauchno-proizvodstvennye ob"edineniya*, or NPOs), that is, associations whose lead unit is a scientific research institute (NII) or design bureau.[84] As with production associations, the administrative apparatus of the lead unit serves as the administrative apparatus for the association as a whole.[85]

These associations accounted for about 50 percent of total Soviet industrial production, although the percentage was much higher in industries such as electronic (100 percent), automobile production (92 percent), light industry (83 percent), tractor production (75 percent), food industry (67 percent), and the machine building and metalworking industries—in which defense industries fall (67 percent).[86]

A diagram of the organization of a "typical" production organization is shown in figure 2.4. As is apparent, it is designed to function as a "mini-ministry." Like the ministry, a plant or association has a Scientific-Technical Council for resolution of technical issues, a direc-

---

FIGURE 2.4. Organization of a Production Association

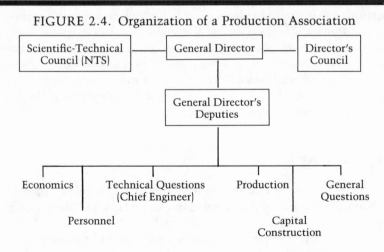

Source: S. Ye. Kamentser and F. M. Rusinov, eds., *Organizatsiya planirovaniye, i upravleniye deyatel'nost'yu promyshlennykh predpriatiy*, p. 202

tor's council (which appears to function as the equivalent of a collegium), and each deputy director has a particular area of responsibility: economics, technology (generally headed by the chief engineer, who also serves as the First Deputy Director), production, "general questions," cadres and social security, and capital construction. (In the second half of the 1980s, the Soviets also established a number of Interbranch Scientific and Technical Complexes, or MNTKs. These MNTKs are designed to integrate organizations from different ministries.)

Each plant also has a Technical Control Department (*otdel tekhnicheskogo kontrolya*, or OTK) to ensure that the enterprise's products reach the minimum standards of quality set by the State Committee on Standards. In theory, products that do not reach the required level are not released to the customer, while products of unusually high quality could be given a "mark of quality" and be sold at a higher wholesale price. This wholesale markup is important, as the Soviet enterprise or association, operating on the *khozraschet* (variously translated as "self-financing" or "profit and loss accounting") system, must cover much of its own costs. It must also be recalled, however, that there is no planned surplus to replace shoddy material, and thus the production of an unacceptable subcomponent can delay considerably the production of a final good.

It is not necessary at this point to describe in greater detail the organization and workings of an association or plant, other than to emphasize that the individuals involved sometimes control enormous organizations and appear to be prominent local or national figures. With such large organizations under his control, the head of an enterprise or, in particular, the head of a production association is also one of a small number of potentially influential individuals within a ministry. He is responsible for setting and meeting the plans at the lower level, and then implementing them.

THE MILITARY

The final participant in any "military industrial complex," of course, is the military itself, and it is necessary to understand where and how the military and military-industry interact.

The Ministry of Defense oversees virtually all military activities for the Soviet Union,[87] serving as the coordinating organization for the five services (the Strategic Rocket Forces, and Ground Forces, the Air Defense Forces, the Air Forces, and the Navy), as well as managing a number of support services and special troops (for example, civil defense or the chemical troops).

The Ministry of Defense typically has three first deputy ministers of defense (for the Wasaw Pact, the Chief of the General Staff, and—apparently—administration of the ministry itself), and ten or eleven deputy ministers. Five of these are always service chiefs. Since 1970, when N. N. Alekseyev was appointed, there has also been a deputy minister responsible for armaments.[88]

Alekseyev's background was in the Army's antiaircraft troops, being involved in the development of various Soviet radar systems. In 1946, he was appointed to the Main Artillery Administration's (GAU) Artillery Committee. He was eventually appointed chief of an administration of the GAU. He also worked for some time in the Council of Ministers.

In 1959, he was appointed deputy chairman of the General Staff's Scientific-Technical Committee, and in 1960 he became the committee's chairman. According to the current deputy minister for armaments, V. M. Shabanov, while chairman of the committee, Alekseyev coordinated the scientific research and design work "for the construction and harmonious development of all means of armed combat."[89]

Alekseyev also served as a military delegate to the first four sessions of the SALT talks.[90] In 1970, Alekseyev was appointed to the post of deputy minister of defense for armaments and called back to Moscow, where he reportedly also continued to keep a close eye on the SALT negotiations.[91]

In the post of deputy minister, Alekseyev was responsible for the long-range development and technical equipping of the armed forces, as well as the training of forces on the new equipment.[92] He also maintained close watch over NIIs, KBs, and defense plants.

V. M. Shabanov, appointed deputy minister for armaments upon Alekseyev's death in 1980, comes from a similar background in electronics and radar development. Prior to his return to the Ministry of Defense in the late 1970s, he served as a deputy minister in the Ministry of Radioelectronics, where he replaced a specialist in electronics for surface-to-air missiles.

The changing backgrounds of the post's occupants is indicative of Soviet objectives and priorities, as the men have changed from specialists in missiles (when this was a high priority item) to specialists in electronics (an increasingly important area in contemporary weapons research).

Despite the return of the post of deputy minister for armaments, the General Staff has not given up its role in armaments development. V. V. Druzhinin was apparently in charge of the General Staff's Armaments Section (or Scientific-Technical Committee [NTK]) from late 1970 until 1978,[93] when he returned to the Air Defense Forces; he may have been replaced by K. A. Trusov, a former SALT delegate.[94]

Chaiko, in his memoirs about this work in the Mil' helicopter design bureau, emphasizes the close ties between the designers and the representatives of the General Staff.[95] It has been suggested that the General Staff's involvement in procurement actually increased in the mid 1960s, in an effort to address three "problem areas: (1) the rising cost of modern weapons, (2) the efficient choice of what weapons to produce, and (3) the need for increased flexibility in weapon R&D."[96] The post of deputy minister for armaments and the parallel position within the General Staff appear to be important in the administration of the Soviet research, development, and production process. The background of the

FIGURE 2.5. Soviet Military Industrial Organization

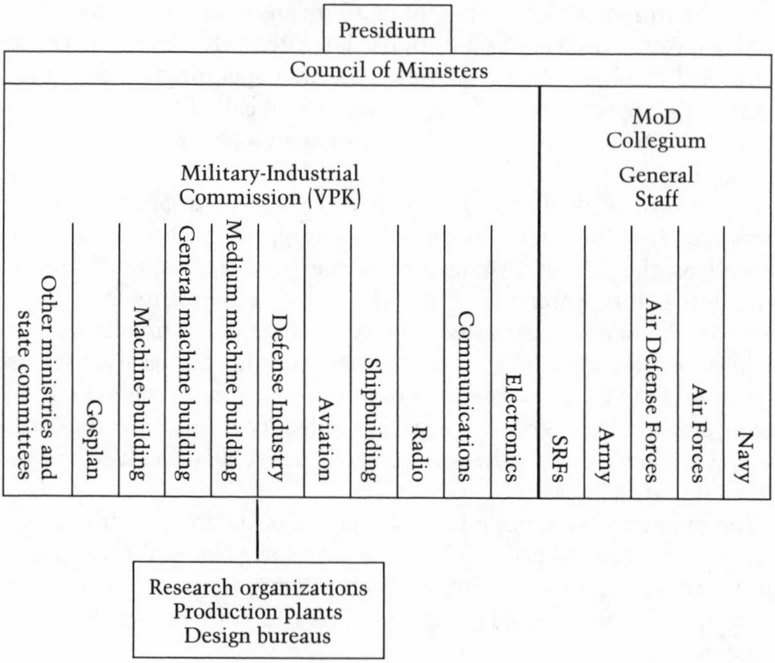

individual holding the deputy minister's position is probably a useful indicator of the immediate technical concerns of the Soviet military, and this has moved from missiles in the 1950s to electronics in the 1970s and beyond.

In addition to the deputy minister for armaments and the chief of the General Staff's Armaments Department, each service has a deputy chief of staff for armaments. The actual contracts between the military industry and the military are apparently between the service's armaments directorate and the production ministry. This day-to-day contract management at the service level may leave the deputy minister for armaments and the General Staff's deputy for armaments to focus on issues of a more general nature (for example, how to increase defense industrial efficiency across the board) and longer-term issues. And both are likely to pay more attention to the production requirements for the ministry of defense *as a whole*, rather than on a service-by-service basis.

FIGURE 2.5. (cont.)

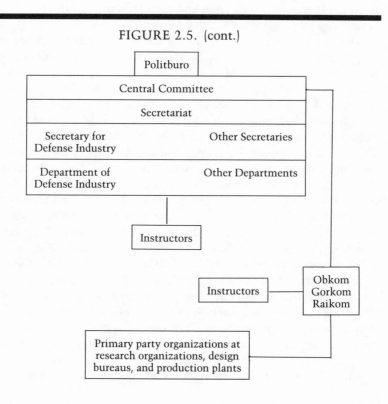

CONCLUSIONS

The importance of the organizational context is twofold, both reflecting the "chain of command" and shaping the potential impact of those occupying various posts.

Understanding the organizational structure and the "official" process helps indicate the important players and the capacity in which they operate. It is well-known that the Politburo is the final arbiter of decisions in the Soviet Union, and thus its members are almost certainly the most important "élite" figures. But deciding *everything* in the Soviet Union is clearly beyond the capabilities (and desires) of the Politburo membership. The issues that reach the Politburo are determined by a combination of the personal desires of its members (an issue certainly takes on salience simply by being of interest to a Politburo member) and the activities of the Secretariat. This is also the probable "entry-way" for Defense Council decisions, which are likely to be made within the Council and then presented to the Politburo for confirmation, rather than detailed discussion.

The Secretariat and its staff in the Central Committee departments play two key roles: "checking" the facts and issues presented to them from the ministries or other originating agencies, including the proposed annual and five year plans; and the monitoring of the implementation of decisions. The Secretariat has the initial right of approval, rejection, or "bumping up" a proposal to the Politburo. In addition, the "checking" function gives the Committees and Secretariat considerable power in shaping the agenda and conclusions of the Politburo; as one Soviet source reported, "the Secretariat *frames* policy decisions. By the time an issue reaches the Politburo, the framework for the decision is usually already there."[97] The Central Committee departments act as a parallel set of monitors, independent of the state organization, with the potential benefits and pitfalls inherent in this role. They observe, comment, and react to policy more than they generate policy.[98]

Membership in the Central Committee appears to reflect the importance *of*, rather than to bestow importance *upon*, its members. The role of the Central Committee is clearly to function as a check upon policy decisions made by the Secretariat and the Politburo, although the independence of the Committee must be questioned; the selection of members is, after all, heavily influenced by the General Secretary and the Politburo itself.

The VPK is certainly a key actor in the making of technical and strategic decisions, and, in fact, appears to have been established specifically to do so. The role of coordinating the production process of the defense industries is perhaps the most clearcut example of strategic decision making available, and Smirnov's role and authority in the SALT negotiations emphasizes the organization's (and his) authority.

The ministries are also designed to address strategic and technical questions, and are well designed to do so. A subsequent chapter will detail their role in the defense industries, but it is clear that the primary function of each ministry is to make these types of decisions, to make recommendations when it is either not competent to make a decision or in controversial areas, and to organize and coordinate the implementation of each decision.

Each of these organizations is designed to make a particular type of decision: the Politburo, the Defense Council, and the Secretariat are responsible for the doctrinal decisions, with integration and some review by the Central Committee; the VPK (and the other, similar, Council of Ministers organizations) make strategic and technical decisions on a broad scale, coordinating the decisions made by its subordinate organizations: Gosplan's decisions are also of a strategic and technical nature, complementing the strategic and technical decisions made elsewhere and attempting to integrate them into the rest of the economy; and, finally, the ministry's role is also to make and implement strategic and technical decisions.

By considering three different professional communities (plant managers, designers, and ministry personnel), it is possible to examine in greater detail how decisions are influenced in these various organizations, which decisions are open to such influence, and how much impact these three specialist-groups have on decisions.

CHAPTER THREE

THE DEFENSE PLANT MANAGER

Perhaps the most striking trait of the defense industrial manager is the similarity he bears, at least in his writings, to his counterpart in civilian industry. Both their backgrounds and professional concerns are very similar, as if the common bonds between the two are greater than any differences arising from their respective specializations. This is not surprising, in that the requirements given to each are generally the same: increase productivity, conserve resources, and ensure quality.

The Soviet industrial manager, whether working in the military or civilian industries, is a member of the Soviet élite. In the military industries, he is one of perhaps 150 key managers of defense plants.[1]

Three key traits were hypothesized for a military industrial complex in chapter 1. The defense industrial manager working in such a military industrial complex would probably have a number of specific characteristics. First, he would likely have as a goal increasing access to and/or control of resources in his area of responsibility. Thus, a plant manager at the Malyshev Tractor (and tank) Plant plant would presumably argue for more resources in the areas of tank development and production, just as the director of the Kazan Aircraft Plant would argue for more resources for bomber development and production.

In making the case for increasing resources, however, the managers (and the designers and the ministry officials) must have some tools with which to make their case. The most obvious one is, of course, an alliance with the military, presumably already inclined to assist the industries.[2] If there are, in fact, complementary interests between the military and its associated industries, one would expect to find the industries attempting to enlist the military in their efforts. Thus, the Malyshev plant's director might enlist the aid of the ground forces, while the Kazan director might rely on that of the air forces.

But it is useful and desirable to have an independent means of making a case. Otherwise, the industries' position vis-a-vis decision makers becomes inextricably linked with that of the military, and the industries risk becoming beholden to the military, almost certainly an undesirable outcome for any plant manager valuing his already limited autonomy and certainly unacceptable to his superiors in the ministry. Presumably, the industrial manager would wish to make a case complementary to that of the military without relying on the military to convey it.

As a result, the military industrialists would be expected to emphasize a potential adversary's militaristic intentions and military capabilities, while at the same time emphasizing their own capacity to counter them. They would seek ways to influence the decision makers independent of the military. Thus, in the United States, the defense industries have a "two-prong" approach to decision makers. First, they support various external "public interest groups," such as the Committee on the Present Danger, which present views emphasizing the military deficiencies of the United States and the potential threat posed by its adversaries. Second, they maintain in-house think tanks, providing an analytic underpinning for the corporation's work.

Finally, to make the argument effectively, the corporations (or managers, designers, or ministries) must have access to a range of both military-technical information (what is each side building, how many each side has, technical advances, etc.) and military-strategic information (how might a particular system be used on combat, how might systems be deployed, etc).

Realistically, there are, of course, limits imposed on any public discussions in the Soviet Union. There are no "political action committees" or independent public interest groups. Discussions in the press are constrained by both the censorship system and the natural conservatism learned through years of living in the system. But there are themes in the Soviet press that are logically related to efforts to influence resource decisions: for example, the need to strengthen the Soviet defensive shield; the need to be ever vigilant in dealing with the west; extolling the role of a particular branch of the armed forces in history (and, by implication, in the present and future); or the importance of the "A" sector of the economy (responsible for capital products) vs. the "B" sector (typically consumer goods). Such discussions are found frequently, and it would be reasonable to expect to find managers using these themes in an effort to shape the views of decision makers. The question is, of course, do they? As detailed below, they do not. It is extremely rare for a defense industrial manager to articulate demands involving foreign or security policy or based on any claim of special position or priority. Instead, their views are indistinguishable from those of their civilian industry counterparts.

WHO ARE THE MANAGERS?

Most managers, whether of the civilian or military industry, come from "the line," i.e., they began as workers, then picked up an advanced degree on the way to the post of manager.

The reports on civilian managers indicate considerable horizontal mobility.[3] In the defense plants, by contrast, those who have become managers remain in one plant unless promoted into the ministry or other more important post. Similarly, there is little evidence of moving from ministry to ministry: the only case in the sample suggest that this happens only at the very highest levels (for example, a deputy minister of aviation becoming minister of instruments, or a deputy minister of milk and meat production becoming a first deputy minister of defense industry), and then infrequently.

Managers of defense plants appear to hold the post for a considerable length of time. While this may simply reflect the fact that only a portion of the managers can be identified, and the longer one is a manager, the more likely he is to be elected to a post or appear in print, it may also reflect the careful screening which is a pre-condition for the defense manager's position.

In the sample used in this study,[4] every manager about whom detailed biographical information is available has a higher education of some sort, and had it prior to becoming manager. Virtually all were graduated from technical institutions, and only one (Lev Zaikov) from an institute that appears to have a specialty in economics and finance. Zaikov directed a major electronics research and produciton facility in Leningrad, served as CPSU secretary for defense industry, and is currently Moscow Party chief.

An intriguing aspect of the educational background of these men is that some may have known each other as a result of being in school together.[5] For example, Yakov Ryabov (secretary for defense industry in the late 1970s), Lev Voronin (Deputy Minister of Defense Industry in the late 1970s), and Yevgeni Varnachev (a director of Uralmash) were all at the Ural Polytechnical Institute in the late 1940s and early 1950s.

Promotion to manager is accomplished, in theory, through use of a mechanism called the "reserve list," a directory of those personnel considered qualified for advancement. The reserve list is part of the *nomenklatura*, which lists positions over which the Party exercises its approval in appointment.[6]

While the training of managers has generally been limited to courses ranging from a few weeks to a few months, it appears that the defense industrial ministries are leaders in the number of officials sent to such programs.[7] The "defense-related ministries" in the early 1980s planned to send the greatest number of trainees to the various management training institutes of the Ministry of Higher Education's six-month program and the third greatest number for the three-month program. The Ministry of Defense itself planned to send 999 individuals to the six-month programs and 547 to the three-month, while the defense industries were, as a whole, sending 1,046 to the six-month and 746 to the three-month.[8]

By areas of specialization, the defense industrial ministries dominate the number of trainees in radioelectronics (83 to 91 percent of the trainees in this area were from the defense industries and the Ministry of Defense), and 40 to 48 percent of those specializing in machine-building were from these industries and the Ministry of Defense.

While Beissinger suggests that the large percentage of defense personnel makes sense only under conditions of a "significant increase of defense industrial production," the pattern would also make sense if the defense industrial ministries placed a higher premium on efficient use of resources and management skills than did the civilian ministries. Such an emphasis may have been prompted by a *tightening* of resources in the defense industries, rather than an increase.

In addition, it should be recalled that most defense industrial plants are dual purpose, producing for both military and civilian customers.[9] There is little information available, however, on the balance between military and civilian production, although it almost certainly varies by plant and product.[10] The civilian component of a defense plant is principally designed to make productive peacetime use of space that would be necessary in the event of mobilization.[11]

The representation of defense industrial managers (indeed, managers in general) on CPSU bodies is limited. There are no current managers of defense industrial plants on the Central Committee.[12] At the republic and lower level, however, participation by defense industrialists is greater, although their importance at this level is not clear. Most defense plants are large industrial structures, and it should not be surprising that the managers of these plants play a role in local politics, just as do managers of large, civilian enterprises. By contrast, the Supreme Soviet contains a number of such managers, although the importance of membership in this organization has been more symbolic than politically important.

ISSUES RAISED BY THE DEFENSE MANAGERS

Several issues appear regularly in the writings of the defense industrial directors. These include planning, supply, cadres, quality control, and links between science and production. While other topics are addressed, these themes comprised a core of issues discussed by the defense managers.

The Challenges of Planning

The view that the plan frequently gets in trouble because of problems with the plan itself is not unique to the defense managers, and they regularly take the plan and those responsible for it to task.[13] For those who believe that there is little internal criticism in the Soviet Union, the treatment of Gosplan and the planners is a revelation.

It should first be emphasized that planning takes place at many levels in the Soviet administrative hierarchy, and refers to much more than simple input/output discussions. There is an often bewildering collection of indicators, some contradictory, that are intended to guide the manager's choices, replacing the presumed vagaries of market mechanisms with "scientific" measures.

Many of the writings detail how various plants have developed a mix of incentives and controls to encourage personal dedication to the plan's objectives. The theme of establishing "personal plans" is one found in the writings of Stepanchenko and Khvedeliyani, both directors of aircraft plants. Other writers emphasize the various problems (and the potential) associated with the so-called "Kosygin reforms" in the economic mechanism implemented from 1965.[14]

Personal plans are those developed for each worker, sometimes with a public display of how each is doing in relation to his or her objectives. Stepanchenko describes a "labor passport," on which one's accomplishments are recorded for evaluation at the end of the year and the determination of "incentives."[15] At the Dmitrov plant, Khvedeliyani describes how at each work station, a card prominently displays each worker's daily output.[16]

But one of the most important developments in the area of personal planning was the further refinement of NOT (*Nauchno-organizatsiya trud*, or scientific organization of labor). NOT is rooted in a belief that labor can be scientifically organized to be more effective. Norms are established, specialization is encouraged, and extraneous (wasteful) effort is eliminated, making the work more productive. In the Soviet context, one of the purposes of NOT is to provide a series of meaningful indicators for the decision maker (for example, the plant manager), indicators that pinpoint weaknesses and make it possible to calculate individual contributions to productivity and improvements. One of the most important contemporary architects of NOT (and winner of a 1969 State Prize for his work in the area) is Pavel Derunov, director of a major motorbuilding plant in Rybinsk responsible for both civilian and military engine production.

Derunov's articles focus on this question of productivity and, more importantly, how to calculate it.[17] The results are, as was the case with the cards in Stepanchenko's aircraft plant, used to determine the level of bonus given to each worker or group.

At a broader level, there are regular reports of dissatisfaction with plan administration, almost identical to those found in the nonmilitary literature. In 1965, O. V. Soyich (who, that same year, became director of a leading Soviet tank plant) attacked the pricing structure and organizations for not encouraging quality production and for not providing sufficient support for necessary basic research.[18] Most western economists agree that the reforms instituted that year to address these concerns were inadequate. Yu. V. Konyshev, director of the aircraft plant in Ulan Ude, complained that the plan for increasing the plant's output of washing machines was increased without increasing the material fund necessary to support it.[19] L. A. Voronin, who in 1985 would be appointed to head the State Supply Agency (Gossnab) after five years in Gosplan, complained in 1967 that the "government department dealing with specific industry sections should also be switched to profit-and-loss accounting [khozraschet]. They would then become not only morally responsible for the enterprises under their juristiction, but also materially, and would therefore adopt a more profit-conscious system."[20]

Voronin may have been referring to the Ministry of Defense Industry, rather than Gosplan,[21] but it is clear that G. Vanag of the Chkalov Aviation Plant in Novosibirsk had Gosplan as his intended target when he argued that the State Planning Committee had to work more closely with the production units rather than "leaving the enterprise alone with difficulties which they are simply not in a position to overcome."[22]

It is clear that the defense industries, despite their important position in the Soviet economy, are not isolated from the problems and complexities associated with Soviet economic planning. It is also clear from the data considered that, while there may be some benefits for the manager working in the defense industries, they are insufficient to buffer the manager from the problems afflicting industry on a wide scale.

Supply

Supply has been the bane of the civilian industrial manager's position for years, but it has often been suggested that the defense industrial manager, because of the priority apparently enjoyed by the defense industries, was somehow immune to supply problems. This does not appear to be the case. If the position of the defense manager is easier than that of the manger responsible for civilian industry, it is not apparent in the writings of the former: there are frequent complaints about the quality, reliability, and planning of supply.[23]

Gossnab, the State Supply Agency, is a popular target for both civilian and defense managers. In 1973, Ye. Sabinin, director of the Tula Weapons Plant since the early 1960s, complained that Gossnab, "doesn't give us the help we need." Requisitions for materials have to be submitted, according to Sabinin, *before* the plan itself is agreed upon, thus leading to potential gaps between supplies and requirements.[24] Another defense manager, Yu. V. Konyshev of the Ulan Ude Aircraft Plant, complained that Gossnab's typical response to complaints about supply is to note that "the apportionment of resources is not guaranteed."[25]

Khvedeliyani's Tbilisi Aircraft Plant kept an "alarm list" of plants that failed to provide promised materials,[26] and G. Vanag, the director of the Novosibirsk Aviation Plant, acknowledged that *every* plant has its *tolkach* (an employee specializing in obtaining needed supplies outside normal channels), and the enterprises have to behave "in unexpected ways" to achieve the assigned tasks.[27]

Presumably in an attempt to improve the supply system for the economy as a whole, Mikhail Gorbachev appointed one of the most prominent defense managers, Lev Voronin, to head Gossnab in 1985. Voronin had moved from plant manger to the post of chief of the Ministry of Defense Industry's Planning-Production Administration, then into Gosplan as the First Deputy Chairman responsible first for defense industry, then for heavy industry.

Cadres

As suggested earlier, cadres policy is an area of concern for the plant manager. Questions of how to find, train, and keep qualified personnel and how to determine the correct mix of incentives and "administrative measures" are frequently reflected in the writings of the defense manager, again, just as in the case of the civilian managers. The defense industries have one advantage in that they offer wages 20 to 30 percent above those offered in unclassified plants.[28] On the other hand, the employees must sign a secrecy vow and are forbidden from meeting foreigners or travelling abroad. As might be expected, the "First Department" (the KGB office at the plant responsible for security) is almost certainly more active at such plants than in civilian production associations.[29]

The typical Soviet machine building plant is large. For example, it is known that the Kiev Aircraft Plant had more than 1,800 party members in 59 Primary Party Organizations (PPOs) and 129 party groups, and relied on "thousands of specialists."[30] The Ministry of General Machine Building's Bolshevik Plant, deeply involved in artillery production, reportedly employes 20,000.[31]

"Cadres" are divided into a number of categories: Laborers, engineering-technical workers, administrative and support staff, etc. The two that received the most attention in the Soviet writings are the laborer and the engineer; administrative staff are hardly mentioned at all.[32]

The continuing education of the workers appears to be a common concern of the plant managers, both in specialized areas and in more general areas. In 1977, the Kiev Aircraft Plant was presented as a model for the assimilation of young specialists into the workplace,[33] and many articles by the director of the Chelyabinsk Tractor Plant (ChTZ, which has in the past produced tank equipment and recently began doing so again) concentrate on clubs and youth, and their utility in nurturing young specialists.[34]

But efforts to provide an education are not always successful. Ya. Khvedeliyani blasted the Georgia Polytechnical Institute for producing too many machine specialists and failing to turn out a sufficient number of aviation specialists. He also argued that too little attention is paid to the *continuing* education of the engineers and specialists once at the plant, allowing them to grow out of touch with the current developments in the field. He bemoans the fact that, although there are more engineers produced in the Soviet Union than in the United States, those in the United States are the more productive, while those in the Soviet Union are often not engaged in creative work. In addition, he notes that many of the new specialists choose not to work at the Dmitrov Plant when given the choice, moving to scientific-research association, (NII) for the better wages and easier working conditions.[35]

Three years later, Khvedeliyani again returned to this theme of how to keep people at the plant once they have received useful training. In his view, they too frequently become "drifters," moving on to another job and taking with them valuable experience gained at the Dmitrov plant. Even worse, they often leave the field completely. Khvedeliyani called for sanctions against these workers, arguing that they were costly to society.[36]

One theme that frequently appeared in the articles on education was the need to increase "economic" education. While this is particularly common in the civilian area, it appears in the writings of various directors involved in military management as well. For example, in 1965, O. Soyich argued that the plants must pay much more attention to training specialists in economics, as well as those in technical skills, and that new technology requires that more young specialists be trained in administrative skills.[37] In 1972, G. V. Zaychenko of the Chelyabinsk Tractor Plant made a similar argument before a conference on administration.[38] Khvedeliyani noted that engineers in particular needed to improve their economics understanding, as they tend to ignore questions of cost in their work, and that this was a national, not just local, problem.[39]

But even a well-educated worker may not be an effective worker, and explaining that difference has led to some awareness of the importance of work environment. Derunov, in his work on NOT, emphasized the "stability of cadres," and noted that one way to promote such stability was through the creation of a constructive "psychic climate" for the individual as well as for the collective.[40] A. A. Lyubchenko, director of the Leningrad Kirov Machinebuilding Plant, noted in a speech about the progress of the plant that simple changes in the psychological environment of the workers increased productivity 20 to 25 percent, making it possible to increase the output of tractors without adding new workers.[41]

A major source of income for director or employee is the bonus.[42] One of the reforms of the mid-1960s gave the manager of a plant greater discretion in how to distribute funds *within* the plant, generally in the form of bonuses. As L. A. Voronin noted, the implementation of the Kosygin reforms at the Krasnogorsk Mechanical Works made it possible for the plant to drop the idea of "equal remuneration" for workers and to distribute funds with more purpose.[43]

The use of bonus funds makes it possible to reward workers who produce quality products, and is credited in part with reducing the number of products that are rejected upon initial submission. Unfortunately, workers cannot be made to pay for unsatisfactory work, according to Ye. Sabinin of the Tula Armaments Plant. When moral pressure and material incentives fail, the alternative appears to be "releasing" workers (apparently firing them) for discipline violations.[44]

V. N. Sivets of the Chkalov Aviation Plant in Tashkent notes that the "master," the level immediately above "worker," can increase his salary by 50 percent through bonuses.[45] The system established at the Chkalov plant for incentives and quality is apparently somewhat more rigorous than that in the Tula plant noted above, for Sivets suggests that the worker who approves a defective piece of equipment can, in fact, be fined.[46]

A slightly different set of incentives was called for by Gleb Vanag of the Novosibirsk Aircraft Plant. He was concerned that the planners were treating Novosibirsk as if it were Moscow, and thus not allowing higher wages to be offered as an incentive to attract qualified workers. It is not known if this changed.[47]

It should also be noted that most Soviet managers who write about incentives do not concentrate exclusively on financial reward. As well as "material" incentives, there are "moral" ones, such as being recorded in the daily log of hero workers of the plant having one's picture posted prominently. But based on the amount of writing devoted to each of these, the directors clearly feel the material incentives are the more important, and the flexibility they have in allocating them is one of their most important and valued rights.

Quality Control

Even when a director's workers are well paid and his supply is secure, quality remains a concern, especially under the Kosygin reforms' emphasis on sales and profitability. Defense industries have the same standards and systems for quality control as the civilian plants, but they are also subject to much greater scrutiny and control by the "consumer." In addition, they have often taken the lead in developing administrative or organizational systems of quality control, perhaps in response to this customer influence.

Every plant, whether civilian or military, has a department of quality control (*otdel tekhnicheskogo kontrolya*, or OTK), which must approve each product before it is released from the plant. The basic task of the OTK is to verify the quality of a finished product, semi-finished product, and overhauled equipment, and, in various cases, to deal with raw materials and components from abroad.[48]

A product can be submitted more than once to the OTK, but it is in the producer's interests to have the product approved upon initial submission. In the event of disagreement over the product's acceptability, the head of the OTK is obliged to report the problems to "higher organs" and the ministry's main inspectorate for quality.[49] But it should also be recalled that the OTK is under the control of the plant within which it operates, rather than an outside agency, and the chief of the OTK is appointed and relieved of duties by the plant director. It would thus not be surprising to find the OTK staff under considerable pressure to approve borderline products, rather than jeopardize completion of the plan.

Besides the establishment of an OTK in each plant, Soviet administrators have developed a number of other administration systems to encourage high-quality production. With only minimal market-type forces pressing for quality, the Soviets generally rely on norms and standards for products, and they have also developed or adapted various administrative systems to encourage quality production. These all involved making the workers themselves responsible to varying degrees for their products, with appropriate rewards and punishments.

One of the first and most important of these was developed at the Saratov Aircraft Plant in 1955,[50] and is known as the Saratov system or the "defectless manufacturing of products" (*sistema bezdefektnoqo izqotovleniya produktsii,* or BIP. A better translation would probably be the name of a similar western development, the "zero-defect system.").[51]

Under the Saratov system, workers, masters, and shop leaders are held strictly responsible for the quality of the product they submit to the OTK. "Suitable" material and moral rewards were allocated upon approval at the first submission.[52]

A modified version of the Saratov system was developed in L'vov, and is known as the "system of defectless labor" (*sistema bezdefektnogo truda* or SBT). It differs from the Saratov system in that responsibility is placed on each category of worker, and the work is evaluated individually. The presumed advantage of such an approach is that each worker has an incentive to actively prevent defects, rather than to be a passive observer. The SBT system is considered particularly useful in industries where especially high quality is required and where the tasks are particularly complex; it has thus been widely used in the radioelectronics, instrument, and machine-building industries,[53] which, in turn, make up the heart of the Soviet defense sector.

What has been characterized as an "engineering system" must also be included in the quality control systems. This is KANARSPI, or "quality, reliability, expected life of equipment from the first piece" (*kachestvo, nadezhnost', resurs tekhniki s pervykh promyshlennykh izdeliy*). KANARSPI was developed at the Gorky Aircraft Plant im. Ordzhonikidze in the late 1950s, and is credited with increasing the reliability of the plant's products from 1.5 to 1.8 times in two years.[54] One source says KANARSPI's superiority lies in its "elaboration and implementation of a complex of measures on guaranteeing the high quality of machines, beginning with the perfection of the design of the products and finishing with their exploitation."[55] KANARSPI, because of its emphasis on each stage in the development and manufacturing process, emphasizes the benefits of automation. It might be suggested that its developers at the Gorky Aircraft Plant may have used it to encourage greater emphasis on improving the technological level of their industry in particular.

Finally, the director of the Tashkent Aircraft Plant reported in 1973 that they had developed and were using yet another system for managing quality: "the system of guarantee of high quality, increasing lifetime, and increasing reliability" (*sistem obespecheniya vysokogo kachestva, uvelicheniya resursa i povysheniya nadezhnosti,* or SOVKURPON), which is yet another derivation of BIP and SBT, and which had reported results similar to those of SBT. It is interesting to note, however, that yet another attempt to develop a new system for quality production originated in an aircraft plant.[56]

Soviet discussions of quality control provide a glimpse of how poor quality had been. For example, before the mid-1960s, the OTK at the Tbilisi Aircraft Plant accepted only about 50 percent of the products submitted. In other words, half of what should have been "final" products were considered below standard.[57] An extreme example is that of the Saratov Aircraft Plant, where *zero* percent of the products submitted in 1955 met minimal standards upon first submission![58] It should be emphasized that these figures were presented to contrast with the high (typically greater than 95 percent) acceptance rate existing from the late 1960s.

The managers of various defense industries have, of course, addressed the problems of quality control, emphasizing the administrative responses to problems of quality. Stepanchenko notes the Kiev Aircraft Plant's reliance on (and successes due to) the BIP system in 1971, reporting that acceptance by the OTK on first submission was at 97 percent or greater and that socialist competition at the plant takes place between shops for acceptance on the initial submission.[59]

Khvedeliyani acknowledges the importance of the Saratov system at the Tbilisi Aircraft Plant, noting that its introduction was preceded by a large-scale review of the plant's plans, technical processes, production and control systems. "Working on the Saratov system disciplined the producers, raising responsibility for quality, [and] having a positive effect on the general increase of quality."[60]

Because of the career of one of the authors, the most interesting discussion of quality control may be that of I. S. Silayev and I. I. Darovskikh.[61] Silayev was director of the Gorky Aviation Plant (where KANARSPI was developed), until he was promoted to deputy minister, then minister of Aviation Industry. In 1985, he was further promoted to the post of deputy chairman of the council of ministers reponsible for all civilian quality control. He has been a clear advocate of the state approval system *(gospriyemka)*, which is based on the *voyenpred* in the defense industries. The reported successes of KANARSPI may have been part of the reason. Their discussion, which appeared in the technical journal *Standards and Quality (Standarty i kachestvo)* and which was apparently directed at an audience of managers, is a clear call for further improvement of the KANARSPI system, but even more a comment on how effective it is in operation. Silayev's promotion under Gorbachev may indicate that there is still considerable emphasis on refining soviet administrative techniques before undertaking more extensive reform efforts.

Derunov also emphasized the benefits of KANARSPI, relying on it at the Rybinsk plant as a means of improving the scientific organization of labor.[62]

Voronin, while director of the Krasnogorsk Mechanical Works, emphasized the link between quality control and the full implementation of the 1965 reforms, instituting a system of "on-line operational testing ('breaking-in') after assembly [and] on-line shock and vibration testing" of the cameras produced at the plant through the use of a new electrical test unit.[63]

But the quality control measure that appears to be unique to the military industries, and which is unmentioned in the writings of the defense plant managers, is the *voyenpred*, or military representative *(voyennyy predstavitel')*. There has been very little written about the voyenpred, but, as is so often the case in the Soviet press, the importance of the subject is inversely related to its frequency of mention in the press.[64]

The voyenpred is an officer or employee of the armed forces (generally with an engineering education) assigned to a plant producing military equipment. His job is to ensure that there are no deviations from the assigned requirements and to act as a monitor of the quality level at the plant, checking the production process and production costs; formally accepting the final product after conducting the appropriate tests and examining its quality and reliability; and organizing training at the plant of representatives of the units who will be using and maintaining the weapon. He also ensures that any required changes are actually made.[65]

The majority of voyenpredy are engineers, working for a particular service. One of the conditions that gives the voyenpred a unique position is that he is paid by his service rather than the plant. Thus, within the Soviet system, the military customer has unparalleled influence over the manufacturing process. The voyenpred is responsible not to the plant or production ministry (as is the case with the staff of the OTK), but to the customer. Every change has to be approved by the voyenpred, after certification by a representative of the laboratory or group that the difference between the planned characteristic and the actual product would not affect performance.[66]

Emigré reports generally agree that the voyenpredy were competent engineers, who engaged in more than just monitoring. The voyenpredy appear to have become at times active participants in the development of the weapons system as well as a means of communicating ideas between the designers and the services.[67]

Science and Industry

Another important theme that appears in the writings of the defense plant directors is the need to strengthen links between production plants and designers. This will be discussed in more detail in the chapter on designers, who wrote more frequently about this issue, but is worth noting here the views of the defense directors.

P. Malofeyev, director of the Uralmash plant (which has produced, among other things, artillery), made a strong case in 1965 for the development of an in-house scientific research institute (NII) or design bureau (KB). In the case of Uralmash, this is the NIITyazhmash (NII of Heavy Machine Building). The benefits flow, in Malofeyev's view, in two directions: the NII or KB has easy access to experimental and production facilities, while the plant has a corps of scientific workers always at hand.[68]

Other managers agree. Again, Stepanchenko and Khvedeliyani are the most direct on the issue. In 1970, Khvedeliyani suggested that the links between the designer and the engineer were weak and becoming weaker. From his experience at the aviation plant and within the industry, he argued that "At the junction of the activities of the designer and of the technologist could be born future technical ideas [and] important innovations."[69]

Stepanchenko noted in one of his articles that Antonov's OKB worked in close contact with the Kiev Aviation Plant, although the plant's own designers, "not infringing on the prerogatives of the OKB," made 1847 proposals of their own in the previous five year plan.[70] Like Malofeyev, Stepanchenko also emphasized the potential symbiotic relationship between plant and institute (not necessarily just a design bureau, but more basic research as well).[71]

F. Ya. Kotov, director of the Siberian Agricultural Machine-building Plant (Sibselmash) until 1976, when he was appointed First Deputy Minister of Machine Building, also emphasized the role of science. During the seven years he was director of the plant, Kotov wrote a number of articles and was interviewed on various subjects, maintaining relatively high visibility. His most important articles noted the importance of close ties between the Siberian Department of the Academy of Sciences and Sibselmash, and he advocated the establishment of a permanent "working-body" to coordinate joint efforts.[72]

DECISIONS AND MANAGERS

The defense plant manager is likely to be most important in the technical and strategic areas of policy making. Only once did a defense plant manager venture into the realm of foreign policy, and that was to report broad support for the SALT 1 treaty, which Brezhnev had just signed.[73]

When one reads the materials these individuals have generated through the 1960s and 1970s, it is clear that few have ventured outside the area of straightforward management issues. If one did not know that these individuals managed key plants in the defense industrial sector, one could not discern it from their writings: their are no claims about the particular importance of their branches of the economy, no linking of their products with national security, and no comparison of their products with those of foreign countries.

Instead, one is struck by how similar these articles are to those written by civilian managers.

TECHNICAL DECISIONS

Three general types of decisions were suggested in Chapter 1: technical, strategic, and doctrinal. The involvement of the defense industrial manager in decisions of each type provides insight into both the potential influence of the defense managers and the constraints under which they operate.

The defense industrial managers, like all other managers, appear to have some flexibility in making technical decisions. For the defense manager, however, this marginal independence is constrained by an institutionalized kibitzer, the voyenpred. The military, unwilling to leave technical decisions completely to the supply ministries, requires that all changes meet with their approval.

The defense manager personally does not seem to be involved in raising technical issues. This is probably left to the plant's chief engineer and designers, and probably takes place informally with the voyenpred.

While it is possible that the manager participates in persuading the military that a change or choice will have no negative impact on the weapon's performance, representing the views of his staff if a question is pushed upstairs to the ministry, there is little reason to expect a manager to be deeply committed to such a decision unless the decision will have an impact on the plant's schedule or productivity.

Technical decisions about the plant's production base will always involve the manager, and these will have an impact on the weapons procurement process. Production of the SS-18 ICBM, for example, was delayed by more than a year as a consequence of decisions made at the production level. Rather than relying on a West German firm which was ready and willing to provide necessary equipment, the task of producing such machine tools was turned over to the the Soviet Institute of Production Technology for domestic development and production.[74]

STRATEGIC DECISIONS

What the managers appear to lose in the technical decision making, they may gain in the area of strategic decision making. While they are not making foreign policy or defense decisions, they are making a number of strategic *economic* recommendations and decisions. In their writings, they raise a wide variety of issues involving, for example, economic planning and incentives, quality control, and cadre policies. They regularly challenge the existing institutional structure's efficacy and propose alternatives, relying on evidence from their own experiences.

And there are clear cases of lobbying, not for specific products, but for changes in the economy's managerial techniques. They frequently appear to experiment with management techniques in an effort to fulfill their assigned tasks, and, if these experiments appear successful, to propagate their views through the press or through the ministry. They also regularly criticize the "central organs" of administration, and argue for changes in the way Gosplan, Gossnab, and the ministry engage in coordination and planning.

The decisions to undertake management reforms also appear to be made at the plant level; the reports of the various systems frequently emphasize that BIP, KANARSPI, or SBT, for example were developed at the initiative of a particular plant, although approval by the ministry was certainly necessary. And the reports by the plants imply considerable flexibility in implementing these experimental programs.

DOCTRINAL DECISIONS

Economic decisions often occupy a borderline realm between strategic and doctrinal decisions. Plant managers are outside any direct involvement with doctrinal decisions, but their participation in strategic economic decisions clearly influences doctrinal decisions. The innumerable economic "experiments" undertaken and promoted by the political leadership and the subsequent efforts to apply more broadly the lessons of these experiments often border on the doctrinal; the underlying logic of the 1965 Kosygin reforms and its variants, for example, had broad implications for Soviet society.

But the plant managers typically lack an institutional base to participate in doctrinal decisions, except through their ministries. There are only two or three plant managers on the Central Committee, and these are from the automobile industry rather than the defense ministry.[75]

Defense plant managers may retain personal ties to various political leaders who have worked in a region, but it is not possible to assess the importance of such ties.

THE DECISION PROCESS

The plant managers are, of course, one of the most important actors in the implementation of any decision, but it is clear that they are also involved frequently in initiation and persuasion. Their articles regularly emphasize the new managerial techniques, for example, pioneered at the plant, and one purpose of the article appears to be to persuade others (either in the leadership or other designers) of how useful the "new" system can be.

There are also several indicators that the managers engage in frequent discussions with Gosplan or the customer (the military) over their assignments, presumably during the persuasion phase. As one designer noted, "the management of the plant will inevitably 'raise hell', claiming that [a] device is unfit for mass production and that the documentation is defective, no matter how well it is actually done."[76] Aware of what will probably be required from their plant, the managers struggle to reduce the requirement and/or increase the resources available.

In general, the manager appears interested not in questions of national security or foreign policy per se, but in how they will affect his plant's ability to complete its assigned tasks. And there appears to be a sense that the "assigned tasks," even when undertaken for national security purposes, are seen as a burden, assigned by individuals often out of touch with the realities of production requirements and capabilities.

ROUTES OF INFLUENCE FOR THE MANAGER

In pursuing his plant's (or his personal) interests, the plant manager can rely on several different means to reach key decision makers. As indicated, the manager is seldom involved in national-level organizations other than the Supreme Soviet. This may be the reason that he appears to rely on both the mass media and the more specialized press to reach other managers and (presumably) their overseers. This use of the press is apparently also acceptable because their writings are almost exclusively on questions of economic management, a generally accepted topic of discussion.

The second route that is officially sanctioned, of course, is the active participation by the managers in decisions made by their ministries, providing input on a range of issues. This is especially true during the planning process. While the plan is formulated initially in Gosplan and the ministry, with the oversight of the Department of Defense Industry, the plant manager, as the "point man" in the implementation of any decision, is able to shape the process by being able to impede implementation unless sufficient resources are made available. The reports by Agursky and Fedoseyev suggest how much independent influence the plants can have, perhaps not in starting or stopping a project, but in delaying its implementation for some time. While it is unlikely that the manager can simply say "no" to a project, the manager is in an excellent position to emphasize the need for increased resources in the event of changes in the plan, etc. And, given the importance of his product, he probably has the ability to call on high-level support in acquiring resources from other, less important facilities.[77]

Personal and unofficial connections are more difficult to assess, as so much of this sort of politicking would naturally take place behind the scenes.[78] The managers are expected to take an active role in community affairs, which would bring them into frequent contact with a number of the leading officials. For example, A. M. Makarov, director of the Urals Southern Machine-Building Plant, has been a member of the Ukrainian Communist Party's Central Committee and has served on various specialized subcommittees, possibly bringing him into regular contact with Politburo member V. V. Shcherbitskiy. But with the scant evidence available, it is not possible to build a case that these ties are systematically used for lobbying purposes.

CONCLUSIONS

When the hypotheses suggested at the beginning of this chapter are compared with the data available, a number of interesting conclusions can be drawn. Specifically, it is clear that the plant managers do lobby for greater resources or, at least, a more reliable supply of already granted resources. There is no evidence of the managers calling upon the military to help press their case, and they appear to rely heavily on the open media (presumably, this is but one visible indicator of the more pointed discussions going on through official channels).

In contrast to the hypothesized behavior of the manager in a military industrial complex, the Soviet defense industrial managers never refer to foreign affairs, defense issues, or "the threat" at all. No director wrote of matters outside his immediate domestic interests, and no director even claimed that his plant and its work had a special "national significance." The evidence from the open media shows no effort by these individuals to influence national security or foreign policy, and the memoir and émigré literature makes no mention of such efforts taking place behind the scenes. While this is not surprising in and of itself, it is interesting to compare it with the more open discussions in the military press of defense economics.

For example, in none of the defense manager's statements can one find the question of balance between the "A" (heavy) and "B" (light) industries. One finds more discussion of this issue in the military press in the late 1960s, as military authors began to suggest that a healthy civilian economy with adequate consumer goods was a necessary prerequisite to a healthy *defense* economy.

This is not to suggest, however, that the managers said nothing of importance. Their public statements serve the useful functions of distilling and distributing what they have learned in their experiences in an industry where higher standards of quality are necessary and in which they must compete more directly with foreign producers. The articles by these professional managers are by no means empty "fluff" pieces or mere rhetoric, but are often interesting and useful (if not always original) discussions of new approaches to problems that have plagued industrial managers in the Soviet Union for years.

There are also clear cases of advocacy, but in areas of management rather than foreign or defense policy. These cases occur both in the media and, to an undetermined degree, behind the scenes.

On the question of supply, the writings of the defense industry managers suggest that the Soviet defense industry may not enjoy the immunity to problems often assumed; it is certainly clear that the managers are not satisfied with whatever degree of special protection they may have. These managers complain just as much as their civilian counterparts about the vagaries of supply and the unpredictability of suppliers. In addition, unpredictable supply hampers rhythmic production, leading to "storming," i.e., the concentration of output at the end of the month (or other planning period). This jeopardizes quality and requires payment of overtime (hardly an efficient use of resources) and threatens the quality of production, and has been a problem in the defense industrial ministries and within the production and repair plants maintained by the Ministry of Defense itself.[79]

It is thus interesting to note the apparent role played by these plants and their directors in the development of various management systems. NOT was improved upon in an engine plant, earning its director a State Prize and, apparently, a two year assignment as a deputy minister of aviation industry. The Saratov and KANARSPI systems were also first developed at aircraft plants. One of the directors involved in implementing KANARSPI (I. S. Silayev) was promoted to deputy minister of the aviation industry, and eventually became minister. In 1985, Gorbachev made him a deputy chairman of the Council of Ministers. Ryzhkov, another key actor in the Gorbachev leadership, directed a plant that produced military hardware and heavy equipment, eventually moving through Gosplan to the Politburo. Voronin moved through the Ministry of Defense Industry's ranks, then through Gosplan until he was appointed head of the Gossnab.

While the men who moved up (and about whom we have detailed background information) wrote about innovations in their plants, they were not alone in this. In fact, others who wrote frequently about their accomplishments or who were used a models for others (for example, Stepanchenko or Khvedeliyani) did not move upwards at all.

The relationship between writings and promotion is, of course, complex, but there does appear to be a discernible trend: those who have moved into more important positions have been involved in innovative and interesting developments such as NOT and KANARSPI, while those who seemed to act more as implementers than as innovators (for example, Stepanchenko or Khvedeliyani) remained in their managerial posts.[80]

In general, the defense plant manager appears in many ways to be *first* a plant manager, and only second a *defense* plant manager. His concerns are those of plant managers in general, applicable to a broad range of management issues.

CHAPTER FOUR

THE WEAPONS SCIENTIST AND THE DESIGNER

The military designer or the scientist involved in weapons development is in a special position in the Soviet Union: he works in the secrecy-shrouded military industries, yet, with his technical expertise and apparent dedication to the defense of the Soviet state, he is an ideal model of the "new Soviet man," for others to emulate and for the state to present.

He is often respected for his expertise by various policymakers, and sometimes given enough prominence to write his own ticket. Because of the nature of his work, he is in frequent contact with the production sector of society, the decision makers, and, of course, the military itself. As a result, he should be aware of both the potential of the Soviet economy and its limitations.

This chapter will discuss the role of the designer (responsible for the engineering of a weapon system) and the scientist (responsible for the basic research employed by the designers) and their impact on policy.[1]

It will discuss the backgrounds of designers and scientists, how they might be able to influence policy through formal and informal procedures, and the issues they have raised or with which they have been associated. The means they have to shape policy include the state's reliance on their technical competence, the informal contacts developed over the years, and their formal position in their ministries. Their prestige and position have made the occasional foray into foreign and military policy possible, but only in exceptional circumstances.

As with the industrial managers, it is useful to suggest the specific indicators that one might expect to find associated with designers and scientists in a military industrial complex. Like the managers, it might be expected that designers and scientists would emphasize the foreign "threat" and the Soviet potential to counter it. Designers and scientists, however, might be expected to emphasize the technical aspects of the west's capabilities. They would also likely emphasize *technical* means of countering any western advantages, rather than arguing, for example, for greater numbers of a particular weapon system or for their operational use in new ways.

As will be discussed in greater detail below, the Soviet designer is pulled in two different directions. On the one hand, the Soviet system is structured in such a way as to reward new designs which can be put into production and enter the inventory quickly. As a result, there is a pressure to make numerous modifications to existing systems, relying, whenever possible, on the creative use of existing technology.

On the other hand, there is likely to be a natural desire to be on the cutting edge of Soviet technology. While this desire is probably especially common among the basic scientists, designers are also likely to find that the more creative and more technically innovative the work, the more interesting it is. This would be reinforced by the perceived need to minimize or negate any surprise that the Soviets might suffer in the event of a *western* technical breakthrough. In addition, the pursuit of high technology allows one to make extensive demands on resources. If such technology is promising and can be successfully promoted to the decision-making elite, it can mean virtually unlimited resources for the designer or scientist.

In a military industrial complex, one would expect to find designers and scientists arguing (in public and in private) for technical solutions to defense and security problems and for the allocation of resources to basic and applied research. Their view of a threat will probably focus on an adversary's *technical* capabilities. This would also seem reasonable in any Soviet military industrial complex, as the military press frequently contains articles discussing the technical capabilities of western military equipment.

There are thousands of designers and scientists participating in Soviet weapons development programs, but all are not of equal stature. A design bureau (KB) or scientific research institute (NII) has a number of designers on its staff, as do production plants, but only a small number of designers in the Soviet Union have the stature (and title) of Chief Designer or General Designer.[2] Soviet military designers have historically been more visible than the scientists responsible for the basic research or the managers responsible for the serial production of the weapons.

According to the U.S. Department of Defense, in 1986 there were fifty-two major design bureaus in the Soviet Union, divided as shown in table 4.1.[3]

It is possible to identify a number of the missile, aircraft, and tracked vehicle design bureaus; data on ship, satellite, and radar design bureaus are relatively scarce.

In general, identifying Soviet military designers is seldom easy. While aircraft have the designer's initials in the aircraft's number, such as the Su prefix indicating a Sukhoi product or the MiG prefix of the Mikoyan and Guryevich bureau, missiles are not, as far as is known, named after their designers. Thus one reason for selecting the designers considered in this study is that they are identifiable through a combination of techniques: some are identified in western sources, some are identified by their position in obituaries of other designers, some by their own obituaries, some through inclusion in various military reference works or memoirs, some through their election to government or party posts. Almost certainly new designers are entering the scene each year. How-

---

TABLE 4.1. Soviet Military Design Bureaus

Specialization	Number
Strategic missiles and space boosters	8
Tactical missile	9
Aircraft	9
Ships	6
Satellites	6
Tracked vehicles and artillery	7
Radars	8

Source: U.S. Department of Defense, *The FY 1987 Department of Defense Program for Research and Development*, p. II-6.

ever, it seems likely that even the new designers have served time in the established design bureaus (just as the missile designers served in aircraft design bureaus), and thus have probably been influenced by their experiences there.

A second reason for using these designers is that they appear to be the most prominent or dominant in their fields. Some are members of the Academy of Sciences, and many are winners of prizes awarded by the state. Some are members of the Communist Party Central Committee, and some are members of the Supreme Soviet. Most have been chief or general designers for many years.

And a third reason is that many of these appear to have been designing through the 1960s and 1970s.[4] The continuity of these designers is at times startling, reflecting how young many were when they began their careers, often before or during World War II.

BACKGROUND

Virtually all the designers about whom biographical information is available received their higher education in technical institutes, the most common being the Moscow Aviation Institute and the Moscow Higher Technical School im. Bauman. It should also be noted that most designers went immediately into design or engineering work upon graduation from school.

It is not the longevity per se of the designers that is important, but the lessons they appear to have learned in the Great Patriotic War. While it is common (and correct) to argue that there are a few basic tenets of Soviet design philosophy (simplicity, producibility, low cost, and reliability), it is useful to note the reinforcement of these guidelines not only through the Soviet incentive structure for designers, but also in the discussions by designers in the 1960s and 1970s of the war experience. Also, as noted in chapter 2, Soviet production and scientific-production associations (POs and NPOs) were being established in the 1960s, and these bear a striking resemblance to war-era design and production combines.

A number of the most important designers have become candidate or full members of the Academy of Science, generally in the Department of Mechanics and Control Processes.[5] These individuals have included several aircraft designers;[6] missile designers;[7] specialists in space and missile computers;[8] as well as a designer of submarines (including the most recent ballistic missile submarine, the Typhoon)[9] and a leading figure in ABM development.[10]

Membership in the Academy is one of the most prestigious honors granted to a Soviet scientist, and with it comes a new status. While it probably does not impart influence to a designer or scientist, it may, like membership in the Central Committee, *reflect* an individual's real or potential impact.

PERSONAL AND PROFESSIONAL TIES

Personal and professional ties take many forms in the Soviet Union, ranging from outright patronage to simple friendship because of neighboring dachas. These relationships, of course, are not fixed in stone, and a professional relationship can evolve into a personal one, and vice versa. For example, two careers may intersect in Dnepropetrovsk, leading to a friendship that continues after the common intersection is over. Or, because of an existing friendship or family ties, an individual may be promoted or otherwise benefit. The best example of these types of relationships, intertwining professional and personal, is probably Brezhnev's Dnepropetrovsk "mafia," the group with whom Brezhnev worked while in that city and whose members were promoted with or by Brezhnev.[11]

Personal or professional ties are one of the important factors that a weapons designer is able to use, and these individuals move in relatively high-level circles. Recognized as an expert in perhaps the most critical areas of Soviet science, engineering and production (and one of the few in which Soviet developments are considered by some to be world class), the Soviet weapons designer is honored with prizes and elected to both important and symbolic positions (for example, the Central Committee, the Academy of Sciences, and the Supreme Soviet). Most are also based in Moscow. Perhaps as important, the CPSU General Secretary during most of the period under study, L. I. Brezhnev, had apparently been closely involved with monitoring defense production, especially in the missile area.[12]

While Khrushchev appears to have known many designers in his capacity as First Secretary (later called General Secretary), Brezhnev knew many of the key designers *before* his appointment as General Secretary and was at least interested in the issues. While this is not to argue that Brezhnev would have given the designers a "free ride" in weapons development, it might suggest that these individuals had relatively easy access to Brezhnev that others did not.

One factor that comes into play in developing personal connections is the intersection of the longevity of the designers and the upward mobility of local Party officials: relationships (professional and personal) established with a local Party official can be expected to bring results if that official moves up in the Party hierarchy. A good example is probably that of M. K. Yangel, whose design bureau in Dnepropetrovsk, brought him into connection with both Brezhnev and Vladimir V. Schcherbitskiy through the 1950s. While Brezhnev's experiences in the area (both technical and geographical) have already been noted, Shcherbitskiy's experience was longer and possibly closer. He served as a Secretary in the Dneprodzerzhinsk Gorkom and Obkom, then the Dnepropetrovsk Obkom before becoming a Secretary for the Ukrainian Central Committee. His move into the Politburo as a Brezhnev ally may have given Yangel two powerful "connections" within the Politburo, as well as giving two Politburo members a source of expertise they had known for twenty or more years.[13]

It is difficult to obtain information on the personal links between Brezhnev and various designers, of course, for the post-1964 period. While it seems reasonable to conclude that the relationships developed during Brezhnev's tenure as Secretary with defense industrial responsibilities continued, it is difficult to find confirming evidence in the Soviet literature. Emigré literature alludes to the importance of links with the political leadership, but provides little first-hand evidence. One émigré author argues that personal connections "are everything, basically everything," in the struggle for resources, because resources are allocated by a small number of people. These individuals are seldom, if ever, technically literate, and thus often unable to make effective decisions. Often, according to Firdman, they must fall back on their personal knowledge of the individual or his or her track record, rather than the potential of any new proposal.[14]

Another émigré, Anatol Fedoseyev, reports that during his tenure as a radar designer (until 1970), "connections to the highest circles of the Soviet power structure gave me a certain clout and weight which I could use to push a specific project."[15] The only examples he provides of using this influence, however, are not in the development of specific weapons system, but were attempts to establish a new ministry for electronics and to increase the wages paid to his scientific workers.[16]

In the area of missile and rocket design, the most important Soviet designer until his death in 1966 was certainly S. P. Korolev. Korolev was able to persuade the leadership of the potential of missiles and rockets, in part by emphasizing their military utility.[17] Khrushchev was so impressed (as was, presumably, Brezhnev, his secretary for defense industry) that not only was a separate service devoted solely to missiles established within seven years, but he also undertook to convert the Soviet armed forces to extensive reliance on missiles, scrapping surface ships in favor of missile-launching submarines, replacing aircraft with land-based missiles, and cutting deeply into the size and missions of the ground forces.[18]

As a measure of his influence, and the confidence vested in him by the leadership, Korolev had an open budget, i.e., he could spend money without prior approval by a potentially stodgy bureaucracy. In addition, he was able to isolate his staff from many of the normal difficulties encountered in Soviet life, including conscription. Other designers, recognizing his special status, attempted to attach their careers to his in order to benefit from the relative independence and prestige he enjoyed.[19] Only with Korolev's death and replacement by V. P. Mishin did these "perks" dry up.[20]

Korolev was able to use his expertise and the potential achievements of rocketry to garner large-scale support for his work. Others were less successful in attracting political patrons. For example, F. G. Staros, an American who defected to the Soviet Union in the early 1950s and who set up one of the leading electronics labs, frequently found himself in conflict with his superiors. Much of Firdman's memoir about the micro-electronics industry in Leningrad revolves around Staros' neverending attempts to gain support, either for the lab or for a particular project, from Khrushchev, Ustinov, the Central Committee Department of Defense Industry, and a panoply of leading designers and ministers.[21]

Firdman notes that Staros was the beneficiary of the competition for leadership of the microelectronics industry then taking place.[22] A. I. Shokin, who promised Staros full support for his microelectronics laboratory, gained Staros' loyalty and was able to enlist Staros in his efforts to lobby the Department of Defense Industry and the Secretariat. With the establishment of the State Committee on Electronics in 1961, Shokin was the victor.[23] Unfortunately, political tides turned against Staros, and he found himself opposed by both Shokin and Leningrad Party chief G. V. Romanov. When the latter was appointed a candidate Politburo member, the Department of Defense Industry could no longer protect Staros or prevent his lab from being absorbed into a larger NPO.[24]

While thus far the focus has been on high-level connections between, for example, designers and members of the Politburo or Secretariat, it should also be noted that personal and professional relationships play a role at lower levels as well. For example, Chaiko reports that a common technique in the helicopter design bureau is to feed ideas to the military through officers from the General Staff's "Helicopter Department"[25] or the voyenpredy, which then incorporates them into future design objectives. At the same time, these officers are said to resist being used in such a way for fear of having their career tied to someone else's untried idea.[26]

In addition to these personal links, formal and informal, there are a number of organizational positions and links both within the ministry and with other organizations that give the designer some influence on decision making.

Membership in the Academy of Science, as already noted, gives a certain amount of prestige and lends a certain weight to a designer's opinions. Another is the formalized access which a handful of designers may enjoy as a result of membership on the CPSU Central Committee. Not only are a number of military and military-industrial figures elected to the Committee, but each Party Congress also elects several military designers: V. P Glushko, P. D. Grushin, V. M. Makeyev, and V. F. Utkin were each full members of the Committee at the 25th and 26th Party Congresses;[27] G. V. Novozhilov (head of the Ilyushin aircraft design bureau) was added at the 27th Party Congress, presumably replacing either Grushin (who was not reelected at the 27th Congress) or Makeyev (who had died).[28]

But for the designer or scientist, the most important post may be membership on a ministry's Scientific-Technical Council (NTS). As noted in chapter 2, this is an advisory body made up of several leading scientists from within and outside the minstry. The NTS has the responsibility for advising the minister on relevant developments in the field and providing guidance for productive avenues to be explored in the future. While very little is known about the actual functioning of these Councils, it is indicative of their role that the NTS for the Ministry of Defense Industry included Zh. Ya. Kotin, N. A. Kucherenko, F. F. Petrov, and V. A. Tyurin.[29] Each of these individuals was a key figure in the design of particular weapons systems: Kotin and Kucherenko in tanks, Petrov and Tyurin in artillery. In addition, it is known that the Ministry of Aviation Industry's Scientific-Technical Council included A. S. Yakovlev.[30]

While the NTS is an advisory organization, it also serves as a forum to bring together the leading designers and scientists (hence the scientific-technical nature of the council) of the ministry. The organization is in a position to promote specific projects or lines of inquiry, of course, but perhaps more interestingly, there is likely to develop a "mutual-support" function. With the leading scientists both in competition within the ministry (over the resources available) and serving on the same board, it seems reasonable to expect that marginal projects will be supported in return for support of other marginal projects. [31] Of course, this does not mean that the minister or his staff will support these projects; the NTS is not a decision making or policy formulation body.

In addition to the permanent Scientific-Technical Council, the Soviets rely on design competitions in pursuit of improved military hardware. Meetings are held between competing designers to hash out new designs, design requirements have been given to more than one organization for development, more than one design is often developed within a design bureau, and prototypes have been tested not only in comparison with the original requirements, but also with each other.[32] Membership on these commissions, reviewing the work of others, clearly has an impact on procurement decisions, and here, too, one finds reports of "mutual guarantees."[33]

There is also the effort throughout Soviet decision making to impose "rationality" wherever possible, eliminating subjective decision making. The establishment of ostensibly objective norms should also limit the amount of ad hoc intervention that can take place, so long as the norms are established by the military. The review commissions seek the best design not only among the competing designs, but also in comparison to established criteria, and the designer's incentive structure is based as much on satisfactory production as on acceptance of the design itself.

The question of bringing in senior officials—in essence, appealing to a higher authority for support—is not discussed in great detail in the Soviet literature.[34] Clearly, it is advantageous to a designer engaged in a competition to enlist the support of senior officials whenever possible. Khrushchev reports numerous cases of lobbying by designers of aircraft, missiles, and nuclear weapons in support of a particular project.[35] It seems likely that Brezhnev and Ustinov, each with much closer ties to the defense production community than Khrushchev had had, would be subject to similar efforts, although perhaps they might have been better able to assess critically any proposals.

And, of course, the Soviet system (like most governments) is designed to minimize the necessity of leadership involvement and intervention in narrow, technical issues better left to the military specialists. With the increasing cost and complexity of prototype development, the system is designed specifically to *resolve* competition as early in the process as possible, and at the lowest level in the hierarchy (although there is almost certain to be the desire at times to kick the problem upstairs).

Under Brezhnev, there also appears to have been an increased emphasis on collective decision making at the Politburo level.[36] It seems unlikely that a single official at the Politburo or other high-level would be able to intervene successfully and systematically without risking the combined wrath of his peers. This was one of the key charges levelled against Khrushchev.[37] In addition to other members of the senior political leadership (the Politburo and the Secretariat), the Central Committee staff still keeps a close eye on the developments of its charges, requiring periodic reports.[38]

In general, there also seems to be nothing comparable to the "pork-barrel" politics that takes place in the Untied States, in which the approval of a new weapons system may mean increased jobs, and increased jobs may mean increased votes for a member of Congress. In a state without democratic traditions or institutions, much of the pressure to accept and produce a particular weapons system is lacking, and, as indicated in the previous chapter, what pressure exists may be in the opposite direction.

From the designer's side, there are also several factors that reduce the incentive to seek intervention outside the normal, established process. First, design bureaus do not appear to operate on a "feast or famine" cycle. Once a project is completed, work is started on the next modification or system, much as on an assembly line.[39] The product of the design bureau, in many ways, is the design and its modifications, and the process of design is a long-term one. A designer and his bureau can be successful while producing only a small number of weapons systems. An extreme example is that of S. G. Simonov, a gun designer of World War II and the postwar era. Although he designed one hundred guns, only three were accepted into the inventory. Yet he is considered a successful leading designer.[40] The leading designer of Soviet solid-fueled missiles, A. D. Nadiradze, has been responsible for a number of marginal weapons systems (the SS-13 and SS-16 in particular), yet he continues to work in the field and receives awards, perhaps for the basic work that is eventually incorporated into his missiles.

This is not to suggest that designers are forever safe. For example,

Myasishchev lost his bureau and was moved to the directorship of the Central Aerohydronamics Institute (TsAGI) after his failed attempts at building an intercontinental bomber. But it does suggest that "new" designs can be years apart in a successful bureau, and the Soviets recognize that the cost of design work are relatively small compared to the potential returns.

Besides the personal intervention of the political leadership, of course, the designer can seek to influence the military. Chaiko reports frequent efforts by designers to generate enough interest in their projects that these ideas will be incorporated in the design of a new helicopter.[41] At the same time, however, there are clearly arguments between the customer and the designers. Chaiko notes that General Staff requirements are

> almost inevitably modified by the designers and builders, who invariably seek more favorable initial conditions for themselves, claiming inferior quality of materials and machine tools technological lag, etc. . . . During negotiations on the military and technical specifications for a new helicopter, which occurs when the Ministry of Defense submits its requirements to the Ministry of Aviation Industry, the General Staff's Helicopter Department usually concedes on questions of quality, insisting only that the mission capability of the new helicopter be met regardless of cost.[42]

The Ministry of Defense (apparently advocating a large production run) and the Ministry of Aviation Industry (apparently arguing for a smaller run) present their cases to the Council of Ministers (presumably through the VPK initially)[43] and the Central Committee, and that "depending on the international situation and the domestic economy, the aviation industry may receive more or less development funding for the design and production of a new helicopter."[44]

While the General Staff might call upon the designers as expert consultants, it should be noted that the General Staff maintains its own staff of technically qualified scientists and engineers and the services each have technical institutes.

There are thus at least two potential avenues of influence open to the designer, and either can be based on personal or professional connections. He can attempt to elicit intervention from the political leadership (either by one individual or, for example, by the Department of Defense Industry), or he can lobby the military itself, attempting to persuade them to share his views.[45]

Debates over strategy and operations are decided by the General Staff (or at a higher level, e.g., the Politburo or the Defense Council). Soviet military thought recognizes, however, that neither doctrine nor strategy is fixed, and that each is shaped by technological changes. But technology is just one factor that shapes military doctrine and strategy, and while a creative technical idea may "bubble up" as the result of a new insight by a designer or scientist or as the result of continuing research, the application of such ideas and its future exploitation are decided from above.

One exceptional case of a military designer actively participating in Soviet strategic policy formulation is the career of Academician Aleksandr Shchukin, a specialist in radio propagation, a general-lieutenant in the engineering service reserves, and a delegate to the SALT 1 and SALT 2 talks since the process began in 1969. Prior to his appointment to the Soviet SALT team, Shchukin was closely involved in the Soviet radio and radio-physics industry, serving as deputy chief of a Ministry of Defense main administration from 1949 and in the staff of the Council of Ministers from 1950. Shchukin had worked on radar and ABM systems, missile accuracy and guidance systems, and submarine communication problems.[46] Through the talks, he was also a deputy chairman of the VPK.[47]

But what appears to make Shchukin unusual was his command of strategic matters in general and US strategic thinking in particular, which was characterized by the chief of the U.S. delegation, Gerard Smith, as "unexcelled in the Soviet delegation."[48] In Smith's view, Shchukin

> seemed to recognize the absurdity of uncontrolled competition in strategic arms. As a major general in the reserves, he knew the military bent of mind that tends to think of weapons in the ways of past wars. He once spoke of people who thought of nuclear weapons in terms of a needed number of wheels of artillery per kilometer of front. Shchukin and Paul Nitze conversed regularly in French. These cautious dialogues were helpful to our understanding of Soviet positions.[49]

Shchukin continued to be a SALT delegate through all of SALT 1 and SALT 2, through June of 1979; he received his second Hero of Socialist Labor citation in 1975.

Opportunities for interaction between designers, political leaders, and military officials clearly exist and, in some cases, are institutional-

ized. In order to assess how the designers may have used these opportunities, it is useful to consider the issues that they raised.

OPEN WRITINGS AND ISSUES

In contrast with the Soviet industrial manager, the Soviet defense
designer writes almost nothing in the open literature about his current
work. While there are numerous memoirs by and about designers, these
generally end their discussion about ten years before the work is actually published. It is not unusual to find a work which provides re-
markable detail about a designer's experiences in the Great Patriotic
war and a paragraph or less about his postwar experiences. This is as
might be expected in any country: working in the military field places
a burden on the designer to keep his work secret. This requirement for
secrecy has reportedly led to some designers declining or minimizing
military-related work.[50]

In the military press, the Soviets frequently appear to discuss their
technical problems and issues in the guise of discussing "foreign developments." But this again does not appear to include the designers
themselves. Rarely does it appear that Soviet *designers* discuss foreign
developments in the open press in anything other than a historical
context.[51]

But this does not mean that designers write nothing of interest. They
frequently detail their design philosophies, as formed in the early years
of their career. They also provide details about their peers and subordinates, many of whom continue designing after the author has retired or
died, and their relationships with high-level military or political officials. Their successors are typically former deputies, nurtured in the
environment established by the Chief Designer.[52] At times, they actually do provide some general information about their more recent
work. And some appear to use their historical reflections as a means of
commenting on contemporary events. Complementing this material,
there are also a few works by émigrés who worked within the defense
design and production system, and who provide a richer (but not contradictory) description of the designer's role and impact.

As was the case with the industrial managers, a number of themes
appear in the open writings of the designers. The most common (and
most important) are the emphasis on producibility and the role of
standardization and unification in production. A third theme, criticism
of the val economic measure will also be discussed.

PRODUCIBILITY

In the 1960s and 1970s, the Soviet press (military and civilian) contained a number of articles by and about weapons designers. They are generally memoirs of the Great Patriotic War, and their common theme is the importance of being able to design and produce weapon systems rapidly.[53] "Producibility" refers to the use of readily available designs and/or equipment in a "new" weapon system, reducing the time (and expense) necessary to begin production of a new system.[54]

This emphasis on producibility came at a time when the Soviets were developing the production associations (POs or VPOs) and scientific production associations described in chapter 2, and the views attributed to the designers are consistent with the views that one might expect to find in support of these associations. In particular, the emphasis on close links between designers and engineers fits with the common theme in the recollections of the military designers.

Typical of the time are the comments by V. G. Grabin, an artillery designer who is frequently lauded for his contributions to production techniques as well as for the actual design of artillery.[55] His fast-production technique relied on close cooperation between the designer and the engineer. "In trying to reduce the time for manufacture, the design bureau of V. G. Grabin began to make wide use of the consultations of technologists in the course of planning. This, it would appear, simple solution immediately led to stunning results."[56] In his own recollections of the experience of the Great Patriotic War, Grabin drew attention to how much the close ties between designer and engineer, established during the war, had substantially degenerated by 1969.[57]

Memoirs of the defense industries under Brezhnev also indicate that producibility plays an important role. In his memoirs on the microelectronics industry in Leningrad, Firdman recalls the sudden emphasis on production over design and development that took place in the early 1960s.[58] There is also evidence that the VPK and the Central Committee's Department of Defense Industry decided at about this time to emphasize copying of foreign technical developments in place of supporting wide ranging domestic research.[59]

Both Fedoseyev and Agursky note the inevitable trouble designers have with producers in persuading them of the producibility of a product. According to Fedoseyev, the state testing commission which approves the new weapon for series production "knows in advance that the management of the plant will inevitably 'raise hell,' claiming that the device is unfit for mass production and that the documentation is defective, no matter how well it is actually done."[60] Mikhail Agursky, formerly in the Soviet missile industry, reports that the contract for the serial production of the new SS-18 ICBM was delayed because insufficient allowance had been made for needed production equipment. The plant's management could have used West German equipment, but instead developed their own equipment, in order to have a justification for any delays in the production program.[61]

As is so often the case, the Soviets have pursued administrative solutions to productivity problems: design bureaus and production facilities are collocated, a process which was common during the war, and designers are expected to pay close attention to the actual production of their product. Designers are generally sent to the plants as series production is beginning, and they continually monitor production as it continues.[62]

UNIFICATION AND STANDARDIZATION

One of the keys to ensuring producibility, apparent in the designers' writings, is the process of unification and standardization (*unifikatsiya i standartizatsiya*).[63] While producibility may be one of the (if not *the*) most important factors in designing new weapons systems, unification and standardization were seen as the basis of that producibility, and their importance grew at the end of the 1960s and early 1970s. As one Soviet author noted, "At the end of the 1960s in our country serious attention turned to the long-range development in industry of standardization and unification as effective means of accelerating scientific-technical progress."[64] This "serious attention" may have been responsible for the prominence given to unification and standardization in the literature by and about designers, especially in the mid-1970s. Codified into law in the early 1970s, unification and standardization refer to the use of similar or identical parts in different pieces of equipment, saving on costs and development requirements, keeping the number of products and the means for their production to a "rational minimum."

Specifically, unification is the use of a piece of production equipment or a component in a number of different applications.[65] It has been most extensively applied in the machinebuilding and instrument-making industries, the two leading sectors of the economy for defense production.[66] In addition to applying to pieces of production equipment, unification also refers to the use of the same military technology in different weapon systems or in different branches of the armed forces.[67]

Design unification is the effort to minimize the numbers of types and designs of products, components, and basic materials used in designing a new product (for example, a weapons system).[68] It is considered especially relevant to the development of new technology and work in scientific research and experimental-design work. It was the *only* topic discussed in the open press by then-chief of the Ministry of Defense Industry's Main Technical Administration (and now chairman of Gosplan) Yu. D. Maslyukov.[69] A discussion of missile design by Korolev's successor illustrates how Korolev's bureau applied standards of unification to the SS-6 and its modifications well before required by law.[70] When the "Unified System of Design Documentation" *(YeSKD)* was finally established by law, it was generally codifying a set of rules that had been operating informally for several years, as reflected in the use of the SS-13 as the base for the SS-14 and SS-15 missiles, for example, or the use of the same antiaircraft missile in different systems for the ground forces and the navy.

Production unification is intended to minimize the varieties of raw material or subcomponents necessary to produce a finished article. In the production of military hardware, unification is considered the most effective means of *standardization,* the latter term referring to the types and basic characteristics of machines and instruments used in a variety of production tasks. Standardization is the establishment of norms and indicators based on contemporary production and design capabilities,[71] and its importance was emphasized regularly in the military press.[72] In discussing artillery development during the war, *Tekhnika i vooruzheniye* emphasized that "the task was set to implement one of the most important principles for design engineering—standardization of the designs of those parts, assemblies, and mechanisms which had recommended themselves well in artillery weapons and ammunition, that is, which had already been proven on proving grounds and in the troops."[73] As artillery designer F. F. Petrov noted in 1965, "I wish to stress once more the important role played by the unification and standardization of all military equipment and armament. This cannot be overestimated, especially in connection with series production."[74] Grabin made the same points,[75] as did Zhosef Kotin ten years later[76] and gun designers G. S. Shpagin and S. G. Simonov.[77] An additional facet of the emphasis on unification and standardization is the potential for applying components to nonmilitary production. One author emphasized the "extreme simplification in production technology, which aids in processing parts with machine tools used in the production of nonmilitary products."[78]

The emphasis on unification and standardization was not simply in the relatively low-technology fields such as artillery, but also in aviation and missiles. Sukhoi had a special unification brigade established in his design bureau,[79] and in his designs, like so many designers, he was already practicing the unification and standardization that was being institutionalized. One western analyst characterizes Sukhoi's designs as "classic examples" of the use of concurrent and previous designs on current prototypes, citing the common wing, tails, and cockpit of two different Sukhoi fighters as but one example.[80] In the missile field, Yangel (who died in 1971) is held up as a model in his judicious experimentation with the use of unification in developing rockets and missiles through the 1960s[81] and the development of the SS-6 has already been noted.[82]

It is clear from the Soviet press of the 1960s and 1970s that a conscious effort to highlight the importance of further standardization in military design and production was being undertaken. Regardless of its immediate origin, the emphasis on standardization and unification that the Soviets embraced, especially from the mid-1970s, is a natural consequence of the new interest in cost-effectiveness noted earlier.[83]

ANTONOV AND VAL

While the emphasis on producibility, unification, and standardization was a theme common to a number of designers, one aircraft designer, O. K. Antonov, concentrated on one theme for a number of years. From his post as chief of an aircraft design bureau in Kiev, Antonov was, until his death in 1984, a sharp critic of the principal indicator used to gauge industrial performance: "val" *(valovaya produktsiya)*. And he was not reluctant to express his views. His publications include a book in 1965[84] and, two years before his death, an article for *Trud*.[85] Val refers to a quantitative measure of gross output, and it is precisely the emphasis on quantity that concerned Antonov. As he put it,

It's high time to understand that indices expressed in tons, meters, rubles and so on, since they ceased to be purely accounting and statistical constants and turned into basic indices used for plans issued for different enterprises, have been converted into sole indicators of the production process understanding neither arguments of sense, nor conscience, nor requirements of the customer.[86]

Val Antonov argued, impedes the introduction of new technology. It creates a disincentive for an enterprise or designer to develop new and more effective products because the plan, "based on the number of units produced, is independent of quality."[87]

In place of val, Antonov argued for the development of a system of planning that would allow or encourage the introduction of new technology without penalizing the plant for consequential slowdowns in immediate production.[88]

Although the planning agencies have attempted to develop an alternative to val,[89] it is difficult to give direct credit to Antonov. He was only one of a number of critics who recognized the same problems and suggested similar solutions. On the other hand, his contribution to the debate should not be minimized. His views were widely known, and, given his prominence in a techology-intensive field and his position in a ministry that has historically been involved in attempts to improve the quality of output, he may have been a particularly influential voice among the many.

ISSUES RAISED (CLOSED)

The Soviet designer can, of course, operate behind the scenes as well, and the public writings are probably only indicators of a more active discussion taking place out of sight. While the incentive structure is designed so that an individual can be a successful designer with only a small number of designs being put into production, design bureaus and posts have been lost.[90] There is a financial incentive to develop successful designs, of course, and there is the natural desire of any designer to see his idea put into production and use. When added to the possibility that the designer and the decision makers will periodically meet in an either official or unofficial capacity, it is difficult to believe that the designer will not take an opportunity to lobby for a pet project. A few such cases have been noted earlier in this chapter. The most dramatic, however, and the one about which the most is probably know, is the private campaign of Andrei Sakharov since the late 1950s.

It should be emphasized the Sakharov was apparently not a weapons designer in the sense that Mikoyan designed aircraft or Yangel designed missiles. Sakharov was a scientist, working in a closed facility and conducting the basic theoretical research that would be incorporated into the design of thermonuclear weapons. While he was aware that the work he was doing was specifically for the development of armaments, he was presumably not involved in the engineering of the actual weaponry.

Sakharov was perhaps the most important scientist involved in the development of the Soviet hydrogen bomb, working with his mentor, Igor Tamm. After the detonation of the first Soviet hydrogen weapon in 1953, Sakharov was made a Hero of Socialist Labor and a full member of the Academy of Sciences, the youngest member in the history of the Academy.

Two years later, however, Sakharov raised questions about the actual utility of nuclear weapons with the officer in charge of developing the Soviet strategic missile forces, M. I. Nedelin. Nedelin reportedly told Sakharov "that the country's leaders could make up their own minds when it came to nuclear weapons."[91] The following year, 1956, Sakharov was awarded a second Hero of Socialist Labor Award and the Lenin Prize for his continuing work in the nuclear weapons program. He also began writing about the dangers of nuclear testing.

In 1957, Sakharov began to argue against continued nuclear testing, and he was able to enlist the support of Tamm and Igor Kurchatov, developer of the Soviet's first atomic bomb, in attempting to persuade the leadership to accept a test ban.[92] In 1958, as a result of a memo written by Sakharov, Kurchatov (then in charge of the nuclear testing program) flew to the vacationing Khrushchev in an attempt to dissuade him from a series of tests.[93]

After the Soviets decided to end their moratorium on testing in 1961, Sakharov wrote Khrushchev, urging that the moratorium be continued: "To resume tests after a three-year moratorium would undermine the talks on banning tests and on disarmament, and would lead to a new round in the armaments race—especially in the sphere of intercontinental missiles and anti-missile defense."[94] According to Sakharov, Khrushchev responded in off-the-cuff remarks that the scientists should "leave it to us, who are specialists in this tricky business, to make foreign policy."[95] In his own memoirs, Khrushchev notes that, at the time, "we were under increasing pressure [to resume testing] from our own military."[96] Khrushchev says that Sakharov's petition was discussed "in the leadership," and it was decided to renew testing.[97]

One year later, Sakharov tried to persuade Yefim Slavsky, the Minister of Medium Machine Building, not to undertake yet another test. Sakharov characterized the test as "useless from the technical point of view," and argued that the Ministry was "acting basically from bureaucratic interest."[98] He tried for several weeks to stop the test, even threatening to resign the night before it was to take place. When Slavsky told him that "We're not holding you by the throat," Sakharov turned to Khrushchev, phoning him and begging him to intervene. The test, which was actually moved up to an earlier hour, took place.[99] That same year, 1962, Sakharov was awarded his third Hero of Socialist Labor.

Sakharov also suggested that the Soviet leadership reconsider a United States proposal for a partial test ban; this was accepted in a treaty in 1963, and Sakharov has written that, "It is possible that my initiative was of help in this historic act."[100]

Sakharov was not unopposed, however, on the partial test ban. Vasili Semyonovich Yemel'yanov, a candidate member of the Academy of Sciences and Soviet representative to the UN International Atomic Energy Agency, reportedly "did everything in his power to persuade Khrushchev not to conclude a treaty on the partial prohibition of nuclear weapons tests."[101]

Yemel'yanov had worked in the Ministry of Defense Industry prior to the Great Patriotic War and was chairman of the State Committee on Standards during much of the war. He also worked in the tank industry during the war, with designer N. L. Dukhov. And, like Dukhov, from 1945 he apparently worked in the nuclear industry. Yemel'yanov went on to become the first chairman of the State Committee on the Use of Atomic Energy (GKAE) from 1960–1962, and he headed the Academy of Science Commission on Scientific Problems of Disarmament from 1966 (which he reportedly failed to convene from 1968 to at least 1978).[102]

It was not until the 1968 publication in the West of Sakharov's *Progress, Coexistence, and Intellectual Freedom* that Sakharov lost his security clearance and his post in a Soviet weapons lab, more than ten years after he started personally lobbying the leadership. As Sakharov put it, "The publication of this volume abroad immediately resulted in my being taken off secret projects (in August 1968)."[103]

The Sakharov case is clearly special, in that Sakharov was one of a small number of leading Soviet scientists and designers and, like Korolev or Kurchatov, his personal impact was magnified by the importance of the project on which he was working. His views demanded attention because of his brilliance and the utility of his work to the state. Presumably, whatever influence a leading weapons designer or scientists has will vary with his or her prestige and value to the leadership, the area of expertise, and the area in which they wish to participate: designers and scientists are expected to participate in technical decisions and some strategic decisions within their field. But once out of bounds, their views probably hold little more weight than any other "peripheral" participant; the difference is that their expertise elsewhere is valued sufficiently to ensure a cordial hearing from those involved in policy.

DECISIONS, DESIGNERS, AND SCIENTISTS

The defense designer or scientist, like the plant manager, is likely to be most important in the technical and strategic areas of policy making, that is, in answering the question of *how* an objective can be achieved, rather than the value of the objective itself. And, also like the managers, few have ventured openly into the areas of foreign or defense policy, except on approved occasions. The most important example of one who did, Andrei Sakharov, demonstrated that the Brezhnev leadership felt it need not tolerate such "advice."

Unlike the managers, however, the designer and scientist are specialized enough that their views are likely to be heard, even if there are no visible results, and one, Shchukin, has been an active participant in arms control and security negotiations between the Soviet Union and the United States.[104]

TECHNICAL DECISIONS

As might be expected, Soviet designers are most important in the realm of technical decisions. Designers are, after all, responsible for developing *technical* solutions to problems presented to them; technical decisions are the day-to-day job of the Soviet designer or scientist. Examples would be questions of choosing a klystron or a magnetron for an ABM radar system, or pursuing solid- or liquid-fueled rockets.

This does not mean that technical solutions are easy or clear-cut. In many ways, it is easier to formulate a problem than to find a satisfactory technical response, and the reported disagreements between the military and the designers over how to achieve a given mission reflects this difference. The fact that the designers appear to win these disagreements, that is, the military acquiesces to the technical limitations indicated by the designers so long as the mission is accomplished, indicates the influence the designers have within their specialized domain. While an individual designer is unlikely to be considered the final authority on technical matters, the specialized designing and scientific community probably is.

STRATEGIC DECISIONS

Designers have also been involved in strategic decisions, both in public and behind the scenes, but typically in an advisory or consultative capacity. Like technical decisions, some strategic decisions are stock-in-trade of the military designer, for he is likely to be confronted with technical challenges that do not have immediately apparent solutions.

The emphasis placed in the public writings of the designers on producibility, standardization, and unification are examples of positions on strategic issues taken by designers, as is Antonov's attempts to eliminate val. These are considered strategic questions because they revolve around how society (or, more specifically, the military industrial community) is to solve a general question: how to use resources more efficiently on an industrywide basis. While it is unlikely that anywhere would one find advocacy of "nonproducibility," the Soviet designer's efforts appear to have been part of a continuing, if inexplicit, debate between those favoring continued reliance on tried and true hardware and incremental development and those favoring investment in weapons systems that may prove more capable, but are technically more complex and of unproven reliability.[105] In this same vein, it is noteworthy that none of the designers, in their writings, argued for improving the technical base, but rather emphasized the need to design within the existing production capability of the state.

This is not surprising, for the designer, in contrast to the scientist, must place greater emphasis on the state's production potential. Scientists typically operate in a more theoretical realm than does the designer, or can afford to rely on unique pieces of equipment in their research. The role of the designer, of course, is to integrate the scientist's theoretical work with the state's defense production base.

DOCTRINAL DECISIONS

There are two cases that might be considered efforts to influence doctrinal decisions, but with qualifications. The first is the decision to emphasize missiles over almost every other type of armament, a decision made by Khrushchev but, to some extent, continued by Brezhnev. The belief that a future war, "if the capitalists unleash it," will be fought primarily with nuclear armed missiles (the dominant perspective through the 1960s and into the early 1970s), was a doctrinal decision: it was a conclusion about a likely future event, providing direction for society as a whole and the military in general, raising major questions about resource and manpower allocation, about civil defense, and about the very nature of victory.

It is, however, not clear from primary evidence how much of a role the various missile designers had in the decision. Clearly, they provided the support work, arguing for the potential that missiles had to counter the U.S. nuclear superiority both on the European continent (in the 1950s and early 1960s) and in the continental United States. It seems likely that the designers were extolling the virtues of missiles over other forms of weaponry, although there is little evidence that they directly compared their weapons with other types.[106]

Of equal importance, however, is that the aircraft designers were able to carve out some role for their products in a political leadership that was skeptical of aircraft's contribution. As already indicated, the Soviet intercontinental bomber program was virtually nonexistent under Brezhnev. But the aircraft designers had been able to reach a compromise which saved their product, arguing that missile-carrying aircraft would be useful, providing the best of aircraft and the best of missiles. Although this debate took place prior to the Brezhnev era, much of it lingered through the 1960s and 1970s.

The second attempt to influence doctrinal decisions is more clearcut, and that is Sakharov's effort to persuade the Soviet leadership to forego nuclear testing. Sakharov, as well as his supporters and opponents in the scientific community, were attempting to persuade the leadership to make a *political* decision, not one over technology or reacting to a foreign challenge, but to take the initiative in what were at the time uncharted political seas.

The difference between the Sakharov and the missile-designer cases (assuming there was advocacy by the latter) is instructive. Those advocating the greater production of, and reliance on, missiles were responding to geographic and technical challenges: the U.S. nuclear threat was based out of the range of Soviet weaponry, and the Soviet Union was very vulnerable. At the same time, missile technology would be a major prestige item for the Soviet Union. The development of missiles made the Soviet Union a superpower.

In contrast, a moratorium on testing would—from the leadership's perspective—probably bring *only* prestige value.[107] And the prestige of appearing conciliatory had to be balanced with the prestige of appearing strong and technically capable. In addition, Khrushchev was under pressure from his own military. When compared, the balance sheet might have understandably tilted towards "security through strength, " rather than "security through negotiations."

But perhaps most important, there is no evidence that any of the missile designers opposed an existing policy, as Sakharov did. Sakharov overstepped the bounds, attempting to move from technical expert to political adivser. Both the military's Nedelin and Khrushchev emphasized that decisions about nuclear weapons and foreign policy were best left to the political leadership; proposals were almost certainly acceptable, but advocacy was not.

THE DECISION PROCESS

Designers clearly have played a role at each stage of the decision process. Korolev, Sakharov, and Fedoseyev each attempted to initiate decisions in areas of their own specialization, and then worked to persuade the decision makers of the correctness of their proposals. Some leading designers also initiate, persuade, and make decisions as a result of their institutional position on the ministry's Scientific-Technical Council. And, of course, they also implement the decisions made by others, attempting, for example, to design a new weapon system to satisfy a new requirement.

CONCLUSIONS

A number of conclusions can be drawn from the available material on the defense industrial designers and scientists. The first, and most important, is that designers, like production personnel, do not write about foreign or military policy, although they may write about historical events and their role in weapons work at the time. They do not venture into open advocacy of changes in Soviet foreign or defense policy without risking their effective excommunication from defense work at best, and internal exile or worse, if they continue to press their perspective.

What influence does exist, it appears, may be based on a combination of their organizational position and connections made with up-wardly mobile officials. A number of the leading designers serve as members of various commissions, where they can shape to some extent the future course of Soviet military technology. Others hold positions in the Central Committee, giving them somewhat greater information, if not actual access to the leadership. A small number participate in arms control negotiations with the United States or other powers. And all regularly deal with the military and various military-industrial organizations.

In fact, of the three specialized "groupings" comprising Soviet military industry (the plant managers, the scientists and designers, and the ministry officials), the designers and scientists are probably the closest to the military in outlook. In contrast to the production officials, who must emphasize relatively short-term results of the monthly, quarterly, and yearly plans, the scientists and designers do not have the same "output pressure." Like the military planner, they must think further into the future, trying to determine which technologies will become possible in the next five years or the next twenty-five.

And it is known that designers have had connections with Brezhnev and other members of his coterie. But the impact of these connections can only be guessed at until the memoir literature expands.

It was suggested at the beginning of this chapter that the weapons designers or scientists in a military industrial complex would, like the manager, emphasize the threat posed by an adversary, especially its technical component, and propose technical solutions. In particular, it was suggested that they might emphasize high technology in their arguments. Surprisingly, this has not been the case. Designers and scientists spend virtually no time discussing the threat (perhaps because this is done in great detail by the military), and, at least in their writings, actually emphasize producibility within current capabilities over promoting high technology solutions to technical problems.

No designer or scientist works in a vacuum, and it is not surprising that at least some of the designers have attempted to use their expertise in military technology as a starting point to address broader policy questions. Economic questions and questions of technology management are an accepted subject for the military designers, as was the case for the military-industrial managers. It would be fair to say that weapon design (and, for that matter, production) is an important domestic concern, only incidentally intersecting with the defense or foreign policy areas. How to improve the product of the military industries, rather than how they are to be used, is the area of specific concern.

Whether participating in decisions through their personal ties or professional position, designers and scientists are, typically, treated by the political leadership as technical experts, addressing questions of what *can* be done, rather than as foreign or defense policy advisers, addressing questions of what *should* be done.

CHAPTER FIVE

THE DEFENSE
INDUSTRIAL MINISTRY

In the previous two chapters, we have examined the managers responsible for the production of military hardware and the designers and scientists responsible for its development. The third leg in what might be considered the "triad" of military-industrial matters in the Soviet Union is the leadership and staff of the various ministries. These are the individuals responsible for coordinating the managers and designers, ensuring their funding, and, perhaps most important, shaping the direction of the ministry as a whole, both internally and in its dealings with its customer (the military) and its overseers (the Council of Ministers and, ultimately, the Party leadership). The focus of this chapter is on the minister, his deputy ministers, and the heads of various main administrations; their writings; the role associated with the post they occupy; and the opportunities for informal "networking."[1]

In a military-industrial complex, ministry officials, like their subordinates in the production and design facilities, could be expected to seek greater resources and autonomy. And, as was the case with the plant managers, they might be expected to rely on links with the military (their customer) and to emphasize the potential and capabilities of the enemy and their own potential. At the same time, they would be cautious of becoming merely an appendage of the military.

One would also expect that, as was the case with managers, the defense industry officials would use their public and private access to pursue these objectives. Again, private communication and behind-the-scenes behavior are difficult to examine, but public statements should provide clues about efforts to influence resource decisions. Thus, the information available from and about ministry officials will be tested against the hypotheses that they seek increased resources through support of the military and that their independent efforts to obtain resources complement those of the military.

Because the concentration of resources and authority was considered an important factor in the industrialization of the Soviet Union in the prewar period, industrial ministries were established *to be powerful*. It might be argued that because of the concentration into these ministries, the Soviets were able to industrialize very quickly, not only before World War II, but also during their recovery from it.

By the late 1950s, however, the ministries appeared to have gotten too powerful and, perhaps more importantly, too "bureaucratized," and Khrushchev attempted to break up the ministries with his Sovnarkhozy reform. Within a year of Khrushchev's ousting in late 1964, the ministries were reinstituted, but a continuing series of reforms was undertaken to constrain the growing power of the ministries.

The ministries were not only powerful in relation to their immediate subordinates. Numerous efforts have been made by the Party and state leadership to restrict the ministry's "petty tutelage" of its subordinates, including the *ob"edineniye* reforms, but the ministries have apparently been able to block their successful implementation for years. "As a result, long-range policy concerns are neglected, poor investment decisions are made, and regional priorities are disregarded."[2]

Both Soviet and western observers credit the ministry with being perhaps the most powerful *administrative* body. Gosplan has the authority to investigate problems, but apparently lacks the clout to make changes unless it falls back on the Party or the Council of Ministers. And the Communist Party's criticism of ministries suggests that the CPSU also views the ministries as the most powerful administrative tool, certainly more powerful than Gosplan.[3]

Two other indicators of the independent power of the ministries are also implicit. The first is the frequent mention of how departmental discord or conflict between ministries has paralyzed a project. The fact that such conflict can preclude implementation of a decision to, for example, build a number of new plants for fifteen years indicates the influence ministries have on implementation.

The second is a more oblique indicator: ministries (and their subordinates) frequently operate outside the law. When the objective and result is fulfillment of the plan, and the laws are at times minor, this is an accepted part of Soviet business behavior, and is considered simply creative zeal in accomplishing an assigned task. These individuals are rewarded for their initiative. Sometimes, however, there are cases where the ministry shields someone who has commited an economic crime for personal gain. A report by the USSR Prosecutor General, after referring to a case in which a ministry attempted to protect an association director ordered removed for embezzlement, complained that "there are a good many instances in which hoodwinkers who have been punished by a court for report-padding continue to hold executive positions or ones of equal authority. One might say that this is the direct result of the parochial and departmental influences."[4] The latter terms are commonly used to refer to ministry positions and relations.

Perhaps the most interesting and important discussion on ministerial influence is that of Tatyana Zaslavskaya, a member of the Academy of Science's Economic Department and head of the Academy's Institute of the Economics and Organization of Industrial Production. Zaslavskaya refers to the "hidden opposition" that retards reform efforts, leading to their slow implementation and "in a compromise fashion." As a result, "the present system of management of the economy stubbornly retains its existing features."[5] One of the problems is "the extent that the reorganization of the existing system of production is given over to social groups that occupy a somewhat elevated position within this system and accordingly are bound to it through personal interest."[6]

The idea that the personal interests of certain groups restricts the implementation of reform is important, especially when coupled with the implications of her argument about ministries. Zaslavskaya implies throughout her report that the influence of Gosplan and the enterprises has diminished, while that of the ministries has increased: "the functions of the intermediate link of management—the ministries and [ministerial] departments (with their territorial organ)—patently suffer from hypertrophy."[7] More importantly, she seems to be associating the bulk of the "hidden opposition" with the ministry personnel—some of whom "occupy numerous 'cosy niches' with ill-defined responsibilities, but thoroughly agreeable salaries."[8]

The *ob"edneiniye* reforms are a good example of ministerial influence. It is apparent that a number of ministries opposed the effort to merge separate production units into larger associations and to have these associations replace the ministry's main administrations. As Holmes notes, "evidence of both lack of enthusiasm for and over opposition to the *ob"edneineya* from higher state organs — ministries, [ministerial departments], [ministerial administrations], and generally all bodies above the associations—is abundant."[9] While the reform was not stopped, it apparently was slowed or in some cases weakened considerably. A common problem in the Soviet system is expecting those organization most affected by reforms to implement those reforms as well.

THE MINISTRY LEADERSHIP

In considering the influence of the ministries, it is necessary to consider the individuals who occupy the "cosy niches" referred to by Zaslavskaya. In Soviet ministries, it is often only the minister who is well known (and in some cases, not even he is), supported by a faceless and nameless bureaucracy. Perhaps as a consequence, it is easy to slip into the assumption that these bureaucrats are simply automatons, following the lead of the party. But by doing so, we risk forgetting that in many ways, these individuals are the "point men" for fulfilling the objectives of the state and party, as well as the senior arbiters, if not experts, on a subject.[10] In addition, the minister and his deputies bear "personal responsibility" for the activities of his or her ministry.[11] This clearly reflects an assumption by the political leadership about the competence of these individuals, and should suggest that considerable authority is granted to them.

But these men and women (again, in the case of the ministries responsible for military production, all identified personnel are men) are unlikely to be only passive observers of policy formulation and implementers of the results. Writing about the pollution of Lake Baikal, Valentin Rasputin asks a pointed question about the Ministry of Timber, Pulp, and Paper, and Lumber Industry that presumably applies to other ministries, including those in the defense industries:

In the ministry, they take refuge in sonorous phrases about the fact that they carry out the decisions of the party and government. But aren't decisions at that level preceded by numerous expert inquiries, computations, and, finally, the approvals of representatives of science, the ministries and the departments? [12]

Unfortunately, in examining the defense industrial ministries, documentation of even the "sonorous phrases" is limited. But there are the writings of some of those who have become administration chiefs or deputy ministers, as well as some information on the impact of the positions these people hold.

The general organization of a ministry has already been discussed in chapter 2. In their dealings with subordinate organizations, it is important to recall that the ministries are responsible for coordinating the financing of research, development, and production within the ministry and with Gosplan; and that decisions appear to reflect the group decision making of the collegium, responsible for making "collective" decisions and ensuring their implementation. In their work with other organizations such as the Central Committee, the Council of Ministers, or the military, however, the ministry has control over much of the information needed to make decisions and, ultimately, control over the implementation of a decision made elsewhere.

ORGANIZATIONAL POSITION

In general, the responsibility of the deputy ministers and administration heads is to oversee a particular branch within the ministry. Subordinate to them are one or more administrations, each with its own set of responsibilities. As noted earlier, these branches might become so self-contained that they can be broken off from their parent ministry and become a ministry in their own right. This was the case with the establishment of the Ministry of Machine Building, formerly a part of the Ministry of Defense Industry. Similarly, the Ministry of General Machine-Building was established, at least in part, due to the belief that the Ministry of Aviation Industry was not providing sufficient support for the missile industry. The dividing line between ballistic missiles (General Machine Building) and air-breathing missiles (Aviation Industry) provided a convenient point of division. [13]

In addition, the deputy ministers oversee the testing of new designs (this may be the role of a deputy minister responsible for the technical administration), and both the deputy minister and the administration head have important roles in managing the resources of their subordinates.

Each deputy minister and administration head, like the minister himself, operates on *yedinonachaliye* (one-man authority), giving him considerable administrative responsibility.[14]

As members of the ministry's collegium, these individuals take part in the ministry's collective decision process.[15] It is likely to be in the collegium (or within the agenda-setting process for the collegium) that each strives for the achievement of his objectives, whether personal or organizational, and where competing claims are resolved or managed. Unfortunately, there is no firsthand evidence of collegium meetings in the defense industries.

The position of the deputy minister or the administration chief carries with it considerable influence; in many ways, the deputy ministers are the minister's inwardly turned eyes and ears. And while the minister's power appears to be rooted in his command of the material (provided to him by his staff) and his position in both the Council of Ministers and the Central Committee,[16] the influence of his deputies presumably is based on who is able to obtain the minister's support and effectively work with the other collegium members. As Ellen Jones has pointed out, "the high value placed on building consensus and promoting participation by all 'interested parties' in the policy process frequently results in compromise solutions."[17]

These ministry personnel also have immediate control over the allocation of resources for projects, which allows them to shape the direction of research. Firdman reports a project which was quashed by a senior ministry official who felt if the Americans weren't doing it, it was not worth the Soviets' pursuing it.[18] Fedoseyev reports that "Form 4," in which the required resources for a project and its timetable are detailed, must go through the main administration and, frequently, to the minister.[19] Even then, the effective designer uses Form 4 to obtain funds for his *next* project because of the time-delays involved: "To rely on equipment supplied in accordance with Form 4 is unrealistic."[20]

In his memoirs of working in the helicopter industry, Lev Chaiko writes of similar frustrations, although he does not lay responsibility at the feet of a particular deputy minister. According to Chaiko, problems with financing arise when a new idea has moved from research to testing.

At this point, the Design Bureau must turn to the Ministry of Aviation Industry to request funding for the research [presumably through the administration—PA]. In other words, the work expands beyond the Design Bureau, which must justify any allocations it receives with positive results. Positive results, in turn, make it necessary for the management to grapple with launching industrial production of the innovation, disrupting established manufacturing processes and creating a situation most Soviet executives strive to avoid. Not only can rewards justifiably be expected to fall far short of off-setting expenditures of resources, even if positive results are obtained; the potential losses resulting from failure are too great to risk.[21]

Fedoseyev and Firdman each make the point that this system gives considerable control to the ministry's planning departments, "which understand nothing about science and technology."[22]

The ministry's (or, more accurately, the ministerial *personnel's*) reluctance to undertake a new project is also fueled by the fear of being tied into a potentially risky project, one that might backfire and fail. Especially when a system emphasizes "personal responsibility," it is understandable that those making decisions will tend towards caution. Firdman, recalling the development of the UM-1 airborne computer system in the late 1950s, points out that the State Committee on Radio Electronics was not interested in moving beyond the prototype stage, despite Ustinov's enthusiasm for it.[23] This immobility was due to several factors: fear of being responsible for the computer in field conditions, a belief that if it failed it could seriously damage the further development of microelectronics, and a lack of desire to undertake large-scale production of the device.[24]

In addition to controlling funding, the ministry personnel also serve as a higher level to which responsibility can be passed. One of the most obvious techniques, of course, is the reliance on commissions to approve proposals and designs. While these serve the real function of evaluating the finished product, they are also established in such a way as to move some responsibility upwards, to the deputy minister responsible for overseeing testing and to the other members of the commission.

But more likely is disagreement over the potential of a new idea. If a project is risky or uncertain, or has no clear-cut application, any decisions are moved upstairs.[25] There is an incentive for each level to attempt to "boot" the problem upstairs. Fedoseyev notes that moving conflicts over proposed projects up into the ministry is very good for managers, as it places responsibility for risky projects at higher and higher levels.[26]

The deputies have earned the confidence of the leadership and the approval of the Department of Defense Industry as managers, and, as has been suggested, many of them worked their way up through the production system. The criteria of scientists (and, perhaps in particular, émigré scientists) such as Fedoseyev or Firdman are likely to be quite different.[27] Their views may be unusually harsh: subordinates who are, in general, disaffected from the Soviet Union should not be expected to sing the praises of their superiors. And they do not.

A criticism that occurs in both Firdman and Fedoseyev's memoirs is that the further from the actual "hands-on" positions—scientist or production staff—the less capable technically become the individuals.[28] Fedoseyev strongly criticizes the deputy minister overseeing his work in the 1960s, K. Mikhaylov, characterizing him as an "alleged" gyroscope specialist and suggesting that Mikhaylov's orders, recognized as stupid by all those involved, were carried out to ensure "Party discipline." Mikhaylov threatened Fedoseyev with both administrative and Party penalties when he questioned the deputy minister's orders.[29]

It is interesting to compare this with the attitude of Ye. P. Slavsky when Sakharov threatened to resign, described in the previous chapter. In both cases, the ministry official was dealing with a, if not *the*, key scientist or designer in a field, and the official felt that his position was strong enough to allow him to be personally abusive, risking resignation in at least one case. Again, the administrative official appears to have held all the cards and the designer or scientist could do little about it, even when he went outside the ministry for support.[30]

It seems reasonable to expect that mid-level personnel may be particularly conscious of "Party discipline," as, given their responsibilities and proximity to the top, they probably risk being scrutinized more closely for orthodoxy. While lower levels might toy with innovation (indeed, they are officially encouraged to be innovative), the mid-level people riding over them are likely to tend toward greater caution.[31] It might be suggested that the further from the center of authority, in administrative as well as geographical terms, the more able one is to experiment at the edges of sanctioned research.

This seems to imply that one of the key roles of the mid-level ministry officials is less to generate innovation and more to ensure that plans are fulfilled. Whatever innovation does take place, while not in spite of these officials, is perhaps best thought of as an incidental result of the ministry's emphasis on production.

Evaluating the informal connections of the mid-level administrators is very difficult. As already noted, the deputy ministers and administration heads seldom find themselves on national, republic, or local organizations. These places seem reserved for either more senior officials (such as ministers) or nominally subordinate, but more prominent, officials (such as designers and plant managers). This arrangement, of course, confuses whatever clear lines of authority might otherwise exist: would cruise missile designer and Central Committee member P. D. Grushin have more influence than deputy minister M. A. Il'in, Grushin's apparent superior, but *not* on the Central Committee?

The new deputy minister or head of a main administration, when it comes to allocating resources, is likely to have a preassembled group of contacts. Firdman in particular emphasizes the importance of personal connections for the scientist or designer applying for funds to the ministry; the flip side is the deputy minister or administration chief who, because of his organizational origin, has close ties to a particular plant or OKB. For example, would it not be reasonable to expect (and equally difficult to prove) that the Sukhoi design bureau benefited from the fact that a close associate of Sukhoi, M. P. Simonov, went on to be deputy minister of aviation industry?[32]

BACKGROUNDS OF THE OFFICIALS

The most striking fact about the ministry officials is their relative obscurity. Military designers and plant managers write more frequently, and, in general, are much more visible, than those responsible for their oversight; it is as if the ministry personnel actually seek anonymity.[33] In addition, managers and designers are often prominent in their geographic area, serving on local organizations at the city, oblast, or republic level. Deputy ministers are seldom, if ever, elected to the Supreme Soviet, the Central Committee, or republican analogues.[34] Often the only way to identify a deputy minister is by his signature on an obituary or his attendance at a conference.[35]

As a result of this minimal participation in the public press, many of the writings by ministry personnel considered in this chapter actually were published prior to their appointment to the ministry. Presumably, the views expressed in the articles were known to the senior officials responsible for the promotion, and they were most likely still held after the promotion.[36]

But first, it is useful to consider the ministers, deputy ministers, and administration chiefs as a group. As complete a list as possible of deputy ministers for the defense industrial ministries is included as appendix B. The sample used in this study in the search for writings emphasizes those ministries most closely associated with military production: the Ministries of Defense Industry, Machine Building, General Machine Building, Medium Machine Building, and Aviation Industry, although some works from the other ministries were examined.

The average age upon appointment to the ministry (as administration chief or deputy minister) was about 46 years old, and, as can be seen in the table (table 5.1) at the end of this chapter, most had held the post of either plant manager or chief engineer. In many ways, the ministry personnel might be considered a select subset of the managers, for a large proportion of the administrators for whom biographical information is available served as managers. In fact, these individuals did *not* work their way up from the bottom of the ministry's administrative hierarchy, but rather moved into administration after frequently long careers in plants, typically after having reached the position of plant directors. Only a very few of the ministry personnel have careers which include work within the ministry at a position lower than that of administration chief.

As with the managers, it appears that most, if not all, deputy ministers and administration heads have a higher, technical education.[37] In fact, it appears that the Soviets may have required such an education as a prerequisite for promotion to the position of plant manager or chief engineer. As virtually all ministry officials about whom biographical information is available served in one of these two posts, it serves as a first filter in the promotion into the ministry. The next stages are typically deputy minister, first deputy minister, then minister.

THE MINISTERS IN THE PRESS

Civilian Goods and Efficiency

The most important occurrence of writings by the ministers of the defense industries took place around the time of the 24th Party Congress, when Leonid Brezhnev emphasized that 42% of the defense industry's output went to civilian production.[38] He also called for greater spin-off from the defense industries to the civilian, due to the former's advanced technical level.[39]

Brezhnev's comments came in March, 1971, but the issue had certainly been raised earlier, and the General Secretary's comments were

TABLE 5.1. Career Outlines for Defense Industry Administrators

Name	Work	Party	Chf Eng	Mgr	Min
Afanas'yev, S. A.	1941 23	1943 25	1941 23		1946 28
Andriasov, S. A.					1974 58
Antropov, P. Ya.	1932 27	1932 27			1945 40
Bakhirev, V. V.	1941 25	1951 35	<1960 <44	1960 44	1965 49
Baklanov, O. D.	1950 18	1953 21	<1975 <43	<1975 <43	1976 44
Bal'mont, B. V.	1952 25	1956 29	<1965 <38	<1965 <38	1965 38
Belousov, B. M.	1959? 25?	1963 29		1976 42	1979 47
Belousov, I. S.	1952 24	1955 27	1967 39		1969 41
Bolbot, A. V.					1978 58
Butoma, B. Ye.	1920 13	1928 21	1944 37	<1948 <41	1948 41
Churin, A. I.	1933 26	na	<1945 <38	1946 39	1957 50
Dement'yev, P. V.	1931 24	1938 31		<1941 <34	1941 34
Derunov, P. F.	1939 23	1947 31		1960 44	1973 57
Dondukov, N. F.	1952 24		1966 38		1974 46
Finogenov, P. V.	1941 22	1943 24	1953 34	1954 35	1965 46
Kalmykov, V. D.	1934 26				1949 41
Kazakov, V. A.	1938 22	1941 25	1951 35		1965 49
Kolesnikov, V. G.	1942 17	1961 36	<1967 <42	1967 42	1971 46
Konyshev, Yu. V.	1950 21	1960 31		1977 48	1982 43
Kotin, Zh. Ya.	1923 15	1931 23	1932 24		1967 59
Kotov, F. Ya.	1949 22	1961 34		1969 42	1976 49

Note: table indicates the year and age when the official began his working career ("Work"), joined the CPSU ("Party"), if and when he became a plant chief engineer ("Chf Eng") and/or plant manager ("Mgr"). The last column ("Min") indicates appointment to the post of deputy minister or above.

TABLE 5.1. (cont.)

Name	Work	Party	Chf Eng	Mgr	Min
Kucherenko, N. A.	1930	1942	1949		1952
	23	35	42		45
Kulov, Ye. V.	1953	1960			1972
	24	31			43
Kurushin, V. I.					1974
					44
Larchenko, O. F.		1961			1968
		33			40
Lobanov, V. V.					1974
					57
Maslyukov, Yu. D.	1962	1966	1970		1974
	25	29	33		37
Mazur, Ye. V.	1929	1949	<1959	1959	1965
	19	39	<49	49	55
Medvedev, D. P.					1968
					51
Mikhailov, M. S.					1972
					43
Mochalin, L. S.	1945	1945	1958		1971
	21	21	34		47
Morokhov, I. D.					1971
					52
Reut, A. A.				<1975	1975
				52	52
Semenikhin, V. S.			1950	1963	1971
			32	45	53
Semenov, N. A.	1940	1942		<1971	1971
	22	24		<53	53
Shkurko, Ye. P.		1942	<1946	<1946	1956
		27	<31	<31	41
Silayev, I. S.	1954	1959	<1971	1971	1974
	24	29	<41	41	44
Slavsky, Ye. P.	1912	1918	<1940	<1940	1945
	14	20	<42	<42	47
Systsov, A. S.	1948	1961	<1975	1975	1981
	19	32	<46	46	52
Voronin, L. A.	1949	1953	1959	1965	1968
	21	25	31	37	40
Yegorov, M. V.	1930	1938			1939
	23	31			32
Zateikin, Yu. A.	1943	1957	1967		1974
	18	32	42		49

almost certainly based on some "behind the scenes" discussion.[40] In fact, the Minister of Defense Industry, S. A. Zverev, had written an article in August 1970 extolling the contribution of his ministry to the Soviet tractor industry.[41] After Brezhnev's speech, Zverev reappeared in the press with an article emphasizing several key areas in which the ministry contributed to the civilian economy, including tractors, photographic equipment, drilling equipment, and medical equipment, and how much this would increase over the next Five Year Plan.[42]

The first article following Brezhnev's speech (and which refers specifically to the speech) was by P. V. Dement'yev, Minister of Aviation Industry, who, like Zverev, wrote about the high quality and varied assortment of goods produced for the civilian economy by his ministry. These include passenger aircraft, of course, but also agricultural products, medical equipment, and automobile engines, for example.[43]

Similarly, *Izvestiya* published an article in June 1971 by the Minister of Machine Building, V. V. Bakhirev, emphasizing *his* ministry's contributions to the civilian economy, in areas such as tape recorders, lamps, and watches.[44] That same month, the Minister of Shipbuilding Industry, B. Ye. Butoma, was interviewed in the agricultural newspaper *Sel'skaya zhizn'* and discussed his ministry's contributions to Soviet agriculture.[45]

While the theme common to each of these articles is the emphasis on the defense ministries' role in the civilian economy, what makes these articles important is *not* so much their content. A call at a Party Congress for action by a ministry should, after all, provoke a response. What is striking is that from 1965 to 1980 these were the *only* articles written by Zverev, Bakhirev, and Dement'yev, and that they all appeared within six weeks of each other.[46] The defensive nature of the articles suggests that there may have been a more than just rhetoric behind Brezhnev's program. Kosygin had been arguing that the levels of military R&D were sufficient, and more attention should be paid to the technical development of the nonmilitary sectors of the economy.[47]

Whether Brezhnev felt compelled to defend the industries as a result of Kosygin's critique (either because he recognized the challenge or because the ministers felt threatened and turned to the former secretary for defense industry for help) or if Brezhnev had reached the conclusion that the Soviet economy required greater spillover from the defense economy cannot be determined. The result, however, was a unique set of articles from the ministers extolling their contributions to the civilian economy, as if to say "we *are* doing our share," and acknowledging (if not accepting) the order to do still more.[48]

Other Officials

The limited information available by and about other ministry personnel reflects only a small number of themes, and these themes appear to be idiosyncratic: each individual has a particular issue he addresses or with which he can be associated. Many of these early articles are narrowly technical, and the topic may be raised only once or twice;[49] a few discuss managerial issues[50] which have been discussed in chapter 3. There are a few cases in which a reasonable case linking the individual's ideas, publicly expressed prior to promotion, might be linked with his subsequent promotion.

The clearest example of a likely tie between an individual's public writings and his promotion is probably the brief appointment of P. F. Derunov to the post of Deputy Minister of Aviation Industry from 1973 to 1974. Derunov's views have been outlined in chapter 4; his prominence is based upon his expertise and advocacy of a systematic application of the "scientific organization of labor," or NOT, for which he won the State Prize in 1969. It seems quite reasonable (although, admittedly, impossible to prove with the available data) that Derunov was promoted into the Ministry to encourage the implementation and improvement of NOT (and its presumed increases in productivity) within the Ministry and its subordinate plants. It may also reflect a reward (his promotion) as a result of Derunov's innovative work. Of course, his removal from that post could reflect either a completion of his task or a dissatisfaction with his work at that level, although the latter seems unlikely.[51]

The promotion of F. Ya. Kotov from the post of director of the Siberian Agricultural Machine-building Plant (Sibselmash) to that of first deputy minister of the Ministry of Machine Building in 1976 may have reflected a similar "reward" system, or a desire to move a director with creative ideas into the ministry. Kotov's writings, as indicated in chapter 3, repeatedly emphasize an important theme in Soviet managerial philosophy: the link between science and production. Such a view, especially when successfully implemented, is certain to appeal to the leadership of a ministry in which the most current technology is very important.

One interesting case of an article by an official of a defense industrial ministry has already be alluded to: the article by Yu. D. Maslyukov, then chief of the main technical administration of the Ministry of Defense Industry, on the introduction of the "Unified System of Technical Preparation of Industry" (YeSTPP).[52] YeSTPP is an effort to systematize and unify the documentation and preparation process for production in order to minimize the required time and resources, and Maslyukov's article is a straightforward presentation of the benefits of YeSTPP within the Ministry of Defense Industry. It is reasonable to suggest that, as chief of the main technological administration, Maslyukov was responsible for the development and introduction of YeSTPP to the Ministry of Defense Industry. The program is reported by Maslyukov to have had an "economic effect" (i.e., savings) of more than 40 million rubles.[53]

It is possible that Maslyukov's success in introducing YeSTPP was in part responsible for his rapid promotions. Other than the obvious emphasis on how successful adoption of the program has proven (he reports that YeSTPP was tried in a few plants in each main administration in 1976, then more broadly introduced in the second half of 1977), there is little in the article that might hint that within ten years Maslyukov would be responsible for *all* defense production as head of the VPK.

There are, however, at least three cases in which a deputy minister was relatively prolific while in the ministry. Surprisingly, these three held or hold the post of deputy minister in the Ministry of Medium Machine Building, the most secretive of the ministries.

P. Ya. Antropov had worked as a deputy to the State Defense Committee (GKO) during the Great Patriotic War. After 1945, he worked in uranium production and exploitation for nuclear weapons with B. L. Vannikov, the head of a Council of Ministers organization "for the creation and development of the atomic industry" and the administrative body overseeing the development of nuclear weapons.[54] According to one biography of Antropov, "from this time to the end of his life, P. Ya. Antropov led the work in creation and development of the resource base of the atomic industry."[55]

Antropov wrote frequently on the subject of uranium exploration. His most frequent theme was the need for Soviet geologists to devote greater effort to finding and mining uranium.[56] He also frequently proposed new ways to predict the location of uranium deposits and how to categorize them.[57]

Perhaps most interesting, although it is not a surprise, is the intensity with which Antropov advocated the expansion and use of nuclear power. In his book on earth's energy potential, he discusses oil, coal, and nuclear power, and argues that the national and global potential of nuclear power will encourage its greater use. In his 1976 edition, he predicts that by the year 2000, 25 percent of U.S. energy will be nuclear, 14 percent of the Japanese, and 32 percent of the Western European, an increasing share for each area.[58]

It seems clear from Antropov's book and articles that he believed that the Soviet Union would also become increasingly dependent on nuclear power, that more needed to be done to exploit effectively the Soviet Union's uranium resources, and that Soviet geologists needed to be more aggressive in their efforts to predict and discover uranium deposits.

Antropov was clearly an advocate of greater reliance on nuclear power, as well as pushing for greater work by the scientific community on the problem of finding and using uranium in the Soviet Union. His work within the Ministry of Medium Machine Building continued this theme, but it is noteworthy that he used public and professional fora for his advocacy. He almost certainly did not encounter disagreement within the ministry; after all, it is dedicated to the use of uranium and nuclear power, too. But his writings do suggest that not enough work was seen as being done in the field of obtaining the raw materials for the Soviet nuclear (weapons?) program, and that he chose public prose-lytizing as a means of increasing the quantity and quality of scientists involved.[59]

A second deputy minister of the Ministry of Medium Machine Building who appeared in print with a specific theme was Aleksandr Ivan-ovich Churin. Churin was First Deputy Minister of the ministry from 1957 to 1970, after a career as director of a number of plants. In 1970, he transferred to the State Committee on Science and Technology (GKNT), and worked, until his death in 1981, on issues of the long-range development of nuclear energy.[60]

Just as Antropov's theme was the effective exploitation of uranium resources, Churin's theme was the use of nuclear power facilities to desalinate sea water. He felt that nuclear power facilities could be used, almost incidentally, to provide potable water in a cost-effective manner in areas where such water was otherwise unavailable.[61]

Churin's case is interesting because of his move from the ministry to the civilian-oriented GKNT. If we can assume that his writings accurately reflect his interests, the case might be made that these increasingly diverged from the purposes of the Ministry of Medium Machine Building, or, at least, that they seemed to fit within the general mandate of the GKNT better than in the Ministry. Churin's writings were published during the second half of the 1960s, and his transfer in 1970 may have reflected his choice—or that of the Ministry.

The third deputy minister of the Medium Machine Building ministry to appear frequently in print is Igor Dmitriyevich Morokhov, who apparently shares a dual appointment to the Ministry and to the State Committee on Atomic Energy (GKAE).[62] Morokhov's portfolio of interests revolves around peaceful nuclear explosions (PNEs) and international cooperation on nuclear issues, and he writes frequently on various international conferences on the subject.[63] Morokhov, as indicated earlier, also served as the chief of the Soviet delegation to the Comprehensive Test Ban (CTB) talks with the United States and Britain from 1977. During these talks, the Soviets announced a moratorium on PNEs and Morokhov reportedly told the chief of the United States delegation, Paul Warnke, that the Soviet Union was prepared to accept monitoring of each side by seismic monitoring stations on the other's territory and on-site inspections in the event of a challenge.[64]

These three individuals appear to have been staking out "advocacy positions": Antropov pushing greater exploitation of nuclear resources (which is in line with official Soviet thinking), Churin arguing that nuclear power plants *could* and *should* be used for more than just power generation (again, in line with official Soviet thinking), and Morokhov making the case repeatedly for the continuing utility of PNEs and the need for international cooperation. Each presumably was making a similar case within his organization, providing him with a forum where his ideas could actually be implemented.

But this does not mean he was able to see them implemented. Antropov may have felt forced to write for the scientific community as a way of encouraging acceptance of his theories as to the nature and location of uranium deposits. Churin's move from First Deputy Minister to an unspecified post in a State Committee was clearly a demotion, but the reasons cannot be discerned from the available data; I am unaware of information confirming that his proposals were implemented (or, for that matter, explicity rejected). And Morokhov's advocacy of continued use of peaceful nuclear explosions and increased cooperation in the nuclear area are apparently not controversial.[65]

The holding of views is not sufficient to demonstrate influence. What it does suggest, however, is that these views may have been taken into consideration at various points and accepted, modified, or rejected by other, more senior, policy makers.

MINISTRIES AND TECHNICAL DECISIONS

As was true with both plant managers and designers, the ministry officials also have responsibility for day to day technical decisions. While this may not be to the same detail as for the directors and designers, and is probably more frequently in the form of approving or rejecting the technical decisions and proposals of their subordinates, it still gives them a "nuts and bolts" influence that designers and plant managers have to be aware of, and which relieves the Party apparatus of much of this responsibility.

What is important about the ministry personnel in technical decisions is their ability to stop projects before they even start by denying them adequate funds or, on the other hand, amply funding other projects. As those responsible for the allocation of funds, these officials also probably are attracted to the least expensive short-term "solutions," even if .there are based on work done elsewhere or are technically inefficient. The first priority of the ministry officials is satisfying the production levels established within the ministry and codified into law by the Council of Ministers; innovative research that does not immediately contribute to the production requirements and may, in fact, take resources away from production, is unlikely to receive much support.

STRATEGIC DECISIONS

Strategic decisions, those that answer the question of how to accomplish an objective, are the bread and butter of the ministry, and it appears that ministry personnel are given considerably leeway in answering the question.

All the work undertaken in any of the ministries is under the direct authority of the responsible ministry official. The establishment of the relevant ministries is, in itself, a strategic decision. For example, Shokin lobbied strenuously (and with the support of some designers) to establish the Ministry of Electronics, in the hope of concentrating Soviet electronics work for greater efficiency. The Ministry of Machine Building broke off from the Ministry of Defense Industry, and it seems reasonable to speculate, although it cannot be demonstrated, that the officials of the new ministry favored its establishment, as it improved their own personal positions and, presumably, filled a void that the new administrators felt existed.[66]

Three deputy ministers of the Ministry of Medium Machine Building published several pieces about their specific interests, presumably in an effort to influence decision makers. Antropov's efforts to persuade more geologists to devote their time to uranium exploitation and Churin's arguments on the benefits of using nuclear reactors for desalination, in particular, seemed clearly intended to rally support for these projects. Morokhov's objectives and intentions are less clear, but his expertise on the issue of peaceful nuclear explosions led to his being placed in charge of the Soviet CTB team, presumably placing him in a position of authority. Derunov's brief appointment as Deputy Minister of Aviation Industry almost certainly had an instrumental purpose: to coordinate and speed implementation of NOT through the ministry. Similarly, it is unlikely that F. Ya. Kotov abandoned his belief that there should be closer links between scientific and production organizations upon being appointed to the post of First Deputy Minister of Machine Building.

While it is regrettable that there is no visible "paper trail," which would make it possible to follow a specific proposal through the ministry, there is enough discussion of a general nature to suggest that the strength of the ministries is in their ability to structure the debates, whether they are taking place in subordinate organizations or in more senior bodies. The ministery typically has control of most of the relevant information and has most of the expertise. It is responsible for determining the allocation of funds and resources, and for implementing contracts with other organizations. It is also, in many ways, the only game in town, since a designer or manager would have a difficult time finding a different employer.

DOCTRINAL DECISIONS

The question of balancing civilian and defense production, whether in the Soviet system as a whole or within the defense industrial ministries, clearly provoked an effort by many players to participate in the decision-making process.

The ministers were apparently participating in a major debate going on behind the scenes in the Soviet political leadership. Beginning in 1974, according to western intelligence estimates, the growth of Soviet military procurement "dropped markedly," apparently as a result of a policy decision.[67] Several factors indicate that the decline was a result of a conscious decision, rather than simply the result of procurement cycles or a temporary problem, including the length of time of the slowdown and the absence of new resources allocated to overcome any bottlenecks that might have been responsible. One other set of indicators should be mentioned: the officials responsible for defense production suffered no repercussions. Some were even moved into problem areas of the civilian economy in an apparent effort to improve the latter.

At the time of any probable decision to slow defense procurement, the secretary of defense industry was D. F. Ustinov, a friend and political supporter of Brezhnev. Also during this period, there was considerable discussion in the military press about the link between a healthy civilian economy and a sound defense. Ustinov would have been in an almost unique position to see the benefits possible through closer ties between the civilian and military economies, and it is unlikely that a decision to cut the procurement rate could have been made without his approval.

While Brezhnev was openly advocating greater reliance on western technology (increasingly available as a result of detente), the VPK was also being geared up to undertake an increased effort to obtain information and material from abroad useful to Soviet industry.[68] Firdman notes that "At the turn of the 1970s, the prevalent opinion in high tech circles in the USSR was that military needs could be best satisfied by clandestine acquisition and subsequent reproduction of Western technologies. This approach was judged to be more effective and efficient than the attempt to develop similar innovations 'in-house.' "[69] By relying as much as possible on acquiring information from the west rather than duplicating it in their own labs, the Soviets appear to have made a conscious decision to conserve resources even at the risk of being somewhat behind the west.

Some in the Ministry of Defense were probably less than happy with these changes. As Fedoseyev points out, relying on emulation means always being behind.[70] Grechko, during this period, was strongly opposed to negotiating with the United States over Soviet security, as was taking place in the SALT 1 negotiations completed in 1972 and the subsequent SALT 2 negotiations.[71] This opposition, coupled with the increased importance of economic management within the armed forces, may help explain the appointment of Ustinov, a defense industrial specialist with no combat or command experience, first to the Politburo in March 1976, and then, one month later, to the post of Minister of Defense upon Grechko's unexpected death.[72]

If there was, in fact, a decision to reduce the standard or programmed increases in defense spending, Ustinov would have certainly been involved.[73] Whether his objectives upon taking the post of minister of defense included increasing the efficiency of the defense sector and/or reducing the rate of growth is difficult to prove, but either seems possible. Ustinov's career had been in the defense industries and their oversight, and his appointment may well reflect the victory over the military of those with broader industrial and economic concerns in the question of defense planning.

THE DECISION PROCESS

Regardless of the stage, much of the information used in making decisions at the national level comes from the ministries, as does most of the analysis. This is true for the initiation of a new proposal as well as for evaluating how well a decision is being implemented.

The professional staff of the ministries, unlike the designers or the plant managers, have as a mandate the making of strategic decisions — from the initiation stage to implementation. Their decisions, of course, have to be approved by their Party overseers and senior government bodies, but it is apparent that a considerable amount of authority has been vested in the ministries already.

Many of the decisions, of course, are fairly routine, or, perhaps more accurately, have become *routinized* through repetition. In particular, the annual and quarterly internal negotiations over the plan have surely settled into a more or less predictable pattern, with most decisions having an impact on the margins, rather than the core, of continuing programs.

But there are requirements and events that fall outside the routine in which the ministry personnel have an interest and, presumably, expertise. The apparent decision to place greater emphasis on civilian production in the defense industries was almost certainly not initiated in the ministries, but the ministry leadership felt it necessary to participate in the discussion. The SALT and CTB negotiations required the participation of technical experts, and the Soviets made two of them full delegates. The result of relying on Shchukin and Morokhov may have been to give these individuals (and, perhaps, the ministries they represented) more direct access and influence on the political leadership in all four phases of the decision-making process.

The ministries are expected to provide current information to their superiors (administratively, the Council of Ministers, but—in fact—the Politburo and the Secretariat) and to develop innovative new ways of solving both new and lingering problems. Certainly the ministry can take considerable responsibility for many of the innovative ideas generated by its subordinates (including plant managers and designers), and when an idea appears to be productive (for example, BIP), the ministry has probably encouraged its dissemination to other plants and may have persuaded the Politburo that the program should be expanded to outside the ministry.

CONCLUSIONS

The hypotheses suggested at the beginning of this chapter, i.e., that the ministries will pursue increased resources through their ties with military production, that they are closely linked with the military, that they will use public and private means to garner support, and that their interests complement those of the military, are not supported by the data. While it is clear that the ministries do seek increased resources, there is evidence that they wish to distance themselves from the responsibilities that often accompany such resources. The information they have about the international military situation is incomplete, rendering them less than fully effective as partners for the military. Their use of the public media is minimal, and appears to be confined to a few individual cases. And, perhaps most important, there is no evidence that the ministries see themselves as having interests which complement those of the military. There appears to be a narrow definition of interests, one in which the ministry sees changes in the military's requirements as a result of long-term objectives as a potential burden, rather than as an opportunity that might be exploited. The ministries' interests are served best by predictability.

The deputy ministers and heads of main administrations typically have their roots in industry and production, eventually making the move from chief engineer or general director to the senior leadership of the ministry. Some managers became deputy ministers after developing relatively creative and easily applicable methods to improve the implementation of policy.

It is striking that the members of the ministry's "inner circle" (the minister, deputy ministers, and heads of administrations) write so infrequently. Those cases in which the ministry officials *do* use the press are very specific. The most dramatic is when the leadership feels compelled to respond to specific charges, as seemed to be the case when the ministers discussed their ministry's contributions to the civilian economy. There are other cases where the purpose of the articles is to generate activity *outside* the ministry that will be to the ministry's benefit, as suggested by Antropov's consistent efforts to interest more geologists in the necessary work of discovering uranium deposits or in Morokhov's discussions of the benefits of peaceful nuclear explosions. Churin's articles also suggest that one might publish outside the ministry to advocate a policy that may have been of little interest *within* the ministry itself.

These writings, however, are probably only indicators of events taking place within the ministry, where there are much more effective tools available to some officials. Control over the purse strings is a key technique used with subordinates, and dragging one's feet is used when dealing with superiors. At the same time, of course, each ministry seeks increased control over its working environment, especially suppliers.

The use of funding to shape the directions of research and production undertaken by the subordinate organizations is indicated in numerous ways, from requiring that proposals for basic research be approved in advance to determining how to distribute rare or valuable equipment among producers or designers. As indicated earlier, the use of resources for control is very difficult to document, as so much of the relevant material would be "for internal use only" in any ministry; when the "national security" qualifier is added, such information is even less likely to appear. But émigré memoirs, in particular, make frequent note of the need to curry favor with the ministry officials who distribute funds and the control these officials have over how the funds are used. While the use of control over resources is fairly clear, it is not possible to be certain about the importance of the control over information. The agendas are shaped in an ostensibly collegial manner, in advance of collegium meetings, as described in chapter 2, presumably ensuring that competing views from within the ministry are dealt with, or at least are expressed, prior to the regular collegium meetings.

The slow implementation of programs, whether technical or administrative, is a time-honored technique in any organization, and the Soviet ministries are no exception. Perhaps the best example is the reluctance with which the ministries implemented the association reforms, dragging the process out for many years and, in some cases, apparently rendering it ineffective.

An important point to recall on this question is that the ministry's objectives are, in many ways, no different from those of its subordinates in dealing with the state's "central planning organs," and the rewards of slow implementation, in many areas, outweigh the risks. Such a system also retards technical innovation. In an independent western corporation, the nature of the reward system is such that the organization's leadership and its subordinates have complementary incentives: rewards depend as much on innovation and optimization as on sheer production.

By contrast, in the Soviet Union an outside agency sets the objectives in consultation with the ministry and rewards are based on achieving those objectives. The ministry has an incentive to establish low (i.e., easily achievable) levels of annual production, while Gosplan is pushing for higher ones. Even if the military industries had first call on all the resources they wanted, there would still be the incentive to seek lower assignments to ensure against the unpredicted and to increase the probability that assignments would be completed on time. This sort of organization virtually institutionalizes an incremental approach to technological development and an emphasis on continuity in production runs, for technical innovation is difficult to predict or order and carries the risk of stripping assets from current production.

Thus, the ministry's mid-level management is unlikely to be a source of pressure for qualitative or quantitative change. While individuals may be interested in new ideas or techniques, those responsible for implementation are unlikely to pursue them unless they have some guarantees that they will not be in financial jeopardy, and the ministry as a whole will likely seek a similar assurance. The stances taken in position papers and proposals, then, are likely to be cautious and familiar.

Innovations in organization or management that are unlikely to jeopardize current production objectives do not seem to meet the "hidden opposition," as Zaslavskaya called it. As noted earlier, the defense industrial ministries appear to be willing to undertake periodic experiments on both small and large scales in the hopes of improving production through improving management.

Ministry officials are responsible for the development of techniques to achieve doctrinal objectives, and thus are responsible for numerous strategic decisions. And just as they favor stability in their relations with the military, it seems reasonable to expect that they favor stability in these doctrinal ∪bjectives. So long as the latter are known and fixed, the ministries' leaders are managing at the margins. But when there has been the threat that these objectives would change, or that the responsibilities placed on the ministries might shift, then the leadership of the ministries have undertaken to minimize the impact of doctrinal and strategic decisions made elsewhere.

CHAPTER SIX
CONCLUSIONS

The preceding chapters detailed the Party and government structures responsible for overseeing the military industries of the Soviet Union, and attempted to indicate the views and political access of the most important nonmilitary participants in the weapons production and acquisition process.

Ascertaining the views of the participants has been, at times, problematic, as there is frequently a paucity of data. For understandable reasons, the individuals who appear most often in the press are the directors of the defense plants and associations. The defense plants are generally large, important facilities within any region, as well as on a national scale. The directors write not as representatives of the defense industry, but as managers of major plants. While this is not necessarily the case in other countries, the Soviet system (and the CPSU in particular) places considerable pressure on the manager to be a social leader and to take an active part in community affairs.[1]

The second reason, already noted more than once, is the preceived importance to the economy of what they write. Not only do they manage large facilities, but they have been given a certain amount of leeway and are creative enough to use it to their advantage. In turn, the techniques developed at these plants can be used to the advantage of other soviet industries.

At the other extreme of visibility lie the administrative personnel of the ministry and other management bodies such as Gosplan. The infrequency with which they appear in the press certainly does not reflect a lack of importance. These are, after all, the officials at the top of the administrative hierarchy, bearing "personal responsibility" for the ministry's successes and failures. It should also be noted that almost 50 percent of the sample worked at some time during their career within the ministry apparatus (see appendix A).

The scarcity of publications is probably due to a number of factors. While a plant manager is able to boast about specifics of his plant, the deputy minister or administrator may not be able to do so without revealing affiliated plants and personnel. The ministry official is not in a senior position of a hierarchy; just as there are fewer articles written by mid-level plant personnel than by directors, there are fewer written by mid-level ministry officials than by ministers. There is likely to be a bureaucratic pressure against ministry staff taking a visible position; recall that even identifying these individuals is often problematic. Finally, most of their work is certainly behind the scenes, with little need or incentive to write articles in the first place.

Between these extremes are the designers and scientists, as frequently the *subject* of someone else's writing as authors in their own right. And while the manager's particular skills can be applied in the civilian sector or described openly, the technical work of the designer, for reasons of national security, often cannot. He is thus left, in his public writings, to comment on history or on themes that have a general industrial applicability: production and design planning, unification, and standardization.

On an informal level, however, it appears that the roles are almost reversed. The military designers have a prominence *within* the Soviet leadership that an administrator, whether a plant director or a ministry official, seldom achieves. Soviet thinking, in general, places an emphasis on the value of science, with an ideology that sees the Soviet Union as the culmination of a historical process that has been scientifically validated. The designer or scientist, placing his talents at the disposal of the state, to *defend* the state, understandably commands respect, if not gratitude. Science is a creative process; administration is much less so.

For the plant manager, there are certain to be considerable informal connections, but most of them will be at a local level. At the city or republic level, he is a prominent person, typically serving on numerous Party and state bodies. But for connections at the national level, he is most likely forced to rely on current, or former, local contacts who have reached a national post (for example, a local secretary who is appointed to the national Secretariat), personal ties through the Department of Defense Industries staff, or his ministry. This, in fact, may be another reason he chooses to use the press as an outlet.

The ministry personnel almost certainly have greater opportunity for "networking" in Moscow, presumably with other administrative-level personnel with whom they regularly come in contact. In addition, recall that most ministry officials have served as plant managers or chief engineers, and whatever connections made while in that post might be useful after their promotion. (Indeed, these ties may be in part responsible *for* the promotion.) While these individuals will have closer ties to the Department of Defense Industries, they are less likely than a director to be elected to either the Central Committee or the Supreme Soviet, two organs which might provide increased informal access to the higher echelons of power.

DECISIONS AND MILITARY INDUSTRY

As suggested in chapter 1, it is useful to consider the process of decision making in a step by step manner, and to consider the type of decisions being made and policies being chosen (see table 6.1). The Soviet leadership, i.e., the Politburo and Secretariat, are certainly not competent to make reasonable decisions at every level, and must rely on a combination of delegation of authority and technical advice.[2] Even if the dozen, or two dozen, senior leaders of the Party and government *were* competent to make every decision, the sheer enormity of the task would make it impossible, and hence the need to delegate authority and to give general orders with specific objectives.

Doctrinal (or policy) decisions are those that set out the broad social objectives and expectations of society. Those that might have involved the defense industries include the decisions to enter the SALT process, the apparent conclusion by Brezhnev that the negative consequences of a nuclear war are likely to outweigh any gains, and the increasing emphasis on conventional forces in the 1970s. Korolev and Sakharov, two of the most important military scientists, played roles in initiating the policy process on two other doctrinal decisions (rocketry and nuclear testing), and each was able to rally a number of other specialist to his cause in persuading the political leadership.[3] Pleshakov, Shchukin, and Morokhov each played key roles in various negotiations with the United States, giving them an opportunity to shape, through their interpretations and evaluations, the view of the leadership they represented and to whom they reported.

But the most important example of industrial involvement in doctrinal decision making for the purpose of this study involves resource allocation. While the Ministry of Defense may feel that several weapon systems are needed, and that these may fall within (or almost within) the technical competence of the defense industrial ministries, it is

TABLE 6.1. Process of Decision Making and Types of
Decision Made

Decision Type	DECISION STAGE			
	Initiation	Persuasion	Decision	Implementation
Doctrinal				
Procurement		Ministry	Politburo	Ministry, VPK
Missiles	Designer	Designer, ministry	Politburo	Ministry
N-Testing	Scientist	Scientist, ministry	Politburo	Ministry
Strategic				
Ass. Reform		Manager, designer	CC and Politburo	Ministry
Mgmt. Techs	Manager	Manager	Ministry	Ministry
Est. Min. of				
Electronics	Manager, designer	Manager, designer	CC and Politburo	Ministry
(Kotov)	Manager	Manager	Ministry, academy	Ministry, academy
(Churin)	Ministry	Ministry		
(Antropov)	Ministry	Ministry		
(Morokhov)	Ministry	Ministry	Politburo(?)[a]	
Technical				
Proposals	Designer	Designer, manager	State Commission(?)	Manager
	Manager	Manager, designer	State Commission (?)	Manager

[a]Decisions on CTB negotiations were presumably made at the Politburo level.

ultimately a Politburo-level decision as to whether the weapons will be built.[4]

The most dramatic example of the intersection of defense and industrial issues is the apparent decision during the Brezhnev era to reduce the rate of procurement spending in the mid-1970s, as discussed in chapter 5. Such a decision would have been a conscious (even if forced by circumstances) policy choice at the highest levels of Soviet decision making, presumably as an effort to trim the resources absorbed by (or earmarked for) the defense effort. Even if the amount actually reallocated would have had a small impact on the economy as whole,[5] the shift may reflect a major change in the commitment of the political leadership towards servicing the needs of the military.[6] Such a decision would be based on each member's personal objectives, his interpretation of the course the Soviet Union wishes to pursue, the "state of the world" that shapes the assessment of need, where the effort to balance military and diplomatic actions will be drawn, and the available resources. These views are shaped by a number of external and internal factors, but the defense industry's position is that of one participant among many, with an expertise in Soviet domestic production capabilities and *not* in foreign or security policy. It is clear that the principal concerns of the military industrialists are primarily industrial, rather than military, and they are disinclined to take on new assignments that may disrupt current production.

Access to decision makers in the area of doctrinal decision making is a right that is given (and which can be taken away), not one that is simply automatic. The doctrinal decision makers remain a small group of individuals in the Politburo and Secretariat, and the best way to reach them, apparently, is to be a leader in the field. Even then, the decision makers appear to consider these leaders as senior specialists, whose views were relevant (and respected) only when they pertained to their field of expertise.

It should not be forgotten that one of the key "rights" of the Politburo and Secretariat is, in effect, to be the *only* organizations allowed to deal directly with doctrinal questions. This monopoly on an entire range of issues is jealously guarded, and those who wish to participate in doctrinal decisions enter the field not as peers or legitimate participants in the debate, but as supplicants. And, once a decision is made, it is expected that visible dissent will be minimal.

This suggests that informal connections, that is, those links established with a key leader outside the normal hierarchy, may actually be the most effective way of influencing doctrinal issues. If one does not have this sort of access, he probably has to fall back upon official channels for proposals or use "indirection," as the ministers of the various defense industries apparently did when writing about the need for them to contribute more to the defense economy.

Strategic decisions lay out plans for achieving doctrinal objectives. In addition, strategic policy is administrative policy, as an effort is made to "operationalize" the variables involved in policy making and to establish concrete steps towards achieving an objective. Thus, a Politburo doctrinal decision to reduce spending on military procurement would provoke a number of other decisions and policies to serve that end: identifying the weapons systems to be reduced or eliminated, determining which plants should have their plans altered, deciding how to compensate for any reductions in military capability, etc.

The role of the ministries and their subordinate organizations is to function precisely as the makers of strategic decisions. They are aware of the technical capabilities of the production and design organizations, the specific requirements of the customers, and the broad doctrinal policy laid down from above. One of the key differences between the defense industries and the civilian industries is the fact that the customer has a powerful position in the former case.

There are several examples of military industrial involvement in strategic decision making. While these include the personal lobbying efforts of Antropov in the area of uranium mining, Antonov on the val system, and Churin on desalination, the efforts to influence how industries are managed is more interesting because it is systematic and pervasive. The numerous managerial techniques (the Saratov system, BIP, KANARSPI, etc.) were initiated in the defense industries, whose managers spend considerable time and effort persuading others (often very successfully) of the general usefulness of the system.

It is interesting to compare the general support for these managerial reforms with the ministry's response to the association reform. The new management techniques were, in general, intra-enterprise developments, independent of the ministry. As a result, the ministry had little reason to become involved unless production declined or to encourage its dissemination to other enterprises. The association reform, however, cut deeply into the relationship between the ministry and its enterprises, in an effort to restrict the "petty tutelage" of the ministry. Thus, the ministries found themselves on the defensive, and in many cases undercut the reform through simply failing to implement it properly.

In attempting to influence strategic decisions, managers, designers, scientists, and ministry officials have a broader selection of tools at their disposal than was the case with doctrinal decisions. Participation in discussions about strategic decisions is tolerated, encouraged, and even expected (at least officially). As a result, there are numerous channels, official and unofficial, by which an individual may make his views known. The most important factor limiting discussion in strategic decisions is probably the military's monopoly on military intelligence (technical and strategic information). This constrains the areas within which the defense industrial officials might participate to basic economic and production issues.

However, outside the purely military area, these same individuals have relied on the press to make a range of claims and counterclaims about everything from the economy and its management to specific technical proposals that they feel are receiving insufficient attention. They have almost certainly relied on private contacts of a more informal nature to press their cases as well. And, of course, there are the official channels within their respective hierarchies, the first within their ministry and the second in the CPSU.

Technical decisions appear to be left as much as possible to the customer and the producer. The Soviet system is well-structured to keep technology and engineering within familiar and well-managed bounds, placing a premium on producibility and, as a result, on encouraging an incremental approach to resolving technical problems. There are, of course, cases of disagreement and dissent within the scientific community over a variety of issues of a technical nature, including those having broader social repercussions and impact on strategic or doctrinal decisions.[7] In this area, the Soviets benefit from the massive basic research effort undertaken in western countries, especially the United States. The Soviets do not need blueprints to benefit from foreign research, as even the knowledge that a particular project is possible is often an important conclusion.

The use of the technical commission to evaluate new weapons and to approve or reject further development at various stages in the procurement cycle also gives considerable influence to the technical specialist. While, under Stalin, senior political leaders intervened frequently in technical decisions, to the point of evaluating the military utility of various shell calibers or proposing modifications to the designs of tank turrets, there does not *appear* to have been the same level of intervention during the Brezhnev era.[8] And it should be recalled that the Scientific-Technical Councils of the various ministries play an important role in shaping the nature of the development of the technology within a ministry, which means they have a significant role within the branch of science as a whole. After the Academy of Sciences lost its "technical sciences" component in the early 1960s, these organizations were absorbed by various ministries and state committees, giving these "consultative" organizations considerable impact on the course of science within an industrial branch.

It is also clear that, in considering the distribution of influence or impact in the Soviet system, one must consider the stages at which this influence might be exercised. Initiation, persuasion, decision, and implementation each invite different participants. (See table 6.1).

In the initiation phase, the data indicate that almost anyone can make proposals, but the perceived legitimacy of those proposals is determined in part by the type of proposal (doctrinal, strategic, or tactical) and how it serves the already existing objectives of the decision makers. Thus, doctrinal proposals by Korolev and Sakharov had considerably different impact, with Korolev's work in rocketry promising to solve a specific Soviet problem and Sakharov's pursuit of a test ban requiring the assumption of moderate risk. The numerous strategic initiatives may have challenged existing strategic policies, but this is considered legitimate so long as the initiatives are designed to satisfy existing doctrinal requirements.

The persuasion phase has been demonstrably played out in the public media and behind the scenes. At the doctrinal level, of course, very little of the process appears in public until *after* the decision is made. What comments do appear, it seems, are consciously obscure. One must often read between the lines and be familiar with the context of an article to recognize an undercurrent of dissent or to recognize subtle, but important, differences. Whether it is aircraft designers acknowledging the general superiority of missiles (*but*, of course, there are some roles for which they are unsuitable) or defense industry ministers emphasizing that they already *are* contributing to the civilian economies, doctrinal decisions are—at most—debated only indirectly in public, *before* the decision is actually reached.

Strategic decisions, on the other hand, appear to be debated openly and frequently, depending on the subject. It should again be emphasized that most participants in strategic discussions have roles as specialists. Their views are respected within the confines of their field and the specialized subject area. Persuasion, that is, relying on recognized expertise to make an argument, is accepted. For the managers and ministry officials, this expertise is in domestic production and management questions, not security or foreign affairs. For the designers and scientists, the expertise is even more specialized and technical.

The actual decision making authority is vested in different organizations and levels. The Politburo has the right to make decisions at any level it wishes, although this might clearly run counter to the Brezhnev promise to give more authority to the technical specialists in making nonpolitical decisions. It should also be noted that one side in a dispute may try to "politicize" it and to seek Politburo intervention, but this is difficult to demonstrate during the Brezhnev era.

The right and responsibility to make strategic decisions have been given to mid-level organizations, such as the ministries, state committees, and the Academy of Sciences. Of course, the leadership of these organizations, that is, the individuals making the decisions, are virtually all members of the Party and have been approved by the Politburo or Central Committee. By having this strong Party representation at these levels, the Party is attempting to ensure that any uncertainties or ambiguities in the decision process, any gaps between available information and complete information, are filled by Party-generated values.

Finally, the implementation phase is handled by several organizations, and it is clear that the implementation often does not meet the standards established by the decision makers for any number of reasons; supply problems, overly optimistic planning, or even by design by those responsible for implementation. (Implementation problems, of course, generate new initiatives.) Implementation brings with it new pressures and problems. In the case of the association reform, for example, the ministries that were to be reformed were charged with carrying out a reform their leadership clearly opposed. Unable to stop the reform through persuasion, they impeded its implementation. At the same time, implementation of the plan often requires extraordinary efforts on the part of the production organizations simply to keep up with the assignments, such as relying on the *tolkach* or seeking resources through the "gray" market. Again, managers also turn to the press and complain of their inability to implement decisions because of the lack of coordination with other responsible organizations.

Each phase is important in understanding how a decision is made and how an idea becomes first policy, then product.

The third variable that clearly needs to be recognized in Soviet decision making is the question of who, in the bureaucratic structure, is allowed to participate (the "openness" of the decision). While it is clear that there is a symbiotic relationship between the three types of decisions, and it is almost axiomatic that an actor will be interested in influencing the decision maker(s) above him, the subject matter constrains how great a role he can play. The debate over the education reforms discussed in chapter 1 was relatively open: the number of participants was large and the availability of information was relatively broad.

By contrast, decisions involving national security are relatively closed: public debate and information are almost nonexistent or confined to a small group of specialists. The subject itself is fraught with security implications and, consequently, secrecy. This degree of closedness is well-understood by most participants, and there are areas into which one ventures at one's own risk. Sakharov's experience is an excellent example, but it should also be recognized that this understanding permeates the military industries as a whole. Each specialist has an area within which he is allowed to vent his opinions, and the military industries comprise economic and industrial specialists, *not* defense and foreign policy specialists.[9]

A MILITARY-INDUSTRIAL COMPLEX?

It is clear that members of the industrial component of any Soviet "military-industrial complex"—the industrial managers, designers, and ministry officials—participate in policy debates and attempt to influence decisions. But, as argued in Chapter 1 mere participation does not define a military industrial complex. Three questions must be answered: first, do the military and the industrialists have complementary interests? For example, does a military interest in high technology equipment translate into potentially desirable objectives for the industries? Second, do the military and the military industries have access to, and influence upon, policy makers, whether through personal connections or political power? And third, is the military highly valued by these policy makers, whether because they perceive a threat or for other reasons?[10]

The evidence examined in this study indicates that the answer to the question of complementary interests is no. As has been indicated in the preceding chapters, the military industries (in the form of its designers, plant managers, and ministry personnel) place great value on the predictability of their industrial assignments and their supplies, with significant changes in the plan neither sought nor desired. The defense industries have the same incentive structure that any industrial ministry does, one which typically encourages conservatism over innovation. "More of the same" is the order of the day for the military industries, as it is for most Soviet industrial ministries.

This is not to suggest that the military and the industries have *no* common interests. The military and the industries, for example, may each desire the continued production of a large number of tanks year after year, with only incremental changes. Both the military and the military industries would be uncomfortable with a sharp, large-scale reduction in weapons production, but for very different reasons. While interests may converge on gradual improvements or on numbers, they diverge on the desirability of rapid change.

In the Sovet case, there are a number of factors working to keep the military and the industries from having complementary or even parallel interests. These factors are visible when one considers the desire for high technology weaponry. For the military, the development and procurement of high technology armaments is important for a number of reasons. The first, of course, is that the more "modern" weapons systems are generally seen as more capable than those they replace. This, and the increased cost effectiveness often associated with more modern, high technology weapons, are two of the key criteria considered when the Soviet military procures a weapon. It should also be added that the cost effectiveness of Soviet weapons is increased by their apparent reliance on much of the basic research and development undertaken in the west.

But even if the Soviets had no independent desire to acquire newer weapons, there would be considerable pressure for them to do so anyway. First, their most important potential adversary (the United States) has developed a force posture that strongly emphasizes high technology and technology-intensive weapons. In order to counter these weapons, the Soviets are often forced to explore high technology counter measures. And, perhaps more important, high technology research and development needs to be undertaken to ensure against the other side's "surprise" development of a key or even decisive breakthrough, one that might take years to counter.[11] This is especially apparent in the recent concern expressed by Soviet writers about "new in principle" weapons.[12] The military, in other words, must be conscious of long-term potential developments by both the Soviet Union and its adversaries.

In contrast, the military industries operate in circumstances that drive them *away* from this interest. There are, as already discussed, disincentives to innovation in Soviet industry and, in fact, the system requires the managers and the ministry officials to concentrate on short-term developments. With production and bonuses linked with the monthly, quarterly and, at best, annual plans, it is not surprising that the immediate concerns of the Soviet industrialist probably do not extend much beyond the next quarter. Long-term planning is not rewarding, and research and development threaten to take resources away from the ministry's or plant's immediate assignment: production. In contrast to the military, the industrialists will be emphasizing a "more of the same" approach to production.

The scientists and designers involved in weapons development, rather than the ministry officials and the plant managers, probably have interests more akin to those of the military. The scientist is, in general, interested in advancing the science itself. Soviet sources emphasize that the role of the scientist is basic research in new and innovative areas. The weapons designer, on the other hand, occupies a middle ground between the military's long-term objectives and the industry's technical limitations. His primary goal is developing new and attainable technologies, neither basic science nor production per se.

While in the United States the costs of high technology research and development can generally be passed on to the Department of Defense, in the Soviet system this is much more difficult to do. The Soviet economic structure does not provide an effective way for a ministry to pass on the costs of research and development to a contractor, and it is difficult for the ministry to structure research and development into its planning. Similarly, marginal improvements and attainable objectives bring rewards comparable to innovation without the risks; it is thus in the interest of the designer or producer to press for minimal changes, not major influxes of funds coupled with potentially problematic responsibilities. Finally, it is difficult to develop an incentive system for innovation based on advance planning.

In Soviet military industry, what is "good" for the industry is typically that policy which increases stability and predictability. The system encourages those responsible for production to associate profits with this stability. This is in marked contrast to the system in, for example, the United States, where the costs for innovation in the defense sector are typically covered by the customer, where they do not conflict with current production programs, and where innovation may, in fact, make the difference between obtaining a contract or not.

At times, of course, factions within the military and the industries do have complementary interests, as when Khrushchev appeared willing to phase out much of the Soviet aircraft inventory in favor of missiles. As a result of this threat, both air force officers and aircraft designers argued for the utility of aircraft in conjunction with missiles. But, as exemplified by the clash between the military's desire for more helicopters and the Ministry of Aviation Industry's desire to keep the number down, the military industries and the military have little reason to work together as advocates and, indeed, probably find themselves at cross-purposes.

A second factor that serves to reduce the role of the military industries in advocating "pro-defense" policies is the lack of specifics they have on the overall picture. As indicated, data about Soviet military capabilities are kept extraordinarily secret and "compartmentalized" within the Soviet Union. In general, it appears that Soviet designers and builders of weapons are told only what is necessary to produce their part of a project. There is no organization within the ministries to assess how the product will be used in combat and how it will perform as part of a large-scale military operation; the ministry's evaluation is based on how well the product matches its design requirements. The Soviet military industries have no defense think tanks to turn to for broad policy analysis or in-house think tanks for the same purpose, as is common in the West. The military effectively controls the evaluation of the Soviet defense position: analysis of the threat and Soviet capabilities is the domain of the General Staff alone.[13] Military industrialists attempting to become involved in such work would most likely be told that their concerns rest elsewhere. It is thus unlikely that the defense industrialists will be able to argue about the necessity of a weapon or how many of a particular weapons system *should* be produced, but only about how many *can* be produced.

This is not to say that the defense industries do not favor increasing their share of national resources, or that this interest is not shared by those responsible for their monitoring, such as the Department of Defense Industry or the VPK. But the combination of minimal incentives and minimal data does suggest that the defense industries are neither natural nor automatic supporters of military programs. While they are the beneficiaries of the concerns of the Ministry of Defense, they are actually likely to attempt to moderate the demands placed upon them.

On the question of access to, and influence on, policy makers, it has been argued through the last three chapters that the individuals who staff the defense industries have such access to, and influence on, both policy makers and the policy-making process at several points, both officially (as a result of their position) and unofficially (as a result of people they know). What should be emphasized here, however, is that while they have access, their influence is based more on their persuasiveness than on their political power. There are no political action committees that they can support (indeed, until 1989 there was not even a recognized opposition). The process by which Politburo leaders are chosen is confined to the Politburo itself, with a pro forma approval by the Central Committee. And the defense industries are only minimally represented at the Central Committee level; Party officials, logically enough, dominate Party decision making.

The individuals who lead the defense industries are also not in a position to go elsewhere, of course. While they could attempt to affect implementation of decisions as a sign of displeasure, in the military realm this would carry with it substantial risks, if only because the military's voyenpredy are perpetually on the scene. And a threat to resign is probably as good *as* resigning: Slavsky's comment to Sakharov that he was not being held by the throat applies to the managers and ministry officials, too. And there is no suitable "alternative employer" in the event one did resign.

Finally, the military is clearly an important component of Soviet planning and thinking. The most visible indicator of this is simply the proportion of resources devoted to it, but there are other indicators as well, including the representation of the military on bodies such as the Central Committee, the repeated emphasis on the military role in the Great Patriotic War, and the constant reference to the "American (or imperialist or NATO) threat."

In conclusion, then, when western analysts refer to a Soviet "military-industrial complex," care must be taken to ensure that the term is, in fact, applicable. If the term is used to mean that the state values its military forces enough to grant certain privileges to the industries supporting them, or that there are industries whose main role is to supply the military, then the Soviet Union, like most developed states, has a military industrial complex.

But using the term to suggest dominance of the decision-making organs in whole or in part by the military and the military industries, which, it is presumed, have common interests and are natural allies, is clearly incorrect. While the military and the military industries are active participants in the Soviet decision-making process, they are but two of several. Even if they were the only two participants in a decision, however, accord would be unlikely. In the effort to create an industrial base for the military, the Soviets have created a system in which the military and the industries are divided by contradictory interests built into the system itself.

APPENDIX A
PUBLIC WRITINGS

The public writings of the following individuals from 1965 to 1980 were identified through the Soviet indexes *Letopis Gazetnykh Statiei* and *Letopis Zhurnalnykh Statiei*. Other articles were found through a review of each article in the *Letopis'* military industry section (typically very small) and through a review of several military journals (in particular, *Voyenny vestnik, Aviatsiva i kosmonavtika, Tekhnika i vooruzheniya).*
Abbreviations used are:

Deputy Minister	DM
Machine-Building	MB
General Machine-Building	GMB
Medium Machine-Building	MMB
Ministry of Defense Industry	MoDI
Department of Defense Industry	DoDI
Trade Union	TU
First Name Unknown	FNU

Detailed biographies were also prepared on more than 500 key officials in the Soviet defense industries.

Name	Post(s)
Abaimov, G. N.	DM, Ministry of MB
Afanasyev, S. A.	Minister of GMB
Andrianov, V. N.	shipyard manager
Antropov, P. Ya.	DM, Ministry of MMB
Bakhirev, V. V.	First DM of MoDI, Minister of MB
Baklanov, O. D.	Plant manager, DM, Minister of GMB
Bal'mont, B. V.	Chief of an administration, DM, First DM of GMB
Belousov, B. M.	plant manager
Bezsonov, N. S.	DM MoDI
Bobrov, A. I.	Gosplan Electronics Industry Dept. Chief
Chechenya, L. S.	plant manager
Chuprin, [FNU]	VPK staff
D'yakonov, V. D.	plant manager
Danilov, B. M.	aircraft plant manager
Denisov, N. S.	aircraft plant manager
Derunov, P. F.	aircraft plant manager, DM, Ministry of Aviation Industry
Dmitriyev, I. F.	Deputy chief, chief, DoDI
Fateyev, P. G.	DM, Ministry of MB
Ferin, M. A.	plant manager
Finogenov, P. V.	DM, Minister of MoDI
Finogeyev, V. P.	DM, MoDI
Georgiyevskiy, P. K.	staff of MMB
Golubev, V. G.	staff, MMB
Grushin, P. D.	aircraft designer, plant manager
Isayev, S. I.	aircraft plant manager
Izgagin, B. G.	plant manager
Izvekov, V.	plant manager
Kalabin, V. B.	probable administration chief, MoDI
Karev, A. T.	Secretary of Aviation and Defense Workers TU
Khvedeliyani, Ya. R.	aircraft plant manager
Kiselev, I. I.	plant manager
Kolsenikov, V. G.	plant manager
Komissarov, B. A.	DM, MoDI; possibly VPK
Konyshev, Yu. V.	aircraft plant manager, DM of Ministry of Aviation Industry
Kornitskiy, I. P.	DM, MoDI
Korotkov, A. V.	chief of a MMB administration
Kotin, Zh. Ya.	designer, DM, MoDI
Kotov, F. Ya.	plant manager, First DM, Ministry of MB
Kovalev, M.	chief of GMB institute
Kovrishkin, I. V.	probable administration chief, MoDI
Kozhevnikov, G. N.	DM, MoDI
Kozlov, V. V.	deputy chief of DoDI
Kritsyn, A. I.	plant manager
Kucherenko, N. A.	chief of an MoDI main administration
Kulov, Ye. V.	plant director, deputy chief and chief of MMB administration, DM, MMB
Kurushin, V. I.	DM, MoDI
Lapshin, V. I.	Secretary of Aviation and Defense Workers TU
Larchenko, O. F.	chief of a MoDI administration, DM, First DM MoDI

Larianov, V. M.	DM, MoDI
Lobanov, V. V.	DM Ministry of GMB
Lozhchenko, N. R.	plant manager
Luzhin, N. M.	chief engineer in shipbuilding plant, deputy chief of DoDI
Makarov, A. M.	plant manager
Makeyev, V. P.	designer, Ministry of GMB
Makhonin, S. N. DM	MoDI
Malashenko, Yu. V.	plant manager
Malofeyev, P. R.	plant manager
Malyshev, V. A.	DM, Ministry of MB
Marakhovskiy, N. P.	Gosplan, probable chief of Defense Summary Dept.
Maslyukov, Yu. D.	chief engineer of a plant, chief of a MoDI administration, DM, First DM MoDI, Gosplan, VPK
Medvedev, D. P.	DM, Ministry of MB
Mezentsev, L. G.	DM, Ministry of MMB
Mikhaylov, A. G.	aircraft plant manager
Mishin, V. P.	designer, Ministry of GMB
Mochalin, L. S.	DM, MoDI
Mordasov, N. K.	DM, MoDI
Nezhlukto, V. Ye.	probable chief of an administration, MoDI
Nikolayev, V. I.	DM, Ministry of MB
Pilyugin, N. A.	designer, Ministry of GMB
Pochernikov, A. A.	probable chief of an administration, Ministry of GMB
Pugin, N. A.	plant manager
Puzyrev, N. G.	DM, Ministry of MB
Rayevskiy, V. N.	DM, Ministry of MB
Rubins, Ya. F.	DM, Ministry of MB
Rudakov, P. N.	DM, MoDI
Ryabev, L. D.	DM, Ministry of MMB
Ryabikov, V. M.	Gosplan
Ryabov, Ya. P.	CPSU Sec for Defense Industry
Ryzhkov, N. I.	plant manager, Gosplan
Sabinin, Ye. N.	plant manager
Semenov, N. A.	plant manager, First DM Ministry of MMB
Serbin, I. D.	Chief of DoDI
Serykh, L. A.	aircraft plant manager
Sharapov, I. A.	probable administration chief, MoDI
Shchukin, V. A.	probable administration chief, MoDI
Shishanov, A. A.	chief of foreign relations for GMB
Shomin, N. A.	tank designer, MoDI
Shorokhov, V. N.	plant manager
Shkurko, Ye. P.	First DM, MoDI
Silayev, I. S.	aircraft plant manager, DM, First DM Aviation Industry
Sivets, V. N.	aircraft plant manager
Slavskiy, Ye. P.	Minister of Medium Machine Building
Smirnov, L. V.	chief of VPK
Sobolev, N. K.	Secretary of Aviation and Defense Workers TU
Solov'yev, P. A.	plant manager
Soyich, O. V.	plant manager
Spirin, S. S.	Gosplan
Stepin, M. N.	DM, Ministry of Aviation Industry
Stroyev, N. S.	deputy chief of VPK
Subbotin, M. I.	plant manager
Suchkov, V. N.	probable administration chief, MoDI

Svirin, Yu. M.	plant manager
Titov, G. A.	Gosplan
Tordiya, P. Sh.	aircraft plant manager
Tsarev, V. P.	chief designer at plant, probable chief of an administration, MoDI
Tyulin, G. A.	DM, MoDI
Tyurin, V. A.	Deputy chairman of MoDI NTS
Udarov, G. R.	DM, Ministry of GMB
Utkin, V. F.	missile designer, Ministry of GMB
Utkin, V. V.	probable aircraft designer
Vanag, G. A.	aircraft plant manager
Varnachev, Ye. A.	plant manager
Vinogradov, N. G.	probable administration chief, MoDI
Volkov, V. M.	DM MoDI
Voronin, L. A.	plant manager, chief of an administration of MoDI, DM MoDI, First DM MoDI, Gosplan, Gossnab
Voronin, P. A.	aircraft plant manager
Vorozhein, L. N.	plant manager
Yakovlev, V. M.	shipyard manager
Zabelin, L. V.	DM, Ministry of MB
Zaikov, L. N.	plant manager, Secretary for Defense Industry
Zaitsev, V. I.	plant manager
Zakharov, M. A.	plant manager, DM, MoDI
Zakharov, N. S.	DM, Ministry of MB
Zaychenko, G. V.	plant manager
Zaychenkov, B. B.	DM, Ministry of MB
Zurabov, R. S.	DM, Ministry of MMB
Zuyevskiy, V. A.	chief designer, MMB plant
Zverev, S. A.	Minister, MoDI

APPENDIX B

THE DEFENSE INDUSTRIAL MINISTRIES OF THE SOVIET UNION

Producing the equipment required by a modern military is a massive job. One need only consider the quantities of various pieces of equipment allegedly produced by the Soviet Union to have some idea of the scale of the task: the DIA estimates that 16,800 tanks, 5,425 fighter aircraft, 60 "major surface combatants," 55 attack submarines, and 2,875 strategic missiles were produced between 1977 and 1983.[1]

The requirements for the Soviet arsenal are satisfied for the most part by fewer than ten of the more than twenty industrial ministries, but these are supported by other, predominantly civilian, ministries and also produce a wide range of civilian goods themselves. Those with primary responsibilities to the defense sector are the Ministry of Defense Industry; the Ministry of Aviation Industry; the Ministry of Shipbuilding Industry; the Ministry of Machine Building; the Ministry of General Machine Building; the Ministry of Medium Machine Building; the Ministry of Electronics Industry; the Ministry of Communications

Equipment Industry; and the Ministry of Radio Industry.[2] These nine ministries are represented on the Military Industrial Commission (the VPK [discussed in chapter 2]).[3]

While a number of smaller plants contribute to the defense effort, there are about 150 major plants that produce the bulk of Soviet military equipment (see table B.1.) These plants are concentrated in a relatively small number of cities.

THE MINISTRY OF DEFENSE INDUSTRY

The Ministry of Defense Industry is responsible for the design and production of ground-forces armament and ammunition (artillery, tanks, vehicles, small arms, fuses, primers, propellants, explosives, and possibly tactical guided missiles), as well as some civilian products (cameras, optical products, petrochemicals, railroad cars, tractors, and motorcycles).[4] The Ministry is rarely mentioned in the Soviet press; when it is, it is generally to comment on a civilian product such as the photographic equipment.

From 1963 to his death in late 1978, the Minister of Defense Industry was Sergei Aleksandrovich Zverev. Zverev had graduated from the

---

TABLE B.1. Soviet Defense Plants

Ground Force Matériel	24 plants
(tanks: 4)	
(other armored vehicles: 7)	
(artillery: 2–9)	
(helicopters: 5)	
Naval Shipyards	24 yards
Aircraft	37 plants
(bombers: 2)	
(tactical aircraft: 3+)	
(cargo: 7)	
Missile equipment	49 plants
("missile systems": 20 plants)	
(SAMs: 5 plants)	
(Medium Machine Building)	(47 plants)
Total	134 plants
(with MMB)	(181 plants)

Sources: *Allocation of Resources in the Soviet Union and China—1981*, p. 12; *Soviet Military Power*, no. 3 (1984), pp. 95–98; Philip Hanson, *Soviet Industrial Espionage: Some New Information.*

Leningrad Institute of Precision Mechanics and Optics in 1936, and worked his way through the defense industrial structure, beginning as an engineer-designer. Zverev joined the Party in 1942. During the war, and until 1947, he was chief engineer at several defense plants, after which he was promoted into the Ministry (then the Ministry of Armaments under D. F. Ustinov), where he was a chief engineer, then chief of a main administration, a deputy minister, and then first deputy minister.

The relationship with Ustinov presumably continued after Ustinov became secretary for defense industrial matters in the early 1960s, and it seems likely that, in order to advance under Ustinov's watch, there must have been a general congruence of views. Zverev oversaw considerable improvements in the ground-forces equipment, including the introduction of new artillery and the development and production of the BMP, an armored fighting vehicle that helped motorize the Soviet army. In 1971, he received a State Prize, and in 1972 he became a Hero of Socialist Labor. In 1976, he was awarded an unannounced Lenin Prize.

Zverev died in 1978, and was replaced by his first deputy, Pavel Vasilyevich Finogenov. Finogenov graduated by correspondence from the Leningrad Military-Mechanics Institute, then worked his way from master (1941) and shop chief to director of the Kovrov Motorcycle Plant in Vladimirsk (from 1954 to 1960). Finogenov had joined the Party in 1943. From 1960 to 1963, he was deputy chairman of the Vladimirsk Sovnarkhoz, after which he moved into the State Committee on Defense Technology as head of an administration. From 1965 to 1973, he was deputy minister of defense industry, and from 1973 to his appointment as minister in 1979, he was first deputy minister. In 1976, while First Deputy Minister, he became a Hero of Socialist Labor.

In 1989, Finogenov was replaced by Boris Mikhaylovich Belousov, former Minister of Machine Building (see below).

Deputy Ministers

There have been, since 1965, about twenty deputy ministers of the ministry (see table B.2).[5] Each of these deputies is responsible for a particular area within the ministry, usually related to the deputy's backgrounds, and including the oversight of one or more main administrations.[6] It seems likely, for example, that Mochalin and Finogeyev were responsible for the area of artillery, for they were the only two deputy ministers to sign the obituary of F. F. Petrov, a prominent artillery designer. Kotin's area of responsibility was almost certainly tank development, as his background was in that area (he was one of the designers of the T-34 tank and continued to design tanks after World War II).

Administration Officials

Administrations in defense industrial ministries are generally identified by numbers (e.g., the Ninth Main Administration), rather than by function.[7] It is thus not especially useful to speculate about the identities and detailed functions of specific administrations except in general

---

TABLE B.2. The Ministry of Defense Industry

Ministers
S. A. Zverev (1963–1978)
P. V. Finogenov (1978–1989)
B. M. Belousov (1989–)

First Deputy Ministers
V. V. Bakhirev (1965–1968)
Ye. P. Shkurko (1968–1973)
P. V. Finogenov (1973–1978)
L. A. Voronin (1979–1980)
O. F. Larchenko (1980–1985)
B. M. Belousov (1985–1987)

Deputy Ministers
N. S. Bezsonov (1965–1974)
B. A. Komissarov (1965–1973?)
A. I. Krytsin (1965?)
N. K. Mordasov (1965–1976?)
V. N. Rayevskiy (1965–1968?)
P. V. Finogenov (1965–1973?)
Zh. Ya. Kotin (1967–1971?)
P. N. Rudakov (1968–1972?)
V. P. Finogeyev (1970–1987?)
L. S. Mochalin (1971–)
L. A. Voronin (1972–1979)
O. F. Larchenko (1974–1980)
V. I. Kurishin (1974–)
I. P. Kornitskiy (1978–)
Yu. D. Maslyukov (1979–1982)
B. M. Belousov (1980–1985)
V. M. Volkov (1980–)
M. A. Zakharov (1982–)
V. N. Demchenko (1985–1987)
G. S. Brevnov (1986–)
V. V. Osekin (1987–)

terms. It is known that Lev Voronin, prior to his 1972 appointment as Deputy Minister, was chief of the Economics and Planning Administration of the ministry.[8] The likely administration heads at the time of Zverev's death were N. G. Vinogradov, V. B. Kalabin, I. V. Kovrizhkin, Yu. D. Maslyukov (head of Technical Administration), V. Ya. Nezhlukto, A. A. Pochernikov, V. N. Suchkov, V. P. Tsarev, I. A. Sharapov, and V. A. Shchukin. Only limited information is available about a few of these individuals: Kalabin's background appears to be in photgraphic equipment, Nezhlukto wrote two articles in the mid-1960s on the development and testing of engines and was associated with the Leningrad Kirov plant, Tsarev was chief engineer as of 1972 at the Krasnyy Barrikady Plant in Volgograd and appears to have worked in the area of drilling and boring equipment, Sharapov's writings indicate a specialization in steel, and Maslyukov was a chief engineer at a subsidiary plant of the Izhevsk Machine Building Plant (formerly the Izhevsk Arms Plant).

THE MINISTRY OF GENERAL MACHINE BUILDING

The Ministry of General Machine Building is responsible for strategic ballistic missiles and space vehicles, and is probably responsible for cruise missiles, some surface-to-air missiles, and cryptographic equipment.[9]

The bulk of the Soviet ballistic missile and space programs fall within the domain of the Ministry of General Machine Building, headed by O. N. Shishkin. As a result of the emigration of at least two individuals who have worked in this ministry, somewhat more information is available about the internal structure than about many of the other ministries.

The ministry was established in 1965, growing out of the State Committee for Defense Technology. Its first minister was Sergei Aleksandrovich Afanasyev, transferred in 1983 to head the Ministry of Heavy and Transport Machinery. Afanasyev's background was in military industry, presumably working on rockets and missiles from the 1940s (he held various posts in the Ministry of Defense Production to 1957, when he was appointed first to be deputy chairman of the Leningrad Sovnarkhoz, then chairman of the Leningrad Sovnarkhoz and ultimately of the RSFSR Sovnarkhoz and deputy chairman of the RSFSR Council of Ministers).

Afanasyev's most important work, however, clearly revolved around the production of ballistic missiles and space boosters. He is a two-time Hero of Socialist Labor (1973, 1978) and a winner of the State (1952) and Lenin (1973) Prizes; three of these awards were made while Afanasyev was Minister of General Machine Building and during the period of rapid growth in Soviet missile numbers and capabilities. His transfer to the Ministry of Heavy and Transport Machinery seems likely to have been an effort to transfer some of the management experience gained in the military sector to one of the most important civilian ministries.

His successor also had deep roots in the General Machine Building ministry, but was fourteen years younger. Oleg Dmitriyevich Baklanov was graduated from the All-Union Energy Correspondence Institute (he also earned a *kandidat* degree, athough it is not clear when or from where) and apparently moved right away into the ministry, working his way up from fitter (in 1950) to chief engineer and eventually director of a Kharkov instrument plant. In 1976, he was appointed deputy minister of the Ministry of General Machine Building and, in 1981, he became first deputy minister. His only two published works after 1965 were

---

TABLE B.3. The Ministry of General Machine Building

Ministers
S. A. Afanasyev (1965–1983)
O. D. Baklanov (1983–1988)
V. Kh. Doguzhiyev (1988–1989)
O. N. Shishkin (1989–)

First Deputy Ministers
B. V. Bal'mont (1976–81)
O. D. Baklanov (1981–1983)
O. N. Shishkin (1988–1989)
V. Kh. Doguzhiyev (1987–1988)

Deputy Ministers
Ye. V. Mazur (1965–1982)
G. R. Udarov (1967–)
B. V. Bal'mont (1983–1976)
V. V. Lobanov (1974–)
O. D. Baklanov (1976–1981)
V. Kh. Doguzhiyev (1983–1987)
A. I. Dunayev (1985?–)
Ye. A. Zhelonov (1984–)
A. S. Matrenin (1985?–)
V. N. Soshin (1985?–)
G. F. Grigorenko (1985?–)
O. N. Shishkin (?)

technical discussions of cylindrical structures. He is also a winner of the Lenin Prize (year not given) and a Hero of Socialist Labor (year not given).

When Baklanov was promoted to the CPSU Secretariat in 1988, he was replaced by Vitali Khusseynovich Doguzhiyev, a deputy minister in 1983 and first deputy minister in 1987. In 1989, Oleg Nikolayevich Shishkin was appointed minister.

First Deputy Ministers

Three first deputy ministers have been identified for the period from 1965 to the present: Boris Vladimirovich Bal'mont (1976–1981), Baklanov (1981–1983), Doguzhiyev (1987–1988), and Shishkin (1988–1989). In 1981, Bal'mont was appointed Minister of Machine Tools and Tool Building.[10] He is a 1952 graduate of the Bauman Moscow Higher Technical School (MVTU im. Bauman). Upon graduation, he first became an engineer-designer, ultimately working his way to the post of senior engineer and then director of a plant in Saratov (perhaps the Saratov Receiver-Amplifier Tube Plant, but this is not certain). In 1965, he was appointed chief of a main administration in the newly reformed Ministry of General Machine Building (and became a member of the Collegium), and in 1973, he was promoted to deputy minister. In 1976, as already noted, he became first deputy minister.

Deputy Ministers

The only deputy minister identified from the mid-1960s is Yevgenii Vasilyevich Mazur, who held the post from 1965 until his death in 1982. Mazur graduated from an unidentified institute in 1936 and worked his way up from engineer-designer to chief engineer of a plant. In 1959, he was appointed director of the Zhdanov Heavy Machine Building Plant, and in 1961, he was appointed deputy chairman of the Ukrainian Sovnarkhoz.

Grigory Rafaelovich Udarov worked within the Ministry of Aviation Industry for a number of years with some of its leading designers, and then appears to have moved into the missile industry.[11] Although he was not identified until August 1967 as a deputy minister of the Ministry of General Machine Building, he was elected to a Party Congress from Moscow and identified in a Moscow newspaper, in 1957, as chief of an administration of general machine building of a Moscow Sovnarkhoz.

There is no information about Vasiliy Vasilyevich Lobanov, except his mention in the CIA directory. Ye. A. Zhelonov, A. S. Matrenin, V. N. Soshin, and O. N. Shishkin appear on a pair of obituaries of missile designers. A. I. Dunayev is also chairman of the State Committee for the Utilization of Space.

Organization of the Ministry

Although there is a serious gap in public information about the senior staffing of the Ministry of General Machine Building, there is (as if to compensate) considerably more information than might be expected about the internal organization. Two émigrés have written about their experiences working in the Ministry at different posts. While it is not possible to verify independently their respective accounts, both are in accord with what is known about the ministry.

The first source is Mikhail Agursky, who worked in the Machine-tool Research Institute (*Eksperimental'nyi Nauchno-issledovatel'skii institut metallorezushchikh stankov,* or ENIMS) from 1960 to 1966, conducted postgraduate work at the Academy of Science's Institute of Control Problems from 1966–1968, and then worked at the Research Institute for Machine-building Technology (*Nauchno-issledovatel'skii institut tekhnologii mashinostroyeniia,* or NIITM) through November 1970, as a leading engineer, and then as a "senior scientific worker." He notes that he was, in fact, at the disposal of the main designer as scientific consultant on various questions of technical progress.[12]

The second source, Victor Yevsikov,[13] worked at the Korolev facility in Kaliningrad (The Central Design Bureau of Experimental Machine Building) as a specialist in the field of coatings for rocket engines and re-entry vehicles from 1964 to 1970, then at the Academy of Science's General and Inorganic Chemistry Institute im. Kurnakov (*Institut obshchey i neorganicheskoy khimii imeni N. S. Kurnakova,* or IONKh). Yevsikov decided to emigrate after completing his candidate of science (roughly equivalent to a western Ph.D.) dissertation sometime later.

It should be emphasized that neither individual was in a position of overall responsibility. Rather, each was employed as a technical specialist in a narrow area. But each is likely to have learned about the organization of the ministry from living and working within it for some time.

According to Agursky, there were four main administrations in the ministry. These were the Main Administration for Ground-based Equipment (such as launch and control facilities), the Main Administration for Rocket Engine Production, the Main Administration for Production of Guidance Systems, and the Main Administration for the Production of Missile Bodies. There was, of course, also a Technical Administration, as well as other functional administrations without production responsibilities.[14] At present, it is not known who might head these administrations, but the more prominent designers within each can be identified. For ground equipment, V. P. Barmin (currently a member of the Academy of Sciences) is the leading designer of missile launch sites.[15] The most prominent designers of guidance systems were N. A. Pilyugin and M. S. Ryazanskiy. Missile engines have been designed by V. P. Glushko, S. P. Izotov, and M. A. Isayev. There are several important missile designers and their bureaus: S. P. Korolev (the best known), M. K. Yangel (probably the most important in the area of military missiles), V. N. Chelomei (ICBMs and SLBMs) V. P. Makeyev (SLBMs) and A. D. Nadiradze (responsible for most of the solid-fueled missiles, although it is not clear whether he has established an independent design bureau or whether it is under the aegis of the Ministry of Defense Industry).

THE MINISTRY OF MEDIUM MACHINE BUILDING

The Ministry of Medium Machine Building is the Soviet agency responsible for development and production of nuclear weapons and the administration of military-related nuclear programs, including the production of fissionable material and the fabrication of nuclear devices and warheads. It is also responsible for high energy lasers and the production of chemical-biological-radiological protective equipment.[16] Presumably because of the secrecy shrouding all nuclear weapons programs, it is also the most obscure of the military-related ministries, and only bits and pieces of information are made public.[17]

According to a number of sources, the ministry supervises the entire chain of production for nuclear weapons, from the mining of the uranium ore through the fabrication of weapons and is responsible for the production of all nuclear materials, reactors, and weapons research, development, testing and production.[18] A 1985 DoD report adds that the ministry is also responsible for high energy lasers.[19]

The ministry was headed from 1957 to 1986 by Yefim Pavlovich Slavsky, when he was replaced by Lev Dmitriyevich Ryabev. The known deputies are noted in table B-4.

Slavsky was one of the longest-serving ministers in Soviet administration, having been born in 1898 and having assumed his minister-
level post in 1957. He served in the Red Army from 1918 to 1928,
graduated from the Moscow Institute of Non-ferrous Metallurgy and
Gold in 1933, and worked his way from shift engineer to plant director.
During World War II, he was director of the Uralsk Aluminum Plant.
From 1945 to 1946, he was a deputy of the Narkom of Nonferrous
Metallurgy, and from 1946 to 1953 the deputy chief of a main administration attached to the Council of Ministers. In 1953, he became deputy
minister of Medium Machine Building, then first deputy minister, and
in 1957, minister of Medium Machine Building. He reportedly was also
the head of the Main Administration for the Utilization of Atomic
Energy from 1956 to 1957. He is one of only a few three-time winners
of the Hero of Socialist Labor award, as well as a two-time winner of
the State Prize. In 1980, he received the Lenin Prize.

Lev Dmitriyevich Ryabev was born in 1933. He worked his way up
in an NII of the Ministry of Medium Machine Building, apparently in
Gorky. He was chief of a department in the Gorky oblast (1969–1972),
institute director in Gorky (apparently between 1972 and 1978) and a
chief of an unexplained "sector R" in the Central Committee appa-

---

TABLE B.4. The Ministry of Medium Machine Building

Ministers
Ye. P. Slavskiy (1957–1986)
L. D. Ryabev (1986–1989)

First Deputy Ministers
A. I. Churin (1957–1970)
N. A. Semenov (1971–1982)
A. G. Meshkov (1982–1986)
L. D. Ryabev (1986)
B. V. Nikipelov (1986?–)

Deputy Ministers
P. Ya. Antropov (1962–1979)
L. G. Mezentsev (1954–1976)
I. D. Morokhov (1971–)
R. S. Zurabov (1975?–)
Ye. V. Kulov (1982–1983)
A. G. Meshkov (1980–)
S. G. Prokof'yev (1982–)
A. N. Usanov (1980–)
A. D. Zakharenkov (1982–)
L. D. Ryabev (1984–1986)
V. F. Konovalev (1989?–)

ratus.[20] Based on the obituaries Ryabev signed, the Gorky institute was almost certainly involved in nuclear weapons work. He next served as a deputy minister until July, 1986, and as first deputy minister for five months before becoming minister in November, 1986. In 1989, Ryabev was appointed deputy prime minister. The ministry was apparently dissolved, although it is not clear who took over its responsibilities.

First Deputy Ministers

Aleksandr Ivanovich Churin, First Deputy Minister from 1957 to 1970, came to the ministry after a career in military industry and energy. After the war, he was the director of "various plants," possibly in the Sverdlovsk area. He went directly from one of these plants to the post of first deputy minister. While first deputy minister, he wrote few articles, and these few were on the subject of using nuclear plants for water desalinization. In 1970, he moved from the ministry to the State Committee on Atomic Energy, working on the long-range development of atomic energy. Churin's career has one intriguing anomaly: despite his responsible position, there is no evidence that he joined the CPSU.

Nikolai Anatol'evich Semenov worked his way up, beginning at various electrical stations and eventually becoming director at "a major enterprise in the Ministry of Medium Machine Building," apparently in Chelyabinsk (he was elected from there as a delegate to the 22nd Party Congress, and identified as an "engineering-technical worker").

The first deputy minister until mid-1986 was reportedly Aleksandr G. Meshkov. He was replaced by Ryabev soon after the Chernobyl disaster.

Deputy Ministers

Pyotr Yakovlevich Antropov, a deputy minister from 1962 to his death in 1979, had been the minister of Geology and Resource Preservation from 1953 to 1962. There were apparently problems in this ministry, and when Antropov lost this post, it was assumed he had simply been ousted. Only at his death was his new post reported. He continued, however, to write about uranium mining and extraction, although his post at the time was not identified. Perhaps more significantly, he was awarded the Lenin Prize in 1978, suggesting that he was not in disfavor. (He also was a Hero of Socialist Labor [1954] and winner of a State Prize [1951].) Antropov's previous work and his writings after his appointment to the Ministry suggest that his area of specialization was in overseeing the mining and extraction side of the Ministry's work. It is also interesting to note that Antropov was graduated from the Moscow Institute of Nonferrous Metallurgy and Gold the year before Slavsky.

Leonid Gavrilovich Mezentsev, deputy minister from 1954 until his death in 1976, was a shop chief and Party organizer during the war at Uralmash, the giant industrial center in Sverdlovsk. From 1945, perhaps until 1954, he was engaged in Party work in the apparatus of the Central Committee, and was then a Secretary of the Crimean Obkom KPSS. He received a number of awards, including the Order of Lenin.

Igor Dmitriyevich Morokhov is an interesting figure, apparently holding two posts simultaneously: since 1960, he has been first deputy chairman of the State Committee on Atomic Energy and, since 1971, a deputy minister in the Ministry of Medium Machine Building. His holding of these two posts suggests that these two state organizations work very closely together in the development and exploitation of atomic energy. He has been a relatively prolific writer, concentrating on the issues of peaceful nuclear explosions (PNEs) and proliferation. The CIA reports that he was born in 1919 and is a Doctor of Technical Science. During the late 1970s, he was also the chief of the Soviet delegation to negotiations over a comprehensive test ban (CTB) with the United States and Great Britain. During these talks, he reportedly told Paul Warnke that the Soviet Union was willing to accept American verification through seismic stations and even through on-site inspections "on challenge."[21]

There is a paucity of data about Robert Sergeyevich Zurabov. A CPSU member since 1930, he attended the 21st and 22nd CPSU Party Congresses, being elected from Irkutsk, where he was engaged at the time in "engineering-technical work." He was identified as deputy minister of Medium Machine Building in January 1975, according to the CIA, and holds the rank of lieutenant colonel.

Aleksandr G. Meshkov served as the deputy minister for nuclear reactors; he lost his post in July 1986, as a result of the nuclear reactor accident at the Chernobyl power station.[22]

Yevgeny Vladimirovich Kulov is the only deputy minister of Medium Machine Building known to have served as the chief of a main administration of the Ministry. After a career (1953 to 1972) "at an enterprise in engineering and leadership posts," he was appointed deputy chief, then chief of an unidentified main administration in the Ministry. In 1982, he was appointed deputy minister, and in 1983 he was placed in charge of the Soviet nuclear safety program, suggesting that his background may have emphasized nuclear power plants; his writings suggest the same. He lost his chairmanship soon after the accident at the Chernobyl power station.

Ye. A. Zhelonov is apparently in charge of the ministry's civilian production. Nothing is known about the other probable deputy ministers: S. G. Prokof'yev, A. N. Usanov, or A. D. Zakharenkov.

Organization of the Ministry

As suggested earlier, the Ministry of Medium Machine Building occupies the blackest of black holes in public information. Most ministries in the Soviet structure are organized on functional lines, and there is no reason to suspect that the Ministry of Medium Machine Building is different. This means that there are, of course, the standard administrations for the day-to-day functions: labor and wages; planning and economics; finance; production and technology; capital construction; material-technical supply, etc. As for the other administrations and responsibilities, however, we must rely at present on speculation.

Given the importance of the nuclear weapons program to the Soviet Union, it seems natural for the Ministry of Medium Machine Building to be responsible for much of the production of nuclear materials. (The State Committee for Atomic Energy is responsible for overall coordination of the Soviet nuclear power program, and a number of other ministries provide support in the form of reactor and component construction, power generation and transmission, etc.) Antropov's background suggests a main administration responsible for mining and producing fissile material. It would also be reasonable to expect there to be an administration responsible for actual nuclear weapons fabrication; Zurabov, given his military rank, would seem a likely official responsible for this area. Morokhov may well have been responsible for an administration coordinating testing and peaceful nuclear explosions (PNEs). The ministry oversees forty-seven (as of 1979) production enterprises,[23] including enrichment plants in Angarsk and Troisk, development labs in Arzamas, Kasli, and Sarova, plutonium production in Beloyarsk and Dodonovo, and weapons assembly in Chelyabinsk, Novosibirsk, and Sverdlovsk.

THE MINISTRY OF MACHINE BUILDING

In 1968, a new ministry was formed from parts of the Ministry of Defense Industry and named the Ministry of Machine Building. Its minister was (until 1987) V. V. Bakhirev, former first deputy minister of the Ministry of Defense Industry. Its responsibilities are in the areas of conventional munitions, projectiles (including antitank missiles), fuzes, solid propellants, antisubmarine weapons, and explosives.[24] Among its civilian products are tape recorders.

Bakhirev was the director of a plant in Kovrov from 1960 to 1965, after a career that went from factory worker to chief designer and deputy director of a plant.[25] Bakhirev had been graduated from Moscow State University im. Lomonosov in 1941, and, while director at Kovrov, won a Lenin Prize in 1964 (he would also win a State Prize in 1978, as minister). He was first deputy minister of Defense Industry until the new Ministry of Machine Building was established in 1968.

Bakhirev was replaced by Boris Mikhavlovich Belousov, former director of the Izhevsk Machine-building Plant (1976–1980) and deputy minister and first deputy minister of defense industry (1980–1987). In 1989, the Ministry was merged into the Ministry of Defense Industry, with Belousov as Minister.

TABLE B.5. The Ministry of Machine Building

Ministers
V. V. Bakhirev (1968–1987)
B. M. Belousov (1987–1989)

First Deputy Ministers
F. Ya. Kotov (1976–)

Deputy Ministers
G. N. Abaimov (1968–)
D. P. Medvedev (1968–)
V. N. Rayevskiy (1968?–1979)
P. G. Fateyev (1969–1985?)
N. S. Zakharov (1973–1978)
L. V. Zabelin (1975–)
B. B. Zaichenkov (1977–)
V. I. Nikolayev (1978–)
N. G. Puzyrev (1979–)
Ya. F. Rubins (1980–1981)
A. A. Kallistov (1983–)
S. N. Antonov (1985?–)
V. A. Malyshev (1985?–)
O. V. Filippov (1986–)
B. M. Sholmov (1985?–)

First Deputy Minister and Deputy Ministers

Since its formation in 1968, the Ministry of Machine has had about fifteen Deputy Ministers (see table B.5).

Fedor Yakovlevich Kotov, First Deputy Minister since 1976, was manager of "Sibselmash," the Siberian Agricultural Machine-building plant, from 1969 until his appointment.

Lieutenant Colonel Dimitri Pavlovich Medvedev had been a member of the Collegium of the Ministry of Defense Industry until 1968, when he was moved to the new Ministry of Machine Building. He was deputy minister until early 1982, when he retired on pension and was replaced by A. A. Kallistov. V. N. Rayevskiy apparently also moved from the Ministry of Defense Industry to the Ministry of Machine Building, and was replaced in late 1979 by N. G. Puzyrev. Puzyrev, in turn, was promoted from the post of head of a main administration to deputy minister. V. Nikolayev is the deputy minister responsible for civilian production. Nothing has been reported about the backgrounds of the other deputy ministers.

THE MINISTRY OF SHIPBUILDING INDUSTRY

The Soviet Union's naval and civilian fleets are both made up of ships produced by the Ministry of Shipbuilding Industry. In addition to ships, this ministry is also responsible for naval fire-control systems, mines, torpedoes, shipyards, electrical assembly plants, storage tanks, pipe, boilers, barrels, chain, and—perhaps—large structural assemblies.[26]

The Ministry was headed by Boris Yevstafevich Butoma from 1957 until his death in 1976. Like most ministers, Butoma had reached his position by working his way up within the ministry, directing a plant in the mid-1940s, heading a main administration from 1948 to 1952, and serving as deputy minister from 1952 to 1957.

Butoma's successor was his first deputy minister, Mikhail Vasil'yevich Yegorov. Yegorov had also worked within the Narkom of Shipbuilding from 1939 to 1955 as deputy chief and chief of a main administration. From 1955 to 1958, he was a deputy minister and from 1958 to 1976 First Deputy Minister of Shipbuilding.

In 1984, Yegorov was replaced by his First Deputy, Igor Sergeyevich Belousov, who fit the same pattern as his predecessors: a career in the shipbuilding ministry from the early 1950s, including a stint as the chief of the economic planning department of the Baltic shipyard and as chief engineer at Leningrad's Admiralty shipyard. He became deputy minister in 1969 and first deputy minister in 1976.

In 1987, Belousov was appointed deputy chairman of the Council of Ministers and chief of the VPK. He was replaced by Igor Vladimirovich Koksanov. Koksanov had been promoted to the post of first deputy minister in 1985, after having worked in the apparatus of the CPSU Central Committee (perhaps in the Department of Defense Industry).

THE MINISTRY OF AVIATION INDUSTRY

The Ministry of Aviation Industry is responsible for aircraft and aircraft components as well as air-to-air and air-to-surface missiles. It

TABLE B.6. The Ministry of Shipbuilding Industry

Ministers
B. Ye. Butoma (1957–1976)
M. V. Yegorov (1976–1984)
I. S. Belousov (1984–1988)
I. V. Koksanov (1988–)

First Deputy Ministers
M. V. Yegorov (1958–1976)
I. S. Belousov (1976–1984)
V. I. Smyslov (1984–1985)
I. V. Koksanov (1985–1988)
G. G. Pulyayevskiy (1988–)

Deputy Ministers
G. M. Chuikov (1965?–1978)
A. A. Khabakhpashev (1965–)
A. M. Fokin (1965?–1981?)
Ye. N. Shaposhnikov (1965–)
Yu. G. Derevyanko (1967–1978?)
M. F. Larioshin (1968?–1979?)
I. S. Belousov (1969–1976)
S. S. Vinogradov (1972–)
L. P. Stefanov (1973–)
L. N. Rezunov (1976–)
G. G. Pulyayevskiy (1978–1988)
V. A. Bukatov (1978–1988)
L. V. Pruss (1979–)
V. I. Smyslov (1981–1984)
Ye. V. Borodulin (1984–)
V. Chmyr (1989–)

also produces various consumer goods (e.g., refrigerators, washers, vacuums, aluminum kitchenware, medical equipment).

The minister of Aviation Industry for almost a quarter century was Petr Vasil'yevich Dement'yev. During the Great Patriotic War, Dement'yev was first deputy commissar of Aviation Industry, and from 1946 to 1953, simply a deputy minister. In 1953, however, he was

---

TABLE B.7. The Ministry of Aviation Industry

Ministers
P. V. Dement'yev (1953–1977)
V. A. Kazakov (1977–1981)
I. S. Silayev (1981–1985)
A. S. Systsov (1985–)

First Deputy Ministers
S. I. Kadyshev (1965–1974)
V. A. Kazakov (1974–1977)
I. S. Silayev (1977–1980)
A. S. Systsov (1981–1985)
A. N. Gerashchenko (1985–)

Deputy Ministers
V. A. Kazakov (1965–1974)
A. A. Belyanskiy (1966?–1973?)
I. A. Salashchenko (1966–1981?)
V. A. Zorin (1967?–1977?)
A. A. Kobzarev (1965?–1970?)
M. A. Il'in (1970–)
A. V. Minayev (1970–1974)
P. V. Derunov (1973–1974)
Ye. V. Vorozhbiyev (1965?–1974?)
Yu. A. Bardin (1974–)
S. A. Andriasov (1974?–1981?)
A. V. Davydov (1974?–1978?)
N. A. Dondukov (1974–1983)
Yu. A. Zateykin (1974–1983)
M. S. Mikhailov (1972–1978?)
I. S. Silayev (1974–1977)
I. M. Burov (1975–?)
A. V. Bol'bot (1978–)
M. P. Simonov (1979–?)
G. B. Stroganov (1983–1984)
Yu. V. Konyshev (1982–1985)
V. M. Chepkin (1984?–?)
Yu. V. Nikitin (1984?–?)
L. M. Shkadov (1984–?)
A. G. Bratukhin (1984–)
V. M. Chuiko (1984?)
V. A. Maksimovskiy (1988?–)
V. B. Sokolov (1988?–)

appointed minister of Aviation Industry, and he held this post until his death in 1977.

Dement'yev's successor, Vasili Alekseyevich Kazakov, worked his way through several posts within the aviation industry, reaching the post of chief of an NII in 1960. In 1965, he was appointed deputy minister, and, in 1974, first deputy minister of Aviation Industry. He served as minister of Aviation Industry from 1977 until his death in 1982, when he was replaced by Ivan Stepanovich Silayev, his first deputy minister. Silayev had worked his way through several posts at the Gorky Aircraft Plant, becoming director in 1971. In 1974, he was appointed deputy minister.

Silayev is unusual in that he spent some time (only a year) as Minister of Machine Tool and Tool Building (1980–1981). With Kazakov's death, he was returned to the Ministry of Aviation until 1985, when he was promoted to deputy chairman of the Council of Ministers.

With Silayev's move to the Council of Ministers, Apollon Sergeyevich Systsov became minister of Aviation Industry. Systsov had directed a plant (or "complex") from 1975 to 1981, when he was appointed first deputy minister.

THE MINISTRY OF RADIO INDUSTRY

The Ministry of Radio Industry is responsible for radios and electronics assemblies, television sets and tape recorders, as well as radars and large computers.[27]

The first minister of Radio Industry was Valeri Dmitriyevich Kalmykov, whose previous career was in the Ministry of Shipbuilding Industry.[28] He worked his way from designer to institute chief in the Ministry from 1934 to 1949, then chief of a Main Administration in the Shipbuilding Ministry, apparently to 1951. In that year, he moved to "responsible work" in the USSR Council of Ministers, probably laying the groundwork for the establishment of the Ministry of Radio Industry. The Ministry itself was formed in 1954.

Upon Kalmykov's death, Petr Stepanovich Pleshakov was appointed minister, after serving for six years as Kalmykov's first deputy minister. Pleshakov may have spent the early years of his career in the Soviet military, working on electronics or communications.[29] In 1964, he was appointed deputy chairman of the State Committee for Radio Industry, which, in 1965, was renamed the Ministry of Radio Industry. It is not clear when Pleshakov became the Ministry's first deputy minister: one source gives 1968 as the year he assumed the post, while another, later, source gives 1965 as the date.[30] Pleshakov was one of six Soviet delegates to the SALT talks from their beginning in 1969 to early 1974.

In 1987, Pleshakov was replaced by V. I. Shimko. Shimko had served in the Party apparat since 1968, probably in the Department of Defense Industry, after a career in the radio industry.

First Deputy Ministers

Little is known about Bogdanov, and Pleshakov has already been discussed. Anatoli Antonovich Reut, Pleshakov's first deputy minister,

---

TABLE B.8. The Ministry of Radio Industry

Ministers
V. D. Kalmykov (1954–1974)
P. S. Pleshakov (1974–1987)
V. I. Shimko (1987–1988, 1989–)

First Deputy Ministers
N. A. Bogdanov (1966–1975)
P. S. Pleshakov (1968–1974)
A. A. Reut (1975–1983)
V. A. Kurochkin (1987–)

Deputy Ministers
S. M. Vladimirskiy (1958–1979?)
I. V. Lobov (1958–1978)
L. I. Gusev (1964?–1979?)
P. S. Pleshakov (1964–1968)
L. P. Kazanskiy (1966–1986?)
V. Ye. Nemtsov (1968?–1973?)
V. I. Markov (1968?–1981?)
N. G. Fedorov (1969?–1978?)
M. K. Sulim (1969?–1979?)
E. K. Pervyshin (1970–1974)
Ye. A. Merkin (1970?–1973?)
V. S. Semenikhin (1971–1974)
V. M. Shabanov (1974–1978)
N. V. Gorshkov (1974–1985)
S. S. Nikol'skiy (1974–1986?)
V. M. Yegoshin (1974–1986?)
I. A. Repkin (1975–1986?)
V. L. Koblov (1979–1986?)
V. I. Gladyshev (1980–1986?)
M. N. Zyabkin (1987?–)
F. P. Kovrigo (1987?–)
A. N. Korotonoshko (1987?–)
G. P. Kutsenko (1987?–)
O. A. Losev (1987?–)

came from a career in economic planning and had been director of the Minsk Ordzhonikidze Computer Works. In 1985, he was moved from his post as first deputy minister to the post of first deputy chairman of Gosplan for General Problems.[31]

THE MINISTRY OF COMMUNICATIONS EQUIPMENT INDUSTRY

The Ministry of Communications Equipment Industry was spun off from the Ministry of Radio Industry in early 1974. It is responsible for electronic systems, radios, televisions, telegraph and telephone equipment, radar, navigation aids, antennae, satellites, and military and space computers.

Its first (and current) minister in Erlen Kirikovich Pervyshin. Pleshakov had worked his way up through engineering posts to become director of an NPO in 1969. The next year, he was appointed deputy minister of Radio Industry, a post he held until the new ministry was created and he was appointed its director.

First Deputy Ministers and Deputy Ministers

No information was actively sought about the deputies in this ministry, given its relatively small role in the defense industries.

TABLE B.9. The Ministry of Communications Equipment Industry

Ministers
E. K. Pervyshin (1974–1989)

First Deputy Ministers
G. D. Kolmogorov (1975–1984)
V. A. Kripaytis (1984–1989)

Deputy Ministers
I. I. Kobin (1974–1984)
V. A. Kripaytis (1974–1984)
L. I. Pankratov (1974–1984?)
G. I. Shirokov (1974–1989?)
G. I. Vasil'yev (1974–1989?)
A. A. Kuzmitskiy (1979–1989?)
V. P. Romanov (1981–1989?)
Yu. P. Khomenko (1983–1989?)

THE MINISTRY OF ELECTRONICS INDUSTRY

The Ministry of Electronics Industry is responsible for electronic components and parts (subassemblies, but not final products, which are apparently the domain of the Ministry of Communications Equipment Industry), including solid-state devices and miniature electronic components. It also is apparently responsible for at least a portion of the ABM radar development and computer work.[32]

The man who formed the Ministry of Electronics Industry was Aleksandr Ivanovich Shokin. Like Kalmykov, Shokin came from the Ministry of Shipbuilding in the 1930s and 1940s, moving to "responsible work" in the radio-technical industry in 1943. He was a deputy and first deputy minister in the Ministry of Radio-Technical Industry, presumably to Kalmykov, until 1961, when he was appointed Chairman of the State Committee of Electronics Technology (from 1965, the Ministry of Electronics Industry).

TABLE B.10. The Ministry of Electronics Industry

Ministers
A. I. Shokin (1965–1985)
V. G. Kolesnikov (1985–)

First Deputy Ministers
K. I. Mikhailov (1968?–1971)
V. G. Kolesnikov (1971–1985)
A. V. Glovatskiy (1985–)

Deputy Ministers
K. I. Martynshov (1965?–1973?)
A. A. Zakharov (1965–1985)
S. V. Il'yushin (1965–)
K. L. Kurakhin (1967?–1979?)
A. A. Rozanov (1967?–1973?)
A. A. Chernyshev (1974–1988?)
G. B. Suvorov (1974–1988?)
A. F. Kazakov (1978–)
M. G. Yazov (1981–)
B. L. Tolstykh (1985–1987)
I. N. Bukreyev (1985–1988?)
V. I. Zhiltsov (1987–)
E. Ye. Ivanov (1988?–)
A. A. Inauri (1988?–)
Yu. A. Kozlov (1988?–)
A. G. Makarov (1988?–)
Ye. V. Mikhailov (1988?–)
Yu. A. Raynov (1988?–)

In 1985, Shokin was replaced by his first deputy, Vladislav Grigor'yevich Kolesnikov. Kolesnikov began his working career during the war in a weapons plant, and was by the early 1950s a deputy chief designer at a radio parts plant. In 1967, he was appointed director of a Voronezh instrument plant (from 1969, a production association). From 1971 to 1985, Kolesnikov was first deputy minister of Electronics Industry. Kolesnikov is unique among the other defense industry ministers in that he is a corresponding member of the Academy of Sciences.

NOTES

Introduction

1. *Pravda,* October 2, 1987, p. 1. During the same speech, Gorbachev criticized the Minister of Shipbuilding Industry, I. S. Belousov. Within six months, however, Belousov was promoted to oversee all Soviet defense industry.

2. "Economist Aganbegian Interviewed on Reforms," *Foreign Broadcast Information Service—USSR National Affairs* [hereafter FBIS], March 10, 1987, pp. S7–S11, at p. S11. For more information on these transfers, see Peter Almquist, "Militarization of Soviet Economy?", *Sovset' News: The Electronic Newsletter of Soviet Studies* (April 7, 1987), 3 (4) and the comments by Julian Cooper, Sovset' Forum message number 476, April 14, 1987.

1. A Framework for Analysis

1. See "Voyenno-promyshlennyy kompleks," *Sovetskaya voyennaya entsiklopediya* (Moscow: Voyenizdat, 1976), vol. 2, pp. 248–250; and R. A. Farama-

zyan, *Voyennaya ekonomika amerikanskogo imperializma* (Moscow: Mysl', 1983), pp. 131–138, 157–163.

2. Bill Keller, "At A Moscow Voter's Meeting, A Surprise Victory for Reform," *The New York Times*, February 12, 1989, p. 1 + .

3. It is important to note an approach not taken in this study. It could be argued that the success of a military industrial complex can be measured by the excess military capability acquired. If the Soviets buy more than they need, does this not indicate a military-industrial complex in action? Unfortunately, such an approach is complicated by the problem of defining the legitimate security needs of the Soviet Union. If it were possible to use internal Soviet assessments of needs, and compare them with actual acquisitions, and control for honest disagreement among experts (military, military-industrial, and civilian) such an approach might be tractable, although I believe it would still be of limited use. A military industrial complex need not be successful to be important, and it may have other means of exercising its influence (in arms control negotiations or diplomacy, for example).

4. The most important early works on totalitarianism are those by Carl Friedrich and Zbigniew Brzezinski. The strongest contemporary exponent of an updated version of the totalitarian model is probably William Odom, former director of the U.S. National Security Agency.

5. The key practitioners of the conflict school are Robert Conquest, Carl Linden, Sidney Ploss, and Michel Tatu.

6. While there are a number of interesting studies of this theme, two volumes neatly frame much of the discussion: the series of essays in H. Gordon Skilling and Franklyn Griffiths, eds., *Interest Groups and Politics in Soviet Politics* (Princeton: Princeton University Press, 1971), and Susan Gross Solomon, ed., *Pluralism in the Soviet Union: Essays in Honour of H. Gordon Skilling.*

7. See Peter H. Solomon, *Soviet Criminologists and Criminal Policy: Specialists in Policy-Making*, p. 128. Solomon attributes the "notion" to William Gamson, *Power and Discontent* (Homewood, Ill. np, 1968), pp. 59–61.

8. Solomon was able to show that the role of specialists, in his case criminologists, changed the probability that certain reforms in the criminal code would be passed. While the criminologists did not "win" every time, that is, their recommendations were not always adopted unchanged, they did have an impact on the issues raised, the decisions made, and the implementation of decisions. See his *Soviet Criminologists and Criminal Policy: Specialists in Policy Making.* See also the critique by David E. Powell, "In Pursuit of Interest Groups," *Soviet Union/Union Sovietique*, pp. 99–124, and Solomon's response in the same journal, pp. 110–118.

9. Zbigniew Brzezinski and Samuel P. Huntington, *Political Power: USA/ USSR* (New York: Viking Press, 1963, 1964), pp. 202–203; see also the chapter by William Potter, "The Study of Soviet Decisionmaking for National Security: What Is To Be Done," in Jiri Valenta and William Potter, eds., *Soviet Decisionmaking for National Security*, pp. 299–307.

10. I should emphasize that this is the author's application of these terms to nonmilitary issues, not one necessarily found in Soviet literature.

11. For the Soviet definition of doctrine, see "Doktrina voyennaya," *Sovetskaya voyennaya entsiklopediya*, vol. 3 (Moscow: Voyenizdat, 1977), pp. 225–229.

12. In Soviet military writings, strategy is one of three "military arts," whose role is to implement doctrine at varying levels of warfare. The other two military arts are operational art (mid-level operations) and tactics (lowest level). Rather than attempt to overparticularize decisions, I have lumped all three of these under the term "strategy," but it should be emphasized that such decisions can be as grandiose as whether to redirect a certain river or as mundane as how to reorganize production at a particular plant. For the Soviet definition of strategy, see "Strategiya voyennaya," *Sovetskaya voyennaya entsiklopediya*, vol. 7 (Moscow: Voyenizdat, 1979), pp. 555–565.

13. A number of case studies have been undertaken of particular Soviet decisions. In particular, see Joel J. Schwartz and William R. Keech, "Group Influence and the Policy Process in the Soviet Union" *American Political Science Review*, 62 (3):840–851; Jiri Valenta, "The Bureaucratic Politics Paradigm and the Soviet Invasion of Czechoslovakia," *Political Science Quarterly* (Spring 1979), 94(1):55–77; A. H. Brown, "Problems of Interest Articulation and Group Influence in the Soviet Union," *Government and Opposition* (Spring 1972), 7(2):229–243; Donald R. Kelley, "Environmental Policy-Making in the USSR: The Role of Industrial and Environmental Interest Groups," *Soviet Studies* (October 1976), 8(4):570–589; Theodore H. Friedgut, "Interests and Groups in Soviet Policy-Making: The MTS Reforms" *Soviet Studies* (October 1976), 28(4):524–547; Donald R. Kelley, "Interest Groups in the USSR: The Impact of Political Sensitivity on Group Influence," *Journal of Politics*, (August 1972), 34(3):860–888; Alexander J. Groth, "USSR: Pluralist Monolith," *British Journal of Political Science*, p. 445–464; A. H. Brown, "Policy-Making in the Soviet Union" *Soviet Studies* (July 1971), 23(1):120–148; T. H. Rigby, "Bureaucracy and Democracy in the USSR," *The Australian Quarterly*, pp. 5–14; Philip D. Stewart, "Soviet Interest Groups and the Policy Process: The Repeal of Production Education," *World Politics*; and Karen Dawisha, "The Limits of the Bureaucratic Politics Model: Observations on the Soviet Case," *Studies in Comparative Communism*, pp. 300–331.

14. For western analyses of this debate, see Schwartz and Keech, "Group Influence and the Policy Process in the Soviet Union," pp. 840–851; Stewart, "Soviet Interest Groups and the Policy Process," pp. 29–50; and Kelley, "Interest Groups in the USSR,"pp. 860–888.

15. Schwartz and Keech, "Group Influence and the Policy Process in the Soviet Union," pp. 840–851.

16. Kelley, "Interest Groups in the USSR," pp. 860–888.

17. Kelley analyzed approximately 350 articles by members of these groups to ascertain their support or opposition to the reforms. See Kelley, "Interest Groups in the USSR," pp. 860–888.

18. Medvedev suggests that Khrushchev's proposals were "informed neither by the findings of educational science nor by the large body of experience that Soviet schools had accumulated between 1953 and 1958. What inspired him, apparently, was his own recollection of the workers' faculties and technical colleges of the early 1920s." See Roy Medvedev, *Khrushchev*, p. 130.

19. Medvedev, *Khrushchev*, p. 128.

20. It might be argued that Khrushchev's efforts actually represent an attempt to reinvigorate existing Soviet views on the role of education in the communist society. This does not detract from the fact that the issue itself was one of both broad and profound importance to the society and was designed to affect the nature of the society itself.

21. See Peter H. Solomon, *Soviet Criminologists and Criminal Policy*

22. Thane Gustafson, *Reform in Soviet Politics: Lessons of Recent Policies on Land and Water* (Cambridge: Cambridge University Press, 1981).

23. See *Izvestiya*, Feb. 17, 1986, pp. 3, 6; also excerpted and translated in *Current Digest of the Soviet Press* (March 19, 1986), 38(7):5–7, 22; and Charles E. Ziegler, "Issue Creation and Interest Groups in Soviet Environmental Policy: The Applicability of the State Corporatists Model," *Comparative Politics* (January, 1986), 18(2):171–192.

24. See Peter Solomon, *Soviet Criminologists and Criminal Policy*, Thane Gustafson, *Reform in Soviet Politics*

25. According to Brezhnev in 1965, "true science takes nothing on faith; it cannot be the monopoly of particular scientists, and still less of administrators, no matter how much prestige they may have. Unfortunately, we have recently had instances in which people incompetent in science at times took upon themselves the role of arbiters in disputes among scientists, and in so doing hampered their initiative and stood in the way of free, creative discussion of scientific topics." *Plenum TsK KPSS*, March, 1965, pp. 25–26, quoted in Thane Gustafson, *Reform in Soviet Politics*, p. 31.

26. Specialists are unlikely to participate in the actual decision making in more than an advisory role. For an example of such participation, see Arkady Shevchenko's memoirs, in which he describes being invited to the Politburo to make presentations and participate when called upon. See Arkady N. Shevchenko, *Breaking With Moscow*, p. 207.

27. See Peter Solomon, *Soviet Criminologists and Criminal Policy*," pp. 160–163.

28. See Joel C. Moses, "Functional Career Specialization in Soviet Regional Elite Recruitment," and Gyula Jozsa, "Political *Seilschaften* in the USSR," both in T. H. Rigby and Bohdan Harasymiw, eds., *Leadership Selection and Patron-Client Relations in the USSR and Yugoslavia* (London: Allen & Unwin, 1983).

29. When Korolev died, his design bureau was taken over by his deputy, V. P. Mishin, and it appears to have rapidly lost much of its influence.

30. The concept of a military-industrial complex, originally put forth by Eisenhower in his farewell speech, has proved troubling to analysts ever since. There is little consensus on what one is, let alone how to determine its pres-

ence. For useful overviews, see in particular Robert D. Cuff, "An Organizational Perspective on the Military-Industrial Complex," *Business History Review*, pp. 251–267; and Charles C. Moskos, Jr, "The Concept of the Military-Industrial Complex: Radical Critique or Liberal Bogey?," *Social Problems* (April, 1974), 21(4):498–512.

31. Of course, at times these things do happen, but it is apparently infrequent and officially proscribed.

32. For example, the U.S. Central Intelligence Agency is forbidden from analyzing United States military capabilities.

2. The Organizational Context

1. See Ned Temko, "Soviet Insiders: How Power Flows in Moscow," in Erik P. Hoffmann and Robbin F. Laird, *The Soviet Polity in the Modern Era* (New York: Aldine, 1984), pp. 167–191, especially pp. 180–181; and Jerry F. Hough and Merle Fainsod, *How the Soviet Union is Governed*, pp. 472–473.

2. Brezhnev makes this point in an interview with *The New York Times*, June 15, 1973. The citation is in the very useful unpublished study by Ben Fischer, "The Soviet Political System and Foreign Policy-Making in the Brezhnev Era," pp. vi–7.

3. See Thomas W. Wolfe, *The SALT Experience* (Cambridge, Mass.: Ballinger, 1979), p. 171; David Holloway, *The Soviet Union and the Arms Race*, p. 109.

4. The aides were were A. M. Aleksandrov-Agentov, A. I. Blatov, and K. V. Rusakov. See Arkady N. Shevchenko, *Breaking with Moscow*, p. 181, and Zhores A. Medvedev, p. 233.

5. See, for example, Shevchenko, *Breaking with Moscow*, pp. 176–181.

6. "Brezhnev," in *Voyennyy entsiklopedicheskii slovar'*, [Hereafter *VES*]. The *Diplomaticheskiy slovar'* (Moscow: Nauka, 1984) states that Brezhnev headed the Council from 1977, when it was first recognized in the Soviet Constitution. This may be an interesting example of how little the diplomatic community actually knows about Soviet military affairs.

7. "Gorbachev Now Heads Key Defense Committee," *Baltimore Sun*, Aug. 2, 1985, p. 5.

8. *Armii stran Varshavskogo Dogovora* (Moscow: Voyennoye Izdatel'stvo, 1985), pp. 64, 88, 111, 131, 155, and 182. For an interesting "inside" perspective on the role of the Defense Council in pre-1968 Czechoslovakia, see Jan Sejna and Joseph D. Douglass, Jr., *Decision-Making in Communist Countries: An Inside View* (Cambridge, Mass.: Institute for Foreign policy Analysis, 1986), pp. 30–40.

9. *Allocation of Resources in the Soviet Union and China—1978*, hearings before the Subcommittee on Priorities and Economy in Government of the Joint Economic Committee, part 4, p. 187. In this source, Ustinov is identified as "probably" on the Defense Council, p. 170.

10. Sejna and Douglass, pp. 30–31.

11. *Armii stran Varshavskogo Dogovora*, pp. 131–132.

12. Kenneth Currie, "The Soviet General Staff," *Problems of Communism* (March–April 1984), p. 38; Coit Blacker, "Military Forces," in *After Brezhnev: Sources of Soviet Conduct in the 1980s* (Bloomington: Indiana University Press, 1983), pp. 125–185, at p. 141; and *Allocation of Resources in the Soviet Union and China—1981*, hearings before the Subcommittee on International Trade, Finance, and Security Economics of the Joint Economic Committee, part 7, p. 209 [hereafter *Allocation of Resources* and year].

13. For example, Marshall Shulman reported that Politburo members not on the Defense Council were denied access to specific military information. See Richard D. Anderson, "The Defense Council, Succession Politics, and Soviet Military Spending," in *Soviet Military Economic Relations: Proceedings of a Workshop*, sponsored by the Subcommittee on International Trade, Finance, and Security Economics of the Joint Economic Committee and the Congressional Research Service (Washington, D.C.: GPO, 1983), pp. 57–68, at p. 59.

14. Dmitri F. Ustinov was a full Politburo member before he was appointed Minister of Defense. His successor, Sergei L. Sokolov, was appointed a candidate (nonvoting) member.

15. Nikolai Vladimirovich Talyzin, appointed by Gorbachev.

16. The term "groups" is used advisedly, for one of the most contentious debates in Soviet studies over the last two decades has been the nature of "groups" and their participation in Soviet politics. In this discussion, the term is used only to indicate individuals engaged in the same or related professions.

17. It is required, under the Rules of the CPSU, to meet at least once every six months, and appears to do so. See Hough and Fainsod, *How the Soviet Union Is Governed*, pp. 460–461.

18. See Temko, "Soviet Insiders," especially pp. 181–182. Also see Hough and Fainsod, pp. 463–465.

19. Shelest's dissent from Brezhnev's détente policy reportedly appeared in Central Committee discussions, paving the way for his eventual removal from the Politburo itself. See Harry Gelman, *The Brezhnev Politburo and the Decline of Detente*, p. 158. Strictly at the Central Committee level, it was rumored that N. G. Yegorychev, first secretary of the Moscow Gorkom, was removed in 1967 for his criticism of Soviet Middle East policy. See Hough and Fainsod, pp. 464–465.

20. See Roy Medvedev, *Khrushchev*, pp. 116–119, 235.

21. Zhores Medvedev provides an interesting discussion of how to interpret public reports of Central Committee decision making, differentiating between decisions adopted by *yedinodushno* and *yedinoglasno*. While both words suggest unanimity, the former applies to the general support apparent in consensus decisions or formal votes in which there has been some dissent, while the latter applies only to formal votes in which everyone casts the same vote. See Zhores Medvedev, *Gorbachev*, p. 16.

22. In fact, the case can be made that the members are often selected *not* because of their personal qualities or achievements, but because of the importance of the position they hold and the desire to ensure that whoever holds the post is kept well-aware of the course of Party thinking as well as contributing a valuable perspective to various discussions.

23. The Supreme Soviet, made up of two chambers and 1,500 deputies, is frequently referred to as the Soviet's "nominal parliament" or in similar terms. It is the chief legislative body and, like the Central Committee, it maintains a smaller body (the Presidium, currently about forty people) to deal with matters between its twice-per-year sessions. Stephen White argues persuasively that the importance of the Supreme Soviet, while still not great, has increased substantially in the last two decades, with its sixteen standing commissions playing an important role in initiating legislation, monitoring the work of the rest of the government, and in consideration of the economic plans and budgets. See Stephen White, "The Supreme Soviet and Budgetary Politics in the USSR," *The British Journal of Political Science*, pp. 75–94.

24. See Peter H. Solomon, *Soviet Criminologists and Criminal Policy*, pp. 110–111.

25. For general information on the Secretariat, see Alexander Rahr, "The Central Committee Secretariat," Radio Liberty Research RL 439/84 (November 16, 1984).

26. It should also be emphasized that there is typically an overlap between the membership of the Secretariat and the Politburo. For example, in late 1976 four (five if one includes former Secretary D. F. Ustinov) of the fifteen full members of the Politburo and one of the seven candidate members were also on the Secretariat of twelve.

27. Donald D. Barry and Carol Barner-Barry, *Contemporary Soviet Politics: An Introduction*, 2d ed. (Englewood Cliffs, N.J.: Prentice-Hall, 1982), p. 127.

28. Michael Voslensky, *Nomenklatura*, p. 267; and Shevchenko, p. 160.

29. Elizabeth Teague, "The Foreign Departments of the Central Committee of the CPSU," p. 3; Abdurakhman Avtorkhanov, *The Communist Party Apparatus* (Chicago: Henry Regnery Company, 1966), pp. 209–210; Hough and Fainsod, p. 424. While in Moscow in November, 1984, I was told by an official of the Committee of Youth Organizations that the professional staff of the Central Committee numbered about 700 people.

30. This post was occupied by D. F. Ustinov (from 1965–1976), then by Yakov P. Ryabov (1976–1979). It appears that no single secretary had responsibilities for the sector until 1983, when G. V. Romanov was appointed to the Secretariat. The current occupant of the post, L. N. Zaikov, had replaced Romanov in Leningrad when the latter was appointed to the Secretariat, and was one of two new Secretaries appointed by Mikhail Gorbachev in July, 1985.

31. Hough and Fainsod, *How the Soviet Union Is Governed*, pp. 411, 425.

32. These include the Ministries of Defense Industry, Aviation Industry, General Machine-building, Machine-building, Means of Communication Indus-

try, Medium Machine-Building, Radio-technical Industry, Shipbuilding, and the State Committee for the Peaceful Use of Atomic Energy. See Hough and Fainsod, p. 413.

33. "D. F. Ustinov," *Sovetskaya voyennaya entsiklopediya* [hereafter SVE] (Moscow: Voyenizdat, 1980), 8:227.

34. Voslensky, p. 94. The Austrian journal *Oesterreichische Militarrische Zeitschrift* reports that 90 to 100 people serve in the Department of Defense Industry. See "Ruestungsbeschaffung in der Sowjetunion," *Oesterreichische Militarrische Zeitschrift* (1982), no. 6, pp. 468–473, at page 470. While in the Soviet Union in November 1984, I was told that the Department of Defense Industry was a bit smaller than average. I have no way of assessing the reliability of this claim.

In comparison, Timothy Colton estimates that the Department of Administrative Organs has "probably no more than fifty men, of whom perhaps twenty are in its military sectors." See Timothy Colton, *Commissars, Commanders, and Civilian Authority: The Structure of Soviet Military Politics* (Cambridge, Mass.: Harvard University Press, 1979), p. 29. The International Department has an estimated 150 people on its staff, while the Propaganda Department may be one of the largest, with several hundred employees. See Lilita Dzirkals, Thane Gustafson, A. Ross Johnson, *The Media and Intra-Elite Communication in the USSR* (Santa Monica, Cal.: Rand, 1982), pp. 14, 20.

35. For the Department of Defense Industry, this was I. D. Serbin from the late 1950s until his death in 1981. He was replaced by his first deputy, I. F. Dmitriyev, who held the post until 1985, when he was replaced by O. S. Belyakov.

36. Hough and Fainsod, pp. 420, 424.

37. For detailed discussions of the Republic departments, see A. V. Chernyak, compiler, *Tovarishch instruktor* (Moscow: Politicheskaya Literatura, 1984).

38. For example, the Ukraine's Department of Defense Industry was headed from its establishment in February 1959 to the mid-1970s by Yakov Kuz'mich Rudenko. See *XXIII s'yezd kommunisticheskoy partii Ukrainy: materialy s"yezda* (Kiev: Izdatel'stvo Politicheskoy Literatury Ukrainy, 1967), p. 177, where his post is listed; and *XXIV s"yezd kommunisticheskoy partii Ukrainy: stenograficheskiy otchet* (Kiev: Izdatel'stvo Politicheskoy Literatury Ukrainy, 1972), p. 278, where he is identified only as "chief of a department." Georgia regularly identifies the head of its Department of Defense Industry, currently A. S. Mikhaylov. See *Zarya Vostoka* (January 26, 1986), p. 1, translated in Joint Publication Research Service (JPRS), *USSR Report: Political and Sociological Affairs* (May 6, 1986), p. 400.

There is a Department of Defense Industry for the Leningrad obkom. See *Krasneya Zvezda*, March 25, 1989, p. 2 and Jerry F. Hough, *The Soviet Prefects*, p. 17. Henry Eric Firdman, in *Decision-Making in the Soviet Microelectronics Industry*, p. 63, describes how the Obkom Department of Defense Industry sided with other local industries against a design bureau with which he was associated. In an interview, Firdman also identified the chiefs of the Leningrad Obkom Department of Defense Industry as B. I. Aristov and R. S. Bobovikov. Its current chief is V. Zolkin. See also *Izvestiya Tsk KPSS*, number 1, 1989, p. 89. I would like to thank Ted Karasik for this reference.

39. *National Policy Machinery in the Soviet Union*, Senate Committee on Government Operations (1960), p. 28.

40. Teague, pp. 3–4.

41. See, for example, Anthony Downs, *Inside Bureaucracy* (Boston: Little, Brown, 1967), pp. 148–153.

42. For example, as discussed in a later chapter, there are cases in which the Department of Defense Industry protected a Leningrad design bureau from the local Party leadership.

43. In fact, some 85 percent of all Council decrees are unpublished, available only to the relevant agencies. See Dietrich A. Loeber, "Legal Rules 'For Internal Use Only'," *International and Comparative Law Quarterly* (January 1970), p. 77, quoted in Thane Gustafson, *Reform in Soviet Politics: Lessons of Recent Policies on Land and Water* (Cambridge: Cambridge University Press, 1981), p. 87.

44. The Council meets about once every three months. See Hough and Fainsod, p. 381.

45. Under Article 17 of the USSR Law "On the Council of Ministers of the USSR," the Council "has special permanent organs for exercising control over large inter-branch complexes and groups of similar branches of the national economy." See Herwig Kraus, "The Government of the USSR," *Radio Liberty Research*, RL 220/86 (June 9, 1986), p. 3.

46. From the early 1960s to 1985, the head was L. V. Smirnov. From 1985 to 1988, it was Yu. D. Maslyukov, who was replaced by I. S. Belousov.

47. Until 1989, the nine were the Ministries of Defense Industry, Aviation Industry, Shipbuilding, Machine Building, General Machine Building, Medium Machine Building, Electronics Industry, Communications Equipment Industry, and Radio Industry. Those with a predominantly civilian role represented on the VPK are the Ministries of Chemical Industry, Petrochemical Industry, and Electrical Equipment Industry. In 1989, the Ministries of Machine Building and Medium Machine Building were eliminated.

48. The current occupant of this position, V. I. Smyslov is a former deputy minister of the Ministry of Shipbuilding.

49. Most of the information on the VPK is drawn from *Défense Nationale* (December 1983), pp. 107–121; translated in FBIS-Western Europe, 18 Jan. 1984, pp. U1–U8; "*Le Monde* Reports on USSR Technological Espionage," in FBIS-WE, April 3, 1985, pp. K1–K6 (translated from *Le Monde*, March 10, 1985, p. 8, and April 2, 1985, p. 7). A U.S. Department of Defense report, "Soviet Acquisition of Militarily Significant Western Technology: An Update," issued in September, 1985, appears to be based on these same documents, and provides more detail about the VPK budget and acquisition programs.

50. It should be emphasized that the State Agro-Industrial Committee absorbed a number of ministries, rather than just coordinating existing ministries.

51. Henry Kissinger, *The White House Years* (Boston: Little, Brown, 1979), p. 1234.

52. Smirnov also apparently played a key role in the SALT 2 talks, meeting with Vance, although in these negotiations Marshal Nikolai Ogarkov, chief of the General Staff," also participated. See Raymond Garthoff, "SALT and the Soviet Military," in Jiri Valenta and William Potter, eds., *Soviet Decisionmaking for National Security*, p. 146.

53. Fyodor I. Kushnirsky, *Soviet Economic Planning, 1965–1980*, p. 83.

54. The Chairman of Gosplan, of course, is a member and, since 1985, another First Deputy Chairman has also been. In 1986, Gorbachev replaced the Chairman of Gosplan, but he has kept his Central Committe membership.

55. Those responsible for defense industries since 1962 have been V. M. Ryabikov (1962–1974), G. A. Titov (1974–1980), L. A. Voronin (1980–1982, when he took over broader industrial responsibilities), Yu. D. Maslyukov (1982–1985), and since late 1985, probably V. I. Smyslov, a former Deputy Minister of the Shipbuilding. A second possible Gosplan overseer for at least part of the defense industries is A. A. Reut, appointed in late 1985 after several years as a Deputy Minister of Electronics Industry.

Only Ryabikov has been identified as having held a military rank (general-colonel-engineer).

56. Kushnirsky, p. 55.

57. The chief of this department from 1977 to his death in 1985 was apparently N. P. Marakhovskiy, who, according to his obituary, had been a Gosplan defense industry specialist for thirty-one years. See *Izvestiya*, Oct. 18, 1985, p. 6.

58. In an interview, former Soviet economist Fyodor Kushnirsky stated that uniformed officers regularly work in Gosplan. In addition, it is known that a former naval officer headed a Gosplan department for several years and then served as a deputy editor of Gosplan's professional journal. See his obituary in *Planovoe Khozyaistvo*, July, 1977.

59. The center for military economics within the General Staff may be the Main Administration for Organization and Mobilization.

There is a large body of Soviet literature from the early 1960s through the early 1970s emphasizing the benefits of systems analysis in planning Soviet military developments and costs, as well as a complementary series of works on the requirements of the military economy and its place in the Soviet economy as a whole.

60. For an interesting discussion of the need to improve coordination between the Soviet economy and its armed forces, see former Chief of the General Staff N. V. Ogarkov's *Vsegda v gotovnosti k zashchite otechestva* (Moscow: Voyenizdat, 1982), pp. 59–60.

61. M. S. Smirtyukov, *Sovetskiy gosudarstvennyy apparat upravleniya*, p. 38. In 1989, these numbers were reduced to 37 ministries and 19 committees.

62. Smirtyukov, pp. 42–43; N. G. Kalinin, ed., *Organizatsiya upravleniya v sisteme ministerstva*, p. 64.

63. For the Eleventh FYP (1981–1985), these were published in early December, 1980.

64. Kushnirsky, p. 59.

65. See Kushnirsky, pp. 58–59.

66. Kalinin, ed., p. 64; also G. Kh. Popov and Yu. I. Krasnopoyas, *Organizatsiya upravleniya obshchestvennym proizvodstvom*, p. 97.

67. Jerry Hough and Merle Fainsod, *How the Soviet Union Is Governed* (Cambridge, Mass.: Harvard University Press, 1979), p. 385. According to Hough, the Ministry of Health had about 1,000 officials in 1965 and the Ministry of Energy and Electrification about 2,000 in 1974.

68. See Popov and Krasnopoyas, p. 97.

69. In the spring of 1973, the CPSU Central Committee and the Council of Ministers announced a potentially wide-sweeping reorganization of industrial management: in an effort to reduce the ministerial bureaucracy, it was decreed that "industrial associations" (*promyshlennoye ob"edineniye*, frequently called *Vsesoyuznoye promyshlennoye ob"edineniye* [VPO] in A-U ministries and *Respublikanskoye promyshlennoye ob"edineniye* [RPO] in the Republic ministries) were to be established to replace a number of administrations *(glavki)*, at the time the middle administrative level.

70. On the collegium, see I. L. Davitnidze, *Kollegii ministerstv;* Popov and Krasnopoyas, p. 97; Ellen Jones, "Committee Decision Making in the Soviet Union," pp. 165–188; and Kalinin, ed., p. 65.

71. Popov and Krasnopoyas, pp. 158–159; Kalinin, ed., p. 180.

72. *National Policy Machinery in the Soviet Union*, p. 38.

73. See, for example, reports of collegium meetings in the *Current Digest of the Soviet Press* (hereafter CDSP): "Expanded Meeting of the Collegium of the Ministry of Railroads," 34 (50):22–23, from *Pravda*, Dec. 14, 1982, p. 3; "Behind the Decisions of the 26th CPSU: A New Branch is Being Born," 34 (48):5–6, 13, from *Pravda*, Nov. 27, 1982, p. 2.

74. Karlik, *Ekonomilka*, p. 51.

75. "Nauchno-Tekhnicheskii Sovet Ministerstva," in *Izvestiya*, Aug. 21, 1966, p. 2.

76. Moskovskiy Gosudarstvennyy Universitet im. M. V. Lomonosova, *Pravovoye polozheniye ministerstv SSSR* (Moscow: Yuridicheskaya Literatura, 1971), p. 225; Kalinin, ed., p. 65.

77. N. D. Tyamshanskiy, *Ekonomika i organizatsiya nauchno-issledovatel-'skikh rabot v mashinostroyenii* (Leningrad: Mashinostroitelniye, 1967), p. 8.

78. Tyamshanskiy, p. 17.

79. Tyamshanskiy, p. 21.

80. For example, the Soviets consider the contribution of the NIIs engaged

in metallurgical research as having made a significant contribution to the artillery industry during World War II, but it is the artillery designers themselves (working at the various artillery design bureaus) who are given the fame and glory. See "Artilleriyskaya Promyshlennost'," in M. M. Kozlov, ed., *Velikaya Otechestvennaya Voyna, 1941–1945: Entsiklopediya* (Moscow: Sovetskaya Entsiklopediya, 1985), pp. 63–65.

Similarly, in the Ministry of Aviation Industry, TsAGI (the Central Aerohydrodynamics Institute, an NII dating to 1918) participates in the evaluation of proposed aircraft designs, provides the basic and applied research to develop handbooks of design criteria for aviation designers, and provides laboratory support for research and testing during the design of new aircraft and the modification of existing aircraft. But it is the KBs of Tupolev, Mikoyan and Guryevich, Sukhoi, and others that design the aircraft and the engines.

81. See Vadim Kirillovich Bekleshov et al, *Organizatsiya i planirovaniye deyatel'nosti otraslevykh NII i KB v priborostroyenii*, pp. 46–55. The book's emphasis is on instrument development, a field in which one might expect there to be considerable basic research.

82. I. G. Zhikharevich et al, *Sovershenstvovaniye organizatsii i upravleniya proizvodstvom v tsvetnoi metallurgii*, p. 31.

83. S. Ye. Kamenitser and F. M. Rusinov, eds., *Organizatsiya, planirovaniye, upravleniye deyatel'nost'yu promyshlennykh predpriyatii*, p. 13.

84. K. I. Taksir, *Upravleniye Promyshlennost'yu SSSR*, p. 191.

85. Taksir, p. 196.

86. Kamenitser and Rusinov, p. 11; P. A. Rodionov et al, *Partiinaya rabota v usloviyakh proizvodstvennykh ob"edineniy*, p. 57.

87. A small military force is also maintained by the KGB.

88. The Ministry does not appear to have had a regular post of "Deputy Minister of Armaments" for some years prior to Alekseyev's appointment. Tukhachevskiy was appointed chief of armaments for the Soviet Army in 1931, with the task of developing a modern military. He established a number of the most important design bureaus or saw to the training of several future designers, including Degtyarev, Tokarev, Shpital'nyy, Grabin, Ivanov, Petrov, Tupolev, Polikarpov, and Mikulin. See V. M. Ivanov, *Marshal M. N. Tukhachevskiy* (Moscow: Voyenizdat, 1985), pp. 280–286.

After the war, the Deputy Minister for Armaments was first Artillery Marshall N. D. Yakovlev (1947–1952), then Artillery Marshall M. I. Nedelin (1952–1953). Both these officers were closely involved with the development of missiles, with Nedelin appointed in 1959 as the first Commander in Chief of the Strategic Rocket Forces. From 1953 to 1964, there was apparently not a deputy minister for armaments, but there was a deputy minister for radar and radioelectronics: A. I. Berg, 1953–1957, and A. V. Gerasimov, 1957–1964. In 1964, Gerasimov became First Deputy Chief of the General Staff for Armaments. See David Holloway, "Innovation in the Defence Sector," in Ronald Amann and Julian Cooper, eds., *Industrial Innovation in the Soviet Union*, pp. 322, 328.

89. V. M. Shabanov, "Marshal voysk svyazi N. N. Alekseyev," *Voyenno-Istoricheskii Zhurnal* (1984), 6:88–90, at p. 90.

90. See Gerard Smith, *Doubletalk: The Story of SALT 1* (Lanham, M.D.: University Press of America, 1985), p. 48.

91. See Smith, p. 48. It appears likely that Valentin Vasil'yevich Druzhinin, another specialist from the Soviet Air Defense Force (PVO), replaced Alekseyev as head of the General Staff's Scientific-Technical Committee and as a deputy chief of the General Staff. See Defense Intelligence Agency, *Soviet Weapons Acquisition Process, with Special Emphasis on the Ground Forces*, DST-1830S-336-80 (partially declassified, 1986), p. 39.

92. Shabanov, p. 90.

93. See Defense Intelligence Agency, *Soviet Weapons Acquisition Process*, p. 39.

94. Trusov's identification is based on commission membership and obituary signatures. Trusov replaced Alekseyev as a Ministry of Defense representative to SALT 1 in 1970, and was identified as a specialist on ABM systems. He was still involved in the SALT negotiations until the end of 1978.

See Smith, p. 49, and Arms Control and Disarmament Agency, *United States and Soviet Participants in SALT I, SALT II, START (1982–1983), and NST (1985–1986)*, provided by ACDA to the author in 1986. Trusov is also identified as a member of the commission on technology and armaments for the preparation of the *Soviet Military Encyclopedia* (1976–1980), but he is dropped from the same commission on the *Military Encyclopedic Dictionary* (1983).

95. Lev Chaiko, "Helicopter Construction in the USSR," pp. 15–21, 69–70.

96. These themes are apparent in a number of unclassified sources that appeared in the late 1960s and early 1970s on questions of procurement, economics, and decision making. The quote is from Defense Intelligence Agency, *Soviet Weapons Acquisition Process*, p. 39.

97. Temko, "Soviet Insiders," p. 180.

98. This appears to be true in the industrial area as well as in more general policy areas, such as foreign policy. At least under Gromyko, foreign policy appears to have been dominated by the Ministry of Foreign Affairs rather than by the International Department. See Shevchenko, and Robert W. Kitrinos, "International Department of the CPSU," *Problems of Communism* (September-October, 1984), 33(5):47–67.

3. The Defense Plant Manager

1. U.S. Department of Defense, *Soviet Military Power*, 5th ed. (Washington, D.C.: GPO, 1986), p. 115.

2. For a useful general discussion of the "military mind," see Samuel P. Huntington, *The Soldier and the State: The Theory and Politics of Civil-Military Relations* (New York: Vintage, 1957), ch. 3.

3. Only 35 to 40 percent of the enterprise directors are promoted from within their own firm, according to one study of a number of branches; the rest are brought in from outside a factory or association, perhaps because they have not been included on the local reserve list. See V. Matriko, "The People in Whom We Place Our Trust," *Literaturnaya gazeta*, Jan. 26, 1977, p. 10 (*Current Digest of the Soviet Press* [hereafter CDSP], 29(6):15).

In general, there is a high turnover rate among Soviet managers. In one study of Volgograd managers, almost 40 percent of the directors and over 56 percent of the chief engineers there were replaced in the course of three years. No more than half the changes involved promotion; the rest were presumably moved aside or down. Of those considered "failed" managers, 20 percent had held the post for less than one year. In the Ministry of Construction, it was noted in 1981 that of the branch's 207 top executives in 1981, only 44 had held their jobs for more than five years. See Aleksandr Levikov, "New Job," *Literaturnaya gazeta*, p. 11 (CDSP, pp. 5–6, at p. 6); and O. Latifi, "Promoted to a Post," *Pravda*, July 17, 1981, p. 2 (CDSP, 33 (29):18–19, at p. 18). These figures support Hough's suggestion of a sense of managerial "tenure," in which officials are more frequently moved around, rather than dropped from the nomenklatura. See Jerry F. Hough, *The Soviet Prefects*, pp. 275–276.

4. See appendix A.

5. It is, of course, not possible to say that these individuals actually knew each other at school. In addition to the size of the institutions, it is not always possible to obtain information about when an individual graduated, or even whether he or she was a correspondence or resident student.

6. This approval is one of the key responsibilities of the Central Committee Department of Defense Industry.

7. It should be emphasized that the discussions in the Soviet press do not distinguish between civilian and defense industrial managers. However, according to one western participant, it appears that the defense manager and the civilian manager participate in the same programs. Shiela Puffer, "Inside a Soviet Management Institute," pp. 90–96.

8. Mark R. Beissinger, *The Politics of Convergence.*

9. Julian Cooper, "The Civilian Production of the Soviet Defence Industry," in Ronald Amann and Julian Cooper, eds., *Technical Progress and Soviet Economic Development*, pp. 31–50.

10. For the most careful assessments, see Julian Cooper, "The Scale of Output of Civilian Products by Enterprises of the Soviet Defence Industry," (Birmingham, England: Centre for Russian and East European Studies, University of Birmingham, 1988).

11. V. Gavrilov noted that this was indicated in the Central Committee report at the 24th Party Congress, presumably referring to Brezhnev's statement that 42 percent of the defense industry output is for civilian use. Gavrilov states that "the defense industry has significant reserves of power which, in the event of war, will be fully employed for producing war materiel." See "The Material Base for Strengthening the Nation's Defense Potential," *Rear and Supply* (Feb-

ruary 1972), p. 14. See also R. Averbokh, "Pressing Questions on the Operation of Production Enterprises," *Rear and Supply* (December 1967), p. 63.

12. There are very few managers of *any* plants on the Central Committee, with only two or three as full members in any Central Committee since 1961. Interestingly, there are a number of "brigade leaders" and other shop-level managers from defense plants on the Central Committee, perhaps elected as representatives of the "working class."

13. For similar comments, see those made nine years apart by V. N. Andrianov of the 61 Kommunar Shipyard and G. Vanag of the Chkalov Aviation Plant. Both men argued that Gosplan was out of touch with both the new economic system (the various reforms implemented at Kosygin's urging from 1965) and with the plants responsible for the plan's implementation. See V. N. Andrianov, "Sovershentsvovaniye Khozrascheta," *Ekonomicheskaya gazeta* (August 1970), 35:6, and G. Vanag, "Upravleniye kachestvom," *Trud*, January 6, 1979, p. 2.

14. The "logic" of the reforms, in the words of Alec Nove, was to reward management "not just for fulfilling quantitative plans (though the amount specified in the plan had to be produced) but for increasing sales and profits." Unfortunately, the results of the reforms did not meet the expectations of the time. See Alec Nove, *The Soviet Economic System*, pp. 90–95 (quote at p. 92).

15. V. Stepanchenko, "V Sodruzhestve s Naukoy," p. 6.

16. Ya. Khvedeliyani and N. Redyukhin, "Rezervy nakhodit kazhdyy," p. 2.

17. One of his articles, "How To Calculate the Level of NOT," consists of a list of seventeen formulae for determining seventeen variables. When summed, these variables give the general NOT level for a shop, and the results can then be used to determine bonuses for the workers. See Pavel Derunov, "Kak Opredelit' Uroven' NOT," *Ekonomicheskaya gazeta* (September 1967), 38:29.

18. O. Soyich, "Dolgoletiye Mashin," *Izvestiya*, Apr. 14, 1965, p. 3. A condensed version of this article, omitting the explicit criticism of Gosplan, was printed in the magazine *Standartizatsiya* (1965), 6:41–42. Also dropped in this version was a call for increased knowledge about world production standards. Both versions noted that about 25 percent of the basic production in Kharkov was not up to contemporary standards.

19. Yu. Konyshev, "Ne Chuzhaya Zabota," *Pravda*, June 16, 1981, p. 4.

20. L. A. Voronin, F. B. Zlotnikov, and P. G. Grodinskiy, "The Krasnogorsk Mechancal Works Operate in a New Fashion," pp. 754–759.

21. If he was, he may have had a chance to change it, for he was soon appointed to head the Ministry of Defense Industry's Department of Production-Planning and eventually became a deputy minister, then first deputy minister before moving into Gosplan.

22. G. Vanag, p. 2.

23. It is, of course, possible that these directors are able to think of their plants as made up of two components, one civilian and one military, and are discussing only the civilian side.

24. Ye. Sabinin, "Vospitaniye distsipliny truda," *Ekonomicheskaya gazeta*, p. 6.

25. Konyshev. It should be noted that this was in the context of an article about washing-machine production.

26. Khvedeliyani and Redyukhin, p. 2.

27. Vanag. Emphasis added because of Vanag's position in a plant that might be expected to receive special treatment because of its military utility.

28. See Mikhail Agursky, *The Soviet Military-Industrial Complex*, Jerusalem Papers on Peace Problems (Jerusalem: Magnes Press, 1980), 31:17–18; and Victor Yevsikov, "Re-Entry Technology and the Soviet Space Program (Some Personal Observations)," p. 5.

29. Yevsikov, p. 5.

30. V. O. Stepanchenko, "V tsentre vnimaniya—Tekhnicheskii Progress," V. A. Stepanchenko, "O samom nasushchnom," p. 28. It should be recalled that CPSU members make up a minority of Soviet workers.

31. Karl Greenburg, "Central Materials Research Institute (TsNIIM) of the Soviet Ministry of Defense Industry," p. 52.

32. The only mention of the administration and support staff in the articles examined is found in an article by V. Stepanchenko of the Kiev Aircraft Plant, in which he notes that "the number of auxiliary [vspomogatelnyy] workers, ITR [engineering-technical workers] and office workers [sluzhashchii] is determined by the norms of maintenance per hundred laborers [rabochii]." Stepanchenko, "Dorogoy poiska i uspekha," p. 12.

33. M. Odinets, "Zdrastvuy, zhizn'!," p. 6.

34. See, for example, G. Zaychenko, "Nashim mal'chishkam v nasledstvo—zavod," p. 1.

35. Ya. Khvedeliyani, "Inzhener, ego rol' i mesto," p. 3. Presumably these are also "closed" (i.e., military) NIIs.

36. Ya. R. Khvedeliyani, "Chem 'pronyat" letuna." *Pravda*, p. 2. There was an article summarizing letters in response to Khvedeliyani's article, also in *Pravda*, Aug. 10, 1973, p. 3, in which the consensus seemed to be that the number of drifters could be reduced by ensuring that work was creative and fulfilling.

37. O. V. Soyich, "Molodoi spetsiyalist," p. 3.

38. G. V. Zaychenko, "Uchit'sya iskusstvu upravleniya," p. 14.

39. Khvedeliyani, "Inzhener, ego rol' i mesto."

40. P. F. Derunov, "Sistema koeffitsiyentov opredeleniya urovnya organizatsii truda."

41. "Rech' tov. A. A. Lyubchenko," *Trud*, Mar. 1, 1968, p. 3. The Kirov plant, with an estimated 30,000 employees, has a long history of military production, especially in the area of armor development. See Greenburg, p. 49.

42. Subbotin detailed what he suggests were typical wages and expenses for both workers and engineering staff. For the worker's family of four, the head of the family earned 1,900 rubles per year, with an additional family member earning 1,660 rubles per year. A bonus of 118 rubles was assumed. Outlays for

the worker's family were assumed to be 1,900 rubles for food, 525 rubles for clothes and shoes, 360 rubles for furniture, 260 rubles for "cultural supplies," 300 rubles for utilities, and the remainder (333 rubles) for miscellaneous expenses.

For the engineer's family, the income is 2,504 rubles for the engineer, 1,037 rubles for an additional member, and a bonus of 1,068 rubles. Expenses were 1,828 rubles for food, 494 rubles for "consumer goods," 285 rubles on books and magazines, 316 on cultural materials, 279 rubles on the theater, movies, and concerts, 350 rubles on household goods, 357 rubles on utilities, and 400 rubles on tourist activities. The remainder is 305 rubles.

Other than the interesting differences in expenditures between the two "typical" families, the differences in bonuses between the two families is striking. That of the engineer's family is equivalent to almost four months of the family's total income, while that of the worker is equivalent to only about two *weeks*.

Subbotin also notes that the average "budget" (income, including bonus) of an office worker at the plant is 2,580 rubles, which he describes as sufficient to satisfy the needs of a family of four or five. See M. Subbotin, "Material'nyye fondy i byudzhet sem'i," p. 3.

43. L. A. Voronin, F. B. Zlotnikov, and P. G. Grodinskiy, "The Krasnogorsk Mechanical Works Operate in a New Fashion," *Soviet Journal of Optical Technology*, pp. 754–759.

44. Sabinin, "Vospitaniye distsipliny truda." According to Sabinin, the plant loses about 8.8 percent of its workers per year, with 1.1% being released for labor violations.

45. V. Sivets, "Nasha zabota o mastere," p. 2. According to Sivets, only about half the master's time is actually spent supervising. Seventeen percent of it is spent in paperwork, 21 percent between shops, and 13 percent in "nonrational production." A master oversees no fewer than twenty-five people. See B. S. Dubko, *Spravochnik inzhenera-ekonomista sudostroitel'nogo prepriyatiya* (Leningrad: Sudostroyeniye, 1978), p. 136.

46. V. N. Sivets, "Sistema obespecheniya vysokogo kachestva, uvelicheniya resursa i povysheniya nadezhnosti," pp. 42–45.

47. G. Vanag, "Upravlenize Kachestvom", p. 2. There is apparently a wage differential that is supposed to provide for greater wages in Siberia. It is not clear why this was not applicable.

48. S. Ye. Kamentser and F. M. Rusinov, eds., *Organizatsiya, planirovanie i upravleniye deyatel'nost'yu promyshlennykh predpriyatiy*, p. 226. For similar discussions of the role of the OTK, see I. M. Gratsershtein and R. D. Malinova, *Ekonomika, organizatsiya, i planirovaniye proizvodstva v tsvetnoy metallurgii*, 2d ed. (Moscow: Metallurgiya, 1985), p. 157, and V. G. Novikov and K. D. Konovalenko, eds., *Organizatsiya i planirovaniye radiotekhnicheskogo proizvodstva*, p. 152.

49. Novikov and Konovalenko, eds., p. 157 and Gratsershtein and Malinova, p. 158.

50. "Put' k vysokomu kachestvu," *Ekonomicheskaya gazeta* (December 1967), 51:24.

51. There is a debate between Soviet and western authors as to who developed the system first. For a good summary of the two views, see Robert W. Campbell, "Management Spillovers from Soviet Space and Military Programmes," *Soviet Studies* (April 1972), 23(4):586–607.

52. S. M. Bukhalo and A. V. Antontsa, eds., *Ekonomika, organizatsiya, i planirovaniye promyshlennogo proizvodstva* (Kiev: Vishcha Shkola, 1984), p. 110; A. I. Marek and A. I. Semenov, *Nauchno-proizvodstvennyye kompleksy: formirovaniye i razvitiye* (Moscow: Nauka, 1985), p. 114; and K. I. Taksir, *Upravleniye promyshlennost'yu SSSR*, pp. 59–60.

53. Taksir, pp. 59–60, and Bukhalo and Antontsa, eds., p. 110.

54. Taksir, p. 61. In the 1980s, the Gorky Aircraft Plant produced the MiG-31 Foxhound aircraft. See also B. V. Vlasov and G. B. Kats, eds., *Organizatsiya, planirovaniye, i upravleniye predpriyatiyem massogo mashinostroyenniya* (Moscow: Vysshaya Shkola, 1985), p. 161.

55. Bukhalo and Antontsa, eds., p. 110–111.

56. Sivets, "Sistema obespecheniya vysokogo kachestva."

57. Ya. R. Khvedeliyani, "Sovremennaya Kontrol'no-Izmeritel'naya Tekhnika," pp. 99–102.

58. N. Denisov, "Garantiya Vysokogo Kachestva," p. 2. This appears to have been one of the major stimuli for developing the Saratov system. See "Put' k vysokomu kachestvu," *Ekonomicheskaya Gazeta*, p. 24.

59. V. Stepanchenko, "O samom nasyshchnom," and "V tsentre vnimaniya —tekhnicheskiy progress," p. 76.

60. Ya. R. Khvedeliyani, "Sovremennaya kontrol'no-izmeritel'naya Tekhnika," p. 102.

61. I. S. Silayev, I. I. Darovskikh, "Osnovyye printsipy sistemy KANARSPI i ikh organizatsionno-tekhnicheskaya realizatsiya," pp. 16–19.

62. P. F. Derunov, "Sistema koeffitsiyentov."

63. L. A. Voronin, A. M. Stesel', and A. P. Afontsev, "Improvement of Reliability of Still and Movie Equipment by Using Modern Electronic Quality Control and Testing Devices on the Assembly Line," *Soviet Journal of Optical Technology*, 35 (3):405–410; and Voronin, Zlotnikov, and Grodinskiy, "Krasnogorskiy . . . ."

64. For one Soviet discussion, see V. A. Silinskiy, "Voyennyy predstavitel'," *Sovyetskaya voyennaya entsiklopediya*, 2:271–272. See also the émigré reports by Mikhail Turetsky, "The Introduction of Missile Systems into the Soviet Navy," pp. 5–6; Lev Chaiko, "Helicopter Construction in the USSR," p. 20; and Anatol Fedoseyev, "Design in Soviet Military R&D," p. 11; and [Igor Genis] "The Role of the Military Representatives in the Soviet Defense Industry—A Case Study of the 3896th Military Representative Group (MRG) in Riga" (McLean, Va.: DBM Corporation, 1981).

Silinsky's position is unknown, but many entries in the encyclopedia are credited to senior officers or officials within a speciality. For example, the head of the Strategic Rocket Forces is credited with the SRF article, and the current director of TsAGI is credited with the article about the Institute. Silinsky is thus likely to be a senior official in the voyenpred system, presumably under the authority of the Deputy Minister of Defense for Armaments (currently V. Shabanov, and until 1980, N. N. Alekseyev).

65. This list is drawn from Silinskiy.

66. Yevsikov, "Re-entry Technology," pp. 41–42.

67. See Turetsky, pp. 5–6; Chaiko, p. 20; and Fedoseyev, "Design in Soviet Military R&D," p. 11.

68. P. Malofeyev, "Zavodskiy institut," p. 3.

69. Khvedeliyani, "Inzhener, ego rol' i mesto."

70. V. Stepanchenko, "Dorogoi poiska i uspekha," p. 12.

71. Stepanchenko, "V sodruzhestve s naukoy."

72. See F. Ya. Kotov and V. D. Dudkin, "Programma dolgovremennogo so-trudnichestva," pp. 91–95; F. Kotov, "Reglamentatsiya truda, pp. 74–77; and F. Ya. Kotov, "Trudovaya estafeta pyatiletok," pp. 12–15. It is not known if such a working body was actually established. Kotov was a graduate of the Leningrad Military-Mechanics Institute.

73. The only exception is the brief speech by Stepanchenko on SALT, in which he indicated that the Ukrainian people, "like all Soviet people and peace-loving humanity of the planet," support the SALT agreements. See V. Stepanchenko's statement in "Politiky partii odobryayem," p. 1.

74. Andrew Cockburn, *The Threat: Inside the Soviet Military Machine* (New York: Random House, 1983), pp. 89–90. Agursky believes the decision to use domestic machine tools was made in order to ensure that the plant could blame the additional years of delay on the Institute of Production Technology. Another possibility, of course, is that the Soviets did not wish to be dependent on a product necessary for weapons production that they could not produce and maintain domestically.

The representative of the Southern Urals Machine Building Plant at the meeting at which the decision was made was the chief engineer, the management official most closely tied with actual production.

75. Defense plant managers do frequently participate in the Supreme Soviet and, perhaps more important, in the various republic and local Party Committees. Their impact at these levels, however, is almost certainly not on a doctrinal level, but on the strategic, following the guidance provided by the national Central Committee.

76. Fedoseyev, "Design in Soviet Military R&D," p. 12.

77. For a report of such an effort, see Alexander Yanov, *Detente After Brezhnev*, pp. 22–26. Yanov emphasizes that having to call for such outside help is unpleasant, as each step of the way the manager is upbraided for poor planning.

78. There is, of course, officially acceptable lobbying out of the public view. The only case I have found of such private contact involving a manager is that of P. A. Voronin, director of the Znamiya Truda Aircraft Plant in Moscow, who was one of two signers of a letter to the Central Committee in 1961 calling for

greater devotion of resources to electronics development. See Mikhail Agursky, "The Research Institute of Machine Building Technology," p. 66–67. This would be a very interesting case to have more information about, but none appears available.

Anatol Fedoseyev, a leading radar designer, also reports writing a letter with a number of other scientists urging the creation of the Ministry of Electronics in the early 1960s. See Anatol Fedoseyev, "Design in Soviet Military R&D" pp. 14–15.

79. Voronin, Zlotnikov, and Grodinskiy reported that in 1967 "our output is not smooth. In the first ten days of each month, only 20 percent of the monthly quota is produced, while 50 percent is produced in the last ten days." P. 758.

In 1976, the military journal *Rear and Supply* contained two articles discussing storming at military enterprises, one noting that in 1974, 20 percent of the monthly production was accomplished in the first ten days and 40 percent in the last ten. In the other, current experience in rhythmic production (31.1 percent in the first ten-day period, 39.3 percent in the second, and 29.6 percent in the third) is contrasted with previous experience, when 5.1 percent of the products were produced in the first ten-day period, 15.3 percent in the second, and 79.0 percent in the third. See O. Andreyev, S. Podgayetskiy, and A. Mironov, "Make Fuller Use of Reserves to Raise the Efficiency of Production,' *Rear and Supply* (June 1976), p. 18; and I. Kauk, "Our Experience in Production Quality Control," *Rear and Supply* (November 1976), p. 55.

80. One of the advantages of studying the Soviet system is that it is reasonable to assume that if a member of the CPSU is promoted, he will, in fact, accept the promotion and move. We can thus assume that those who remained in the manager's post for several years probably were not pressed to move into a more responsible position.

4. The Weapons Scientist and the Designer

1. Much of the discussion will revolve around designers because they are the most closely involved in converting theoretical developments into weapons technology. Most theoretical developments have application in both the civilian and military realms. However, the role of the scientists, frequently working in the more general scientific research institutes *(nauchno-issledovatel'skiy institut*, or NII) and responsible for establishing many of the boundaries within which the designers work, should not be ignored or minimized. (Male pronouns will be used, as virtually every military designer identified is male.)

2. It appears that each plant with a design bureau has a Chief Designer, while the title "General Designer" is of greater stature, perhaps reflecting an industrywide standing. For example, most of the leading designers of Soviet aircraft were Chief Designers, apparently at a plant or KB, for many years before becoming General Designers of the Ministry of Aviation Industry.

3. Two years earlier, the Department of Defense reported forty-four major design bureaus, with the difference being that eleven design bureaus are reported responsible for "Strategic and Tactical Missiles," rather than the breakdown in the more recent table. See Department of Defense, *The FY 1985 Department of Defense Program for Research, Development, and Acquisition,* p. II-4, reprinted in John Sheerer, ed., *USSR Facts & Figures Annual,* (Gulf Breeze, Fla.: Academic International, 1985), 9:111.

4. This is, of course, not always the case. But often even retired designers appear in the press to note their experiences and offer their expertise on various issues.

5. Many of the military designers originally joined the now disbanded "Technical Sciences Department," an Academy of Sciences department that emphasized connections with industry and production or engineering expertise. The Department played an important role in mobilizing scientists during the war, but by the late 1950s, the closeness of some of its institutes to industry and its lack of involvement in the "specifics of academic work" provoked a rebuke from the president of the Academy. A split within the Academy between "engineers" and "theoreticians" was resolved in 1961 with the elimination of the Technical Sciences Department and the distribution of its institutes to ministries or other government agencies. Within a year the Academy had lost one-half its institutes and one-third of its scientific personnel. See Alexander Vucinich, *Empire of Knowledge: The Academy of Sciences of the USSR (1917– 1970)* (Berkeley: University of California Press, 1984), pp. 199–203, 298–311; and Loren R. Graham, "The Place of the Academy of Sciences System in the Overall Organization of Soviet Science," in John R. Thomas and Ursula M. Kruse-Vaucienne, eds., *"Soviet Science and Technology: Domestic and Foreign Perspectives* (Washington, D.C.: National Science Foundation, 1977), p. 47.

6. Oleg Antonov, Rotislav Belyakov, Aleksei Il'yushin, Nikolai Kuznetsov, Georgi Svishchev, and Aleksandr Yakovlev.

7. Vladimir Chelomei, Petr Grushin, Viktor Makeyev, Viktor Mishin, and Aleksandr Nadiradze.

It is interesting to note that one rocket-engine designer, A. M. Isayev, refused to join the Academy, reportedly on the grounds that he was an engineer, not a scientist. Mikhail Agursky, *"The Research Institute of Machine-Building Technology: A Part of the Soviet Military-Industrial Complex,"* Soviet Institutions Series Paper (Jerusalem: The Soviet and East European Research Centre of the Hebrew University of Jerusalem, nd), 8:25.

8. Svyatoslav Lavrov, Vsevolod Burtsev, and Boris Chertok.

9. Sergei Kovalev.

10. Vladimir Semenikhin.

11. For two useful studies of patronage in the Brezhnev era, see Joel C. Moses, "Functional Career Specialization in Soviet Regional Elite Recruitment," and Gyula Jozsa, "Political *Seilschaften* in the USSR," both in T. H. Rigby and Bohda Harasymiw, eds., *Leadership Selection and Patron-Client Relations in the USSR and Yugoslavia* (London: George Allen & Unwin, 1983).

12. For Brezhnev's own recollections of his work with various weapons designers, see *Novyy Mir* (January 1983), 1:26–51. Others have also noted Brezhnev's close involvement with the Soviet missile industry while a secretary. See, for example, V. P. Platonov and V. P. Gorbulin, *Mikhaylo Kuz'mich Yangel* (Kiev: Naukova Dumka, 1979), p. 64, in which a visit by Brezhnev and Ustinov to Yangel's design bureau in 1959 is mentioned, and note that it was probably Brezhnev who approached Yangel about establishing his own design bureau. See V. Gubarev, *Konstruktor*, pp. 72–73. The former chief of the Strategic Rocket Forces also recalled that Brezhnev's office was the focal point for the development of the Soviet missile industry. See V. Tolubko, *Nedelin*, p. 183. Kuz'mina, in her biography of P. O. Sukhoi, describes a visit to the series production plant by Brezhnev, then a secretary of the Central Committee with responsibility for "questions of new technology," and his help in smoothing out certain production problems. L. Kuz'mina, *Generalnyy konstruktor Pavel Sukhoi*, p. 181.

13. For a brief note on Shcherbitskiy and Yangel, see Platonov and Gorbulin, p. 97.

14. Author's interview with Henry Eric Firdman.

15. Fedoseyev, "Design in Soviet Military R&D," pp. 14–15. As an example, Fedoseyev refers to a letter he wrote advocating the establishment of the Ministry of Electronics. In another example, he was less successful. In his book *Zapadnya*, he reports that he and some other scientists wrote to Kosygin in the hope of raising the basic salary level of their lab staffs. Kosygin wrote back that the funds were not available, and Fedoseyev states that a Gosplan official told him that the "official" figures on income were fraudulent anyway. See A. Fedoseyev, *Zapadnya*, pp. 183–184.

16. Fedoseyev discusses his most important competition, that with Mints over the development of the ABM radar system, without mentioning using any of the "clout and weight." Indeed, he emphasizes that it was the superiority of his magnetron "which had no equivalents in the West," over that of Mints' "American-style klystron." Both were presented at the VPK meeting over which Ustinov (then a secretary) presided. According to Fedoseyev, "the discussion did not end in any formal decision, but later on General Kisun'ko [developer of the ABM system] called me and said that I would be the developer of the tube for his radar system." See Fedoseyev, "Design in Soviet Military R&D," p. 14; Anatol Fedoseyev, "Draft of remarks prepared for a colloquium at the Harvard Russian Research Center," February 29, 1983, p. 16.

17. Khrushchev reports that soon after Stalin's death, Korolev came to the Politburo to report on his rocketry research. According to Khrushchev, "I don't want to exaggerate, but I'd say we gawked at what he showed us as if we were a bunch of sheep seeing a new gate for the first time." See Khrushchev, *Khrushchev Remembers*, p. 46. For a useful overview of Korolev's career, especially in the early development of military rockets, see the introduction by V. P. Mishin and B. V. Raushenbakh to M. V. Keldysh, ed., *Tvorcheskoye naslediye akade-*

mika Sergeya Pavlovicha Koroleva: Izbrannyye trudy i dokumenty (Moscow: Nauka, 1980), especially pp. 14–18.

18. One indicator that Brezhnev may have agreed with the general thrust of emphasizing missiles over aircraft or ships is to consider how the Soviet arsenal grew during the Brezhnev era. According to the U.S. Defense Intelligence Agency (DIA), from 1964 (when Brezhnev became General Secretary) to 1982 (Brezhnev's death), the intercontinental bomber inventory actually declined marginally, from 163 to 145. (The Tu-22M Backfire theater bomber, entering the inventory since 1975, is not included in this total.) During this same period, the number of intercontinental ballistic missiles deployed on land and in submarines increased from fewer than 300 to more than 2,300. See DIA, "Intercontinental Strategic Forces Summary, USSR," (DDB-2680-253-85), August 1985.

Additional DIA data on production shows a similar trend, with bomber production actually peaking in 1964 (at 180) and then declining dramatically, bottoming out in 1973 and 1974 at 15 (where these bombers went while the force inventory was static is not clear). ICBM and SLBM production increased and declined with each new generation of missiles. See DIA, "Soviet Military Materiel Production, 1960–1985," (U-45, 542/DB-4).

19. Yevsikov, "Re-entry Technology," pp. 11–12.

20. Yevsikov, pp. 3, 11–12. See also Henry Eric Firdman, "Decision-making in the Soviet Microelectronics Industry," p. 58. Firdman notes this in the context of discussing the efforts of an electronics designer to attach himself to Korolev's coattails, to ensure support for his own projects.

21. See Firdman, "Decision-making in the Soviet Microelectronics Industry."

22. Shokin and chief engineer Smirnov of NIIRE (a leading electronics scientific research institute in Leningrad), in competing to gain control over the Soviet microelectronics industry, chose different paths. While Smirnov tried to influence several leading Soviet designers, including Korolev, Kurchatov, and Tupolev, Shokin attempted to gain influence through pushing for the establishment of a State Committee on Electronics and gaining a seat on the Council of Ministers as its chairman.

23. Firdman, "Decision-making in the Soviet Microelectronics Industry," pp. 25–27.

24. Firdman, "Decision-making in the Soviet Microelectronics Industry," pp. 41–43.

25. Presumably actually a department within the General Staff's Administration for Technology and Armaments.

26. Chaiko, "Helicopter Construction," pp. 21, 69–70.

27. It is interesting that each of these men had been involved in rocket or missile development in some capacity.

28. It should also be noted that, while Novozhilov and the Ilyushin design bureau are part of the Ministry of Aviation Industry, their work has emphasized civilian and cargo aircraft for many years.

29. See the obituaries of Kotin *(Pravda,* Oct. 24, 1979, p. 3), Kucherenko *(Izvestiya,* Sept. 15, 1976), p. 4), and Petrov *(Pravda,* Aug. 23, 1978, p. 6). Tyurin is identified in the CIA's *Directory of Soviet Officials: National Organizations* (August 1984).

30. *Deputaty verkhovnogo soveta SSSR: odinnadtsatyy sozyv* (Moscow: Izvestiya, 1984).

31. This is especially common on the evaluation boards (see below).

32. For typical discussions of such competition taken from the aircraft industry, see D. Gay, *Nebesnoye Prityazheniye,* especially pages 118–119, in which Myasishchev takes on the task of building an intercontinental bomber that Tupolev deemed impossible; and Kuz'mina, *Generalnyy Konstruktor Pavel Sukhoi,* in which Sukhoi often compares his work with that of Mikoyan. Gubarev's *Konstruktor,* pp. 72–73 discusses the decaying relationship between Korolov and Yangel, and the offer by an unidentified Central Committee Secretary (presumably Brezhnev) to establish a new design bureau for Yangel in which he could determine his own course. See also Lev Chaiko, "Helicopter Construction in the USSR," p. 23, for an interesting discussion of competition *within* the helicopter design bureau. Competition in artillery is discussed frequently in the context of the Great Patriotic War. For general western discussions, see David Holloway, "Innovation in the Defence Sector: Battle Tanks and ICBMs," in Ronald Amann and Julian Cooper, eds., *Industrial Innovation in the Soviet Union;* Holloway, *The Soviet Union and the Arms Race.*

33. Both Firdman and Chaiko discuss the close relations between the designers and the commissions responsible for evaluation and assessment. According to Firdman, evaluation of scientific-technical work or design work is undertaken by a commission staffed at the suggestion of the project leader, and "often includes his friends, colleagues, and associates, and operates according to what is known in the USSR as the policy of 'mutual guarantee,' whereby members of a particular commission readily support a given project, knowing that the group leader's backing will one day be needed for their own project." Firdman, "Decision-making in the Soviet Microelectronics Industry," pp. 88–89. Chaiko also makes the same point. Chaiko, "Helicopter Construction," pp. 53–55. An unusual case of the "mutual guarantee" phenomenon is Yakovlev's designing of the early Soviet vertical takeoff and landing (VTOL) aircraft in the early 1960s. Reportedly concerned that he had been saddled with an impossible task, he accepted on the condition that other designers be involved also, to ensure that the risk was not his alone. See Arthur Alexander, "Research in Soviet Defence Production," *NATO's Fifteen Nations* (October–November, 1981), pp. 52–60+; and *Aviation Week and Space Technology* (June 24, 1968), pp. 210–211.

34. One extreme case involved artillery designer F. F. Petrov. During the war, Petrov found that the Main Artillery Administration of the Ministry of Defense (responsible for overseeing artillery development) was delaying the testing and production of his howitzer in favor of another, inferior, design.

Finally, the Central Committee itself was forced to intervene in favor of Petrov. See F. F. Petrov, "V poiskakh konstruktirovanogo sovershenstva," pp. 2–4, at 4.

35. See N. Khrushchev, *Khrushchev Remembers*, chaps. 3 and 4. Firdman reports of attempts to lobby Khrushchev in favor of a particular computer system with military use. See Firdman, "Decision-making in the Soviet Microelectronics Industry." The interesting case of Andrei Sakharov in particular will be discussed below. It is also useful to recall that Khrushchev's son, Sergei, was an electronics specialist and, according to an interview with Firdman, deputy chief designer to Chelomei. Khrushchev notes that his son "had something to do with missiles." See Nikita Khrushchev, *Khrushchev Remembers*, p. 49.

36. See Hough and Fainsod, *How the Soviet Union is Governed*, pp. 473–478.

37. While, according to Roy Medvedev, none of the "indictments" levelled against Khrushchev included his intervention in military decisions per se, he was accused of ignoring his fellow Presidium (now Politburo) members in "collective" decisions and considering himself an expert in all matters. See Medvedev, *Khrushchev*, chap. 21.

38. See, for example, Yevsikov, "Re-entry Technology," p. 16, where he describes such calls from the Central Committee; Fedoseyev, *Zapandnya*, p. 114; and Firdman, "Decision-making in the Soviet Microelectronics Industry," p. 39, where Firdman describes how representatives of the Department of Defense Industry protected a designer from the Minister of Electronics Industry.

39. For an example of this approach, see V. Nikolayev, "Tanki" pp. 14–16, in which as one tank enters production, a second is on the drawing boards, and a third is in the initial conception stages.

40. "Oruzhiye, dostoynoye boytsa," *Voyennyy vestnik*, (April 1977), pp. 25–29, p. 29.

41. Chaiko, "Helicopter Construction" p. 21, pp. 69–70.

42. Chaiko, pp. 19–20.

43. Fedoseyev reports VPK intervention in resolving general disagreements over designs and procurement. See Fedoseyev, "Design in Soviet Military R&D," pp. 13–14.

44. Chaiko, p. 19.

45. Note Firdman's opinion that "Though the defense establishment was often manipulated, its interest in a given project was decisive; if the designer failed to attract the military's attention, he would rarely have access to the kind of funds and equipment necessary for experimentation." Firdman, "Decision-making in the Soviet Microelectronics Industry," p. 20.

46. Smith, *Doubletalk*, p. 47.

47. Shchukin is identified by Raymond Garthoff as a deputy chairman of the VPK. See Garthoff, "SALT and the Soviet Military," in Valenta and Potter, eds., *Soviet Decisionmaking*, p. 144.

48. Smith, p. 47.

49. Smith, p. 47.

50. Dunskaya and Agursky each argue that there is a strong incentive for scientists to avoid classified military work on the grounds that their results cannot be published, and claims of discovery cannot be confirmed. See Irina Dunskaya, "Security Practices at Soviet Scientific Research Facilities," pp. 115–127; and Mikhail Agursky and Hannes Adomeit, "The Soviet Military-Industrial Complex and its Internal Mechanism," pp. 27–36. Fedoseyev cautions that serious designers are usually unable to publish anything in the classified ministry magazines and that "the open technical literature is actually devoid of anything which is 'important.' " See Fedoseyev, "Design in Soviet Military R&D," p. 7–8. It should also be noted that at times designers have been quoted or written articles under pseudonyms, generally for the popular press. The best known case is probably Sergei Korolev's interviews and writings under the name "K. Sergeyev" in the late 1950s and early 1960s.

51. This is not to say that they do not closely follow the foreign press. An interesting case of this is Myasishchev's following of the development of the B-52 in various western magazines. See Gay, pp. 130–131. It is also interesting to note that information on Soviet military equipment is so compartmentalized that the Soviet designers seldom have access to the work of their peers.

52. And at times the chief designer can choose his successor, as Il'yushin reportedly did in recommending the appointment of his deputy G. V. Novozhilov to head the Ilyushin design bureau. See V. Lebedev, "Akademik Il'yushin," *Aviatsiya i kosmonavtika* (March 1984), pp. 39–41.

53. This theme also appears in writings on contemporary weapons development. For example, S. Bartenev and S. Klyuyev argue that "under modern conditions, particular significance is acquired by the factor of time, [and] the ability to set up military production rapidly;" S. Bartenev and S. Klyuyev, "Economy and Government Defense Might," *Tyl i snabzheniye sovetskikh vooruzhyonnykh sil* (June 1970), pp. 8–15, at p. 13. Similarly, I. Kauk argued that the development of blueprints had to be carefully supervised to ensure that, in innovation, "use would be made of existing gear, reducing time, and assuring the quality of parts, assemblies, and items as a whole which are to be produced." I. Kauk, "Nash opyt upravleniya kachestvom produktsii," *Tyl i snabzheniye sovetskikh vooruzhyonnykh sil* (November 1976), pp. 41–45, at p. 45.

54. This emphasis appears to be greater in the military production sphere than in the civilian, possibly because there is a strong customer (the Ministry of Defense) pushing for actual production of the weapon system.

55. See, for example, V. G. Grabin, "Usovershenstvovannaya divizionnaya," pp. 16–17; L. Karnozov, "Designer of Artillery Equipment," *Tekhnika i vooruzheniye* (January 1970), pp. 43–44; V. Grabin, "Vklad v pobedu," p. 7 (and the series of articles in the same issue on the development of the F-22 gun); I. Tsygankov, "Sovetskaya voyennaya tekhnika: razvitiye konstruktorskoy mysli," *Tekhnika i vooruzheniye* (February 1978), pp. 6–13.

56. L. Karnozov, "Konstruktor artilleriyskogo vooruzheniya," *Tekhnika i vooruzheniye*, January 1970, pp. 43–44.

57. Leonid Kudrevatykh, "Konstruktor V. G. Grabin," pp. 168–174.

58. Firdman, "Decision-making in the Soviet Microelectronics Industry," p. 40.

59. Firdman, "Decision-making in the Soviet Microelectronics Industry," p. 40.

60. Fedoseyev, "Design in Soviet Military R&D," p. 12. Fedoseyev argues that this concern ensures that the commission will very carefully evaluate the proposed product for its producibility, a process which may take several months.

61. Agursky, *The Research Institute of Machine-Building Technology,* pp. 29–30, p. 46; and Cockburn, pp. 88–91.

In addition, the plant (the Southern Urals Machine Building Plant in Dnepropetrovsk) had trouble obtaining sufficient labor forces and was already so overworked that it only accepted a few orders.

62. See, for example, L. Yevtukhov, "Dykhaniye goryachey broni," p. 4., in which the author visits a contemporary tank design bureau and notes that one-third of the design bureau staff are at the plant.

63. Both words can be translated as "standardization," but to emphasize the difference between the two, "unification," and "standardization" will be used.

64. Kuz'mina, *Pavel Sukhoi,* pp. 219–220.

65. See "Unifikatsiya," in *SVE,* 8:199–200.

66. "Unifikatsiya" in the *Bol'shaya Sovetskaya entsiklopediya,* 27:23–24.

67. "Unifikatsiya," in *SVE,* 8:199–200.

68. Vlasov and Kats, eds., *Organizatsiya, planriovaniye, i upravleniye . . .* p. 96.

69. Yu. D. Maslyukov, "Vnedreniye yednoy sistemy tekhnologicheskoy podgotovki proizvodstvo," pp. 15–16. For other articles on the subject, see A. Nikoforenko, "Kachestvo cherez standarty," pp. 4–6; I. Saksonov, "Razrabotka konstruktorskoy dokumentatsii," p. 27.

70. V. P. Mishin, ed., *Osnovy proyektirovaniya letalel'nykh apparatov (transportnyye sistemy),* pp. 295–296.

71. Vlasov and Kats, eds., pp. 96–97. See also *SVE,* (Moscow: Voyenizdat, 1980), 8:199–200, and "Standartizatsiya," in *SVE,* (Moscow: Voyenizdat, 1979), 7:525. The latter article is attributed to N. N. Alekseyev, then Deputy Minister of Defense for Armaments.

It should also be noted that there are four levels of standards: State (GOST), Branch (OST), Republic (RST) and local (i.e., at the plant or organization—[fjSTP).

72. See, in particular, F. F. Petrov, "Tak kovalos' oruzhiye," pp. 12–19; V. Grabin, "Vklad v pobedy," p. 7; "Po planu perevooruzheniya," *Tekhnika i vooruzheniye,* May, 1974, p. 18; "Period perevooruzheniya," *Tekhnika i vooruzheniye* (June 1974), pp. 18–19; "Proizvodstvo artillerskiyskogo vooruzheniya, 1941–1945," *Tekhnika i vooruzheniye* (December, 1974), pp. 12–13; N. Kurin, "Po resheniyu GKO," pp. 10–11; M. Kruglov, "Sistemy upravleniya kachestvom produktsii," p. 7; "Sila artillerii—v ogne," *Voyennyy vestnik* (June 1977), pp. 20–23; and I. Tsygankov, "Sovetskaya voyennaya tekhnika: razvitiye konstruktorskoy mysli," *Tekhnika i vooruzheniye* (February 1978), pp. 6–13.

Each of these articles seems to go out of its way to emphasize the importance of standardization and unification of parts and documentation.

73. "Period perevooruzheniya," pp. 18–19. The article is a discussion of the contribution of V. D. Grendal', commander of the Main Artillery Administration (or Directorate) during the Great Patriotic War. The administration continues to exist, but it has incorporated tactical missiles into its responsibilities and is now known as the Main Rocket and Artillery Administration, under the command of P. Kuleshov since 1965. It is interesting to note that much of the discussion of standardization and unification seems rooted in the artillery industry, presumably because of the large numbers involved and the importance placed on artillery by the Soviet military. For another example, see "Proizvodstvo artillerskiyskogo vooruzheniya, 1941–1945," pp. 12–13.

74. F. F. Petrov, "Tak kovalos' oruzhiye," p. 18. Petrov repeatedly emphasized the use of the same or similar equipment in different situations, for example, the same basic gun barrel being used in a number of different pieces of artillery.

75. V. G. Grabin, "Usovershenstvovannaya divizionnaya," p. 16.

76. I. Saltykov, "Konstruktor i pobeda," *Standarti i kachestvo,* (May 1975), pp. 5–7, at page 7. Kotin was a leading Soviet tank designer.

77. Yu. Sergeyev, "Samoye massovoye oruzhiye," p. 27; and "Oruzhiye, dostoynoye boytsa," *Voyennyy vestnik,* April 1977, pp. 25–29.

78. Ye. Kosyrev, "Razvitiye strelkobogo oruzhiya," pp. 8–11.

79. Kuz'mina, *Generalnny, Konstruktor Pavel Sukhoi,* pp. 219–220.

80. Richard D. Ward, "Soviet Practice in Designing & Procuring Military Aircraft," *Astronautics and Aeronautics* (September 1981), pp. 24–38, at p. 32. Ward also cites a number of other examples from various design bureaus. See also Frederick P. Biery, "Converging Lines," *Defense & Foreign Affairs* (May 1983), pp. 11–15, 49; and Arthur J. Alexander, "Research in Soviet Defence Production," *Nato's Fifteen Nations* (October–November, 1981), pp. 52–60, 74.

81. Platonov and Gorbulin, *Mikhaylo Kuz'mich Yangel,* pp. 78–81.

82. Mishin, *Osnovy proyektirovaniya,* p. 17.

83. Soviet authors cite a number of reasons for standardization and unification of equipment, but the two that are the most important are that it speeds up production and reduces cost. See, for example, the article by P. Sigov and V. Lysov, in which they emphasize that production costs of a weapon can be reduced "if one uses structures and individual technical resources left over from models of equipment no longer in use." P. Sigov and V. Lysov, "Economy and Operation," *Tekhnika i vooruzheniye* (September 1978), pp. 93–97.

84. O. K. Antonov, *Dlya vsekh i dlya sebya: O sovershenstvovanii pokazateley planirovaniya sotsiyalisticheskogo promyshlennogo proizvodstva* (Moscow: Ekonomika, 1965).

85. O. K. Antonov, "Chto vmesto 'vala'?" p. 2. The article was even translated in *Aviation Week and Space Technology.* Gleb Vanag, the director of the Novosibirsk Chkalov aircraft plant, replied to an earlier article by Antonov on this subject which also appeared in *Trud,* December 15, 1978. Vanag suggested

that the real problem was that the planners were out of touch with the needs and capabilities of the plants. See G. Vanag, "Upravleniye Kachestvom," p. 2.

86. Antonov, "Chto vmesto 'vala'?"

87. Antonov, *Dlya vsekh i dlya sebya*, p. 81. Antonov was not, of course, alone in this argument, as others made the same argument both in the Soviet Union and outside of it. It is, however, interesting that someone involved in *military* production should feel obliged to complain about val, suggesting that at least a portion of the defense industries rely on this indicator.

88. Perhaps coincidentally, Antonov was an admirer of A. G. Aganbegian, one of the most influential economists in the Gorbachev leadership.

89. For example, "net normative output," in which the difference between the cost norm and the actual cost of the product is kept (or made up by) the producer.

90. The example of Myasishchev has already been noted. It is, unfortunately, difficult to obtain information on other design bureaus that have been closed or designers who have been replaced. One of the legacies of the Brezhnev era may have been the establishment of permanent design bureaus whose leaders serve until their death and are then replaced by deputies. As new problems arise, new design bureaus are established.

91. Kevin Klose, "Sakharov and the Bomb," in Edward D. Lozansky, ed., *Andrei Sakharov and Peace* pp. 61–87, at p. 69.

92. This trio was also part of the intellectual opposition to Brezhnev's proposed rehabilitation of Stalin in 1966. Andrei Sakharov, *Sakharov Speaks* p. 14.

93. Sakharov, *Sakharov Speaks*, pp. 10, 32. Harrison Salisbury states that this was Sakharov's first effort to influence a major Soviet policy decision. At the same time, Sakharov took a public stand on a controversial educational reform package.

Kurchatov was an excellent choice to present a proposal to Khrushchev, given the respect Khrushchev claims to have had for him. In particular, Khrushchev praised Kurchatov for recognizing "that government funds must be expended according to a system of priorities . . . [and] first and foremost we had to think about the defense and security of our country." See N. Khrushchev, *Khrushchev Remembers*, pp. 59–60.

94. A. Sakharov, *Sakharov Speaks*, p. 33.

95. A. Sakharov, *Sakharov Speaks*, p. 33. Khrushchev's account does not differ from Sakharov's on the basic themes.

96. N. Khrushchev, *Khrushchev Remembers*, p. 69. Khrushchev also noted the military's influence in weapons' procurement decisions. See pages 411–412. An anonymous reviewer of the manuscript of this book indicates that the actual transcript of Khrushchev's memoirs attributes opposition to both the military and scientists. One of the opponents in the scientific community, V. S. Yemel'yanov, is discussed below.

97. N. Khrushchev, *Khrushchev Remembers*, p. 71. Some analysts have suggested that Khrushchev opposed renewed testing, and that the decision was imposed upon him by his domestic opponents. See Christer Jonsson, *Soviet*

Bargaining Behavior: The Nuclear Test Ban Case (New York: Columbia University Press, 1979), chap. 12.

98. A. Sakharov, *Sakharov Speaks*, p. 33.

99. A. Sakharov, *Sakharov Speaks*, p. 34. It is interesting to speculate as to whether the military and/or the Ministry of Medium Machine Building moved the test up specifically to ensure that Sakharov could not stop it.

100. A. Sakharov, *Sakharov speaks*, p. 34.

101. Igor S. Glagolev, "The Soviet Decision-Making Process in Arms-Control Negotiations," pp. 767–776, at p. 770.

102. Glagolev, "The Soviet Decision-Making Process," p. 770. Yemel'yanov was replaced as head of the GKAE by Andronik Melkovich Petrosyants, who had also been in the tank industry in the war and who had been deputy minister of the Ministry of Medium Machine Building from 1955 to 1962. Interestingly, biographical information about Petrosyants does not appear in the standard Soviet sources. This information is from *Prominent Personalities in the USSR* (Methuen, N.J.: Scarecrow Press, 1968).

103. A. Sakharov, *Sakharov Speaks*, p. 38. The manuscript had been widely circulated in samizdat by May and June within the Soviet Union.

104. Two other participants in arms control negotiations have been identified as associated with the Academy of Sciences. Viktor P. Rozhkov of the Academy's Institute of Space Research was an Expert on the Soviet delegation from January to July 1973. V. P. Pavlichenko, identified only as an adviser or expert from the Academy of Sciences, has participated in the Negotiations on Nuclear and Space Arms (NST) since 1985. Strobe Talbott identifies Pavlichenko as a KGB official. See Strobe Talbott, *Deadly Gambits*, p. 95.

105. This sort of debate is not unique to the Soviet Union. In the Department of Defense, there has for years reportedly been a debate between the fighter "mafia," favoring more and simpler fighter aircraft, and opponents who favor the multipurpose, technologically advanced aircraft.

106. Military writers, on the other hand, frequently emphasized the advantages of missiles over aircraft.

107. The arguments of Sakharov and others was based on health effects of nuclear testing, but the political leadership was apparently not impressed with the argument at the time.

5. The Defense Industrial Ministry

1. It is striking that there are almost no references to individuals working in the ministries below the level of administration chief. Few of those about whom biographical information is available spent time in the ministry at a post below that of administration head. The message seems to be that if one wishes to become a minister, he or she must start in production; starting in the ministry's mail room is insufficient.

2. Alice C. Gorlin, "The Power of Soviet Industrial Ministries in the 1980s," p. 354.

3. Gorlin, pp. 358–359.

4. See *The Current Digest of the Soviet Press*, 37(29):5.

5. Zaslavskaya's comments appear in a report apparently prepared for delivery to a closed meeting of economists from the Central Committee, the Academy of Sciences, and Gosplan, which was leaked to the western media. See [Tatyana Zaslavskaya], "Doklad o Neobkhodimosti Bolee Uglublennogo Izucheniya v SSSR Sotsial'nogo Mekhanizma Razvitiya Ekonomiki," AS 5042, August 26, 1983. The report is translated in *Survey* (spring 1984), 28(1):88–108, with comment by Philip Hanson, "The Novosibirsk Report: Comment," pp. 82–87. For the citation, see p. 96.

6. [Zaslavskaya], p. 98.

7. [Zaslavskaya], p. 98.

8. [Zaslavskaya], p. 99.

9. Leslie Holmes, *The Policy Process in Communist States* p. 219.

10. For an ironic example of this tendency, see the report by Valentin Rasputin, a Soviet writer, on his meeting with the leadership of the Ministry of Timber, Pulp and Paper, and Lumber Industry, to discuss the environmental damage being done to Lake Baikal. In it, he states that "The Minister resembled a Minister, and his deputies resembled Deputy Ministers. What I mean is that my prior conception matched up easily with my first impression and was subsequently confirmed . . . by the diplomacy of the ministry chief and the monumentality of his assistants' views." See *Izvestiya*, Feb. 17, 1986, pp. 3, 6; also excerpted and translated in *Current Digest of the Soviet Press* (March 19, 1986), 38(7):5–7, 22.

11. See, for example, the October 2, 1969 decree on the Ministry of Aviation Industry (no. 135), in *Sobraniye postanovleniy pravitel'stva*, 1969, pp. 597–603.

In fact, there is a paucity of information on how a Soviet ministry "really" works, as most Soviet discussions do not extend beyond details of the "wire diagrams" frequently presented. An interesting complement, however, is A. Doak Barnett's detailed study of an unspecified "Ministry M" in the late 1950s and early 1960s in the People's Republic of China, organized on the Soviet model and having a "Staff Office for Soviet Experts." See A. Doak Barnett, *Cadres, Bureaucracy, and Political Power in Communist China* (New York: Columbia University Press, 1967), part 1.

12. V. Rasputin.

13. M. Agursky, "The Research Institute of Machine-Building Technology," p. 32–33.

14. Hough persuasively argues that this authority is in *administration*, rather than in policy *formulation*. See Jerry F. Hough, *The Soviet Prefects*, pp. 82–86.

15. See also E. Jones, "Committee Decision-Making."

16. See P. Solomon, "Soviet Policy-Making," pp. 110–117.

17. E. Jones, "Committee Decision-Making," p. 184.

18. Author's interview with Henry Eric Firdman.

19. A. Fedoseyev, *Zapadnya*, pp. 162–165. Firdman suggests that if a scientist seeks a small amount of money, approaching the main administration is the usual route, especially if one has personal contacts there. If, however, the sum is large, it is better to work through the Central Committee's Department of Defense Industry, bypassing for the moment the main administration. (Interview with author.)

The general route for funding requirements was outlined in chapter 2.

20. A. Fedoseyev, "Design in Soviet Military R&D," p. 9.

21. Chaiko, "Helicopter Construction," p. 69.

22. A. Fedoseyev, *Zapadnya*, p. 165.

23. In 1957, Khrushchev implemented the sovnarkhoz reform, which abolished most industrial ministries and turned their assets over to regional authorities. The exceptions were the defense industrial ministries, which were renamed "State Committees." With Khrushchev's ousting in 1964, these State Committees were soon renamed Ministries, with little real impact on their organization or personnel.

24. Firdman, "Decision-making in the Soviet Microelectronics Industry," p. 50.

25. This complements the Soviet emphasis on copying foreign developments, as such a process not only reduces the costs, but also, the uncertainties involved. In effect, the Soviets are conducting original research when necessary, and when presented with the opportunity, they following the path of least resistance, requiring the least speculative (and costly) initial research. See the U.S. government report *Soviet Acquisition of Militarily Significant Western Technology: An Update* (September, 1985).

26. A. Fedoseyev, "Design in Soviet Military R&D," pp. 7–8. For an interesting western summary of the techniques subordinates use to influence their superiors, see Warren K. Schlit and Edwin A. Locke, "A Study of Upward Influence in Organizations," *Administrative Science Quarterly* (1982), 27:304–316.

27. It is perhaps not surprising that the little information available comes from people who worked under deputy ministers or administration heads. To my knowledge, no administration head or deputy minister has emigrated or defected from the Soviet Union. In addition, within Soviet sources there is little discussion by deputy ministers in the memoir literature; most is by more "noteworthy" figures.

28. Firdman interview.

29. A. Fedoseyev, *Zapadnya*, pp. 179–180, 200.

Fedoseyev also has few kind words for the Minister of Electronics Industry, Shokin, whom he characterizes as a man without principles. It is interesting that Fedoseyev feels that he may have had some influence on the *establishment* of the Ministry, but apparently could do nothing to determine who headed it. See Anatol Fedoseyev, "Design in Soviet Military R&D," pp. 14–15.

30. Fedoseyev's clout did not help him remove Mikhaylov, and Sakharov's appeals do not seem to have had any impact on Slavskiy's career.

31. For one example, see H. E. Firdman, "Decision-making in the Soviet Microelectronics Industry," pp. 10–11, where he describes how research on transitors took place at the lower levels of the state committee on electronics, despite its official disfavor.

32. See L. Kuz'mina, *Generalnyy Konstruktor Pavel Sukhoi*, pp. 211, 224. On page 211, Kuz'mina refers to an "M. P. Semonov" as director of the experimental plant, and on p. 224, she identifies "Mikhail Petrovich Simonov" as a deputy to Sukhoi. M. P. Simonov is included in the acknowledgements. In 1979, Mikhail Petrovich Simonov was appointed a Deputy Minister for Aviation Industry.

33. This is especially true in the defense industrial ministries. In addition, often a ministry official (an administration head or even a deputy minister) will not be identified as such. The most extreme case of this of which I am aware is the case of Petr Ya. Antropov, who was deputy minister of Medium Machine Building for seventeen years until his death in 1979. Antropov was a prolific writer, publishing—while a deputy minister—a number of articles on uranium and two editions of a book on global energy reserves, yet his post was never acknowledged. Even in a ninety-page biography of Antropov in the Scientific Biography Series of the Academy of Science, the Ministry is identified by name only once in a chronology of Antropov's life that appears as an appendix. See F. I. Vol'fson, N. S. Zontov, G. R. Shushaniya, *Petr Yakovlevich Antropov, 1905–1979* (Moscow: Nauka, 1986), p. 87.

34. This may be, in part, because most deputy ministers presumably are based in Moscow, at the Ministry.

35. This may also be a useful way to determine the area of responsibility for a deputy minister or the relative status within the ministry. In the case of "Tank Day," the Ministry of Defense Industry representative in 1980 was L. A. Voronin, then First Deputy Minister of Defense Industry, and in 1981, it was O. F. Larchenko, also First Deputy Minister. For the last several it years has been Deputy Minister M. A. Zakharov.

36. See Glenn H. Snyder and Paul Diesing, *Conflict Among Nations: Bargaining, Decision Making, and System Structure in International Crises* (Princeton, N.J.: Princeton University Press, 1977), chap. 5, especially pp. 352, 359.

37. The few exceptions appear to have had long practical experience in their field. While almost every ministry official's biography notes that he "completed" or "graduated" a higher technical institute, a deputy minister of defense industry who died in 1965, Amo S. Yelyan only "attended" the Azerbaidjan Polytechnical Institute from 1923 to 1926.

38. See M. Cherednichenko, "Sovremennaya voyna i ekonomika," *Kommunist vooruzhennykh sil* (1971), 18:20–27; and A. Kormil'tsev, "Rol' otrasley narodnogo khozyaystva v sovremennoy voyne," *Kommunist vooruzhennykh sil* (1971) 20:9–17. See also Julian Cooper, "The Civilian Production of the Soviet Defence Industry," in Ronald Amann and Julian Cooper, eds., *Technical Progress and Soviet Economic Development*, pp. 31–50. The 42 percent figure may

refer to the Ministry of Defense Industry, as opposed to defense industry as a whole, but the Soviet sources are not clear on this question.

39. See Bruce Parrott's discussion in his *Politics and Technology in the Soviet Union*, pp. 247–255, especially pp. 248–249. This is in contrast with Brezhnev's earlier views, and may have reflected a partial victory by Kosygin in his effort to contain Soviet defense spending. See Parrott, pp. 183–185 for a discussion of the earlier "debate."

40. Breslauer claims that Brezhnev came to the July 1970 Plenum "armed with promises from the heads of seven ministries associated with the military-heavy-industrial complex that they would produce agricultural equipment at their plants 'without reducing the volume of production of their basic output.' " While such a claim is not unreasonable, the meaning of such "promises" is difficult to evaluate. Such a statement by Brezhnev was presumably prepared well in advance of the Plenum, but it would be more interesting to know how such promises were extracted from the ministers. See George W. Breslauer, *Khrushchev and Brezhnev as Leaders: Building Authority in Soviet Politics* (London: George Allen and Unwin, 1982), p. 180.

41. See S. Zverev, "Nasha pomoshch' selu," p. 2. The subject was apparently interesting enough to merit the reprinting of the article in the national press, as it appeared in *Sotsiyalisticheskaya industriya,* under the title "Dlya kolkhoznykh niv" (October 1, 1970), p. 2.

42. S. Zverev, "Vosmozhnosti otrasli," p. 1.

43. P. Dement'yev, "Ne tol'ko samolety," p. 1.

44. Bakhirev's article appeared in two editions of *Izvestiya*. The first edition is for evening distribution in Moscow, while the second edition receives broader (national and international) circulation. In fact, the first edition is apparently not available outside the Soviet Union and is not loaned out by Soviet libraries to libraries in the United States on an "inter-library" basis. The difference between the versions of the Bakhirev article is only in the greater level of detail in the first edition version: there are more specific identifications of his ministry's consumer goods and specific promises about increasing, for example, tractor production. See V. Bakhirev, "Shirokiy assortiment, vysokoye kachestvo," *Izvestiya*, June 30, 1971 (Moscow evening edition), and excerpts from it under the title "Vysokoye kachestvo," *Izvestiya*, July 2, 1971, p. 3. I am indebted to Paul Josephson for his hand-copying of the Moscow evening edition version while he was in Moscow.

45. "Vklad sudostroiteley," *Sel'skaya zhizn'* (June 26, 1971), p. 1.

46. The other ministers investigated, Afanas'yev (Ministry of General Machine Building) and Slavskiy (Ministry of Medium Machine Building), did not publish anything from 1965 to at least 1980.

47. See Parrott, *Politics and Technology*, pp. 183–185; Gelman, *The Brezhnev Politburo*, pp. 82, 182; Breslauer, *Khrushchev and Brezhnev*, p. 279.

48. Another result, equally interesting, was a flurry of articles by military authors appearing in *Kommunist vooruzhennykh sil* emphasizing how the United States was committed to increased defense spending, especially in the areas of

research and development. See, for example, A. Sukhoguzov, "Problema zhivu-zhesti ekonomiki v sovremennoy voyne," *Kommunist vooruzhennykh sil* (1972), 3:9–16; M. Gladkov and B. Ivanov, "Ekonomika i voyenno-tekhnicheskaya politika," *Kommunist vooruzhennykh sil* (1972); 9:10–17; and V. Rut'kov, "Voyenno-ekonomicheskoye mogushchestvo sotsialisticheskikh stran—faktor bezopasnosti narodov," *Kommunist vooruzhennykh sil* (1974), 23:18–25.

49. See, for example, V. I. Kazas, Yu. V. Konyshev, A. G. Laktionov, "Poto-chnyy Samoletnyy Pribor Dlya Izmereniya Razmerov i Kontsentratsii Krupnykh Kapel' v Oblakakh." pp. 1212–1215; Yu V Konyshev, A. G. Klakionov, "Same-letnyy Fotoelektricheskii Izmeritel' Oblachnykh Kapel'," pp. 766–769; O. D. Baklanov et al, "Transformator polnykh soprotivleniy na tsilindricheskom vol-novode," pp. 11–15; O. D. Baklanov et al, "Metodika rascheta transformatorov polnykh soprotivleniy na pryamougolnykh volnovodakh," pp. 15–22; V. Ya. Nezhlukto, "Osnovnyye rezul'taty ispytaniy pervoy otechestvennoy gazotur-binnoy ustanovki (GTU-20) dlya morskikh sudov," pp. 22–36; V. Ya. Nezh-lukto, "Opyt dovodki i rezul'taty zavodskikh ispytaniy gazoturbinnykh dviga-teley ustanovki GTU-20 LKZ," pp. 1–5; V. Yu. Torochkov, V. B. Kalabin, V. S. Usov, "Stabilizatsiya opticheskaoy osi aerofotos'emochnoy," pp. 125–128; G. I. Zubovskiy, V. B. Kalabin, V. V. Makartsev, G. K. Klimenko, "Kinoapparatura na vystavke 'Fotokina-72,' " pp. 72–80; V. B. Kalabin, V. A. Babenko, A. V. Burav-tsev, "Girostabiliziruyushchaya ustanovka dlya kinos'emok s dvizhushchego-sya avtomobilya," pp. 55–56.

50. See, for example, I. S. Silayev and Darovskikh's article on KANARSPI or the Voronin et al articles on production at the Krasnogorsk Mechanical Works. It is interesting to note that those who have been promoted to posts outside or above the ministries tend to be those whose articles emphasized managerial, rather than technical, issues.

51. It seems unlikely, given his prominence, that the move was even a true *demotion*. Derunov has had a long track record within the ministry (he was appointed director in 1960), and would thus have been a well-known figure prior to his move up. There is also no evidence that someone else took his place as director of the Rybinsk Engine Plant during this period, suggesting that he may have held both posts (director and deputy minister) simultaneously.

For a suggestion of how serious such a demotion would be, see Irina Dun-skaya, "Security Practices at Soviet Scientific Research Facilities," p. 14, where she discusses the "serious demotion" of an administration chief to the post of plant director.

52. For a good summary of YeSTPP, see Yu. D. Amirov, *Organizatsiya i effektivnost' nauchno-issledovatel'skikh konstruktorskikh rabot* (Moscow: Ekonomika, 1974), pp. 143–147.

53. Maslyukov, "Vnedreniye yedinoy sistemy." It is, unfortunately, not pos-sible to provide the Ministry of Defense Industry's budget. By way of compari-son, however, in Zverev's 1971 article, he noted that production of consumer goods by the MODI in 1971 would be 10 million rubles over the plan. See S. Zverev, "Vozmozhnosti Otrasli," p. 1.

54. F. I. Vol'fson, N. S. Zontov, and G. R. Shushaniya, *Petr Yakovlevich Antropov, 1905–1979* (Moscow: Nauka, 1986), p. 30.

55. Vol'fson, Zontov, and Shushaniya, p. 30. Apparently, Antropov's career was not without its problems, however. He was criticized for his performance as minister of geology and resource preservation, and lost this job in 1962, when he was appointed deputy minister of medium machine building. It may also be relevant that Antropov and the Minister of Medium Machine Building, Ye. P. Slavsky, were in school together at the Moscow Mining Academy in the early 1930s.

56. See P. Ya. Antropov, "Perspektivy poiskov promyshlennykh mestorozhdeniy urana v depressionnykh zonakh zemnoy kory," *Geologicheskiy zhurnal*, pp. 75–82; P. Ya. Antropov, "Perspektivy poiskov promyshlennykh mestorozhdeniy urana v depressionnykh zonakh zemnoy kory," *Izvestiya Armyanskoy SSR. Nauki o zemle*, pp. 37–43. This had been a popular theme with Antropov since the mid-1950s. See also Vol'fson, Zontov, Shushaniya; and Arnold Kramish, *Atomic Energy in the Soviet Union* (Stanford, Cal.: Stanford University Press, 1959), pp. 171–172.

57. See Antropov, "Perspektivy poiskov," and Antropov, "O nekotorykh geologicheskikh kontseptsiyakh v svyazi s toplivno-energeticheskim potentsialom zemli," pp. 139–143. Antropov's proposals for *how* to identify uranium deposits were apparently not universally accepted, and these two articles contained an editors' note stating that some of Antropov's views were controversial and were presented "for discussion."

58. P. Ya. Antropov, *Toplivno-energeticheskiy potentsiyal zemli*, 2d ed. (Moscow: Energiya, 1976), p. 10.

59. Khrushchev notes that there was a lack of the "raw material" needed for nuclear weapons, apparently in the late 1950s, when asked by Grechko to develop a tactical nuclear missile, See N. Khrushchev, *Khrushchev Remembers*, p. 52.

60. The GKNT is responsible for formulating the central state plans for research, design, and innovation and ensuring the integration of the plans of other organizations (for example, ministries and republics) with the state plan. See Louvan E. Noulting, *The Structure and Function of the USSR State Committee for Science and Technology*.

61. See A. I. Churin and V. A. Klyachko, "Sovremennoye sostoyaniye problemy opresneniya vody," pp. 34–47; A. I. Churin, et al, "Sovmeshcheniya krupnykh atomnykh elektrostantsiy s opresnitel'nymi ustanovkami," pp. 394–402; and Aleksandr Churin and Viktor Smagin, " 'Zhivaya vlaga' Kazakhstana," p. 3.

62. Polikanov states that the GKAE grew out of the Ministry of Medium Machine Building and remains informally subordinate to it. See Sergei Polikanov, "Nuclear Physics in the Soviet Union," p. 8. In general, the GKAE is responsible for civilian nuclear power and research.

63. Morokhov is perhaps the most prolific writer surveyed. Typical articles, of which Morokhov is the author or coauthor, include "International Cooperation of the USSR in the Field of Peaceful Uses of Atomic Energy," *Soviet*

Atomic Energy, 31(4):1186–1195; "New Progress for the Peaceful Use of Atomic Energy," *Soviet Atomic Energy,* 17(3):879–885; and "International Cooperation and the Development of Nuclear Reactor Projects," *Soviet Atomic Energy,* 17(4):982–988. In the article "New Progress for the Peaceful Use of Nuclear Energy," Morokhov makes the interesting point that Khrushchev had ordered "releasing from military purposes 'fissionable materials to be used for peaceful purposes.' " See p. 879 of that article.

64. See Raymond Garthoff, *Detente and Confrontation: American-Soviet Relations from Nixon to Reagan* (Washington, D.C.: Brookings, 1985), pp. 756–757.

65. I. D. Morokhov, V. S. Kandaritskii, and Yu. V. Arkhangel'skii, "International Cooperation and the Development of Nuclear Reactor Projects," *Soviet Atomic Energy,* 17(4):982–988.

66. In the case of the Ministry of Machine Building, it was presumably to separate much of the work being done on explosives, fuses, and conventional ammunition from the Ministry of Defense Industry's work on tanks and artillery pieces.

67. See the CIA and DIA report, "The Soviet Economy Under a New Leader: A Report Presented to the Subcommittee on Economic Resources, Competitiveness, and Security Economics of the Joint Economic Committee," March 19, 1986, in which the agencies note that the drop in procurement "held overall defense growth (measured in dollars) to about 2 percent per year during the 1974–1985 period—about half the rate of the previous decade" (p. 5); and the testimony of Robert Gates of the Central Intelligence Agency before the Subcommittee on International Trade, Finance, and Security Economics of the U.S. Joint Economic Committee, in which he states that "from 1976 to 1982, outlays on military programs increased on the average by about 2 percent a year. This rate was about half that of the previous decade. Growth slowed in most categories of defense spending, but the main source of the reduction in growth was a leveling off of military procurement." *Allocation of Resources in the Soviet Union and China—1984, part 10,* p. 7.

68. See the U.S. Government report, *Soviet Acquisition of Militarily Significant Western Technology: An Update* (September, 1985).

69. Firdman, "Decision-making in the Soviet Microelectronics Industry," p. 68–69. He also reports that by the early 1970s, the Department of Defense Industry allegedly advocated "reproduction as a principal means for innovation" (p. 69). Not surprisingly, the emphasis appears to have been in the areas that the Soviets find the most difficult: electronics and communications. See U.S. Government, *Soviet Acquisition of Militarily Significant Western Technology: An Update* (September, 1985), p. 7.

70. Fedoseyev, *Zapadnya,* pp. 116–117.

71. For evidence on the collision course that appeared to be developing between Brezhnev's advocacy of détente and Grechko's concerns, see, for example, Gelman, *The Brezhnev Politburo,* pp. 46–47, 95, 160–161, and Michael J. Deane, *Political Control of the Soviet Armed Forces* (New York: Crane,

Russak, 1977), chap. 9, especially pp. 249–254 and pp. 270–272. For a more personal (if at times dubious) memoir, see Shevchenko, *Breaking with Moscow*, pp. 162–163, 205.

72. It is difficult to characterize confidently the views of Ustinov. For two interesting attempts to do so, see Dan L. Strode and Rebecca V. Strode, "Diplomacy and Defense in Soviet National Defense Policy," *International Security* (Fall 1983), 8(2):91–116, and the correspondence between Gerhard Wettig and George G. Weickhardt in *Problems of Communism*, (May–June 1985), 34(3):91–96. One of the few points upon which Wettig and Weickhardt agree is the hard-line stance taken by Grechko. While Ustinov may not have been the strongest advocate of Soviet arms control, he may have been a reluctant advocate, recognizing the problems that were beginning to appear in the Soviet economy.

73. Given that the slowdown appeared in about 1974, it most likely was planned somewhat earlier. Richard Kaufmann suggests that it was the result of decisions included in the Ninth Five Year Plan (1971–1976). Regardless of when it was planned, Ustinov would have been a key actor in the decisions. See Richard Kaufman, "Causes of the Slowdown in Soviet Defense," *Soviet Economy*, (January–March, 1985) vol. 1, no. 1, reprinted in Subcommittee on International Trade, Finance, and Security Economics of the U.S. Joint Economic Committee, *Allocation of Resources in the Soviet Union and China—1984*, part 10, pp. 202–224, at p. 221.

It is also interesting that Ustinov's biography makes note of Ustinov's contribution to "the long-range strengthening of the *economic* and defense potential of the nation." (emphasis added) See *Sovetskaya Voyennaya Entsiklopediya*, (Moscow: Voyenizdat, 1980), 8:227.

6. Conclusions

1. See, for example, Ye. Sabinin, "Vremya khozyaistvennika," *Sotsialisticheskaya industriya* (July 22, 1970), p. 3; and M. Subbotin, "Gorizonty Vliyaniya," p. 2.

2. Brezhnev himself warned against intervention by political figures in technical decisions, noting in 1965 that "true science takes nothing on faith; it cannot be the monopoly of particular scientists, and still less of administrators, no matter how much prestige they may have. Unfortunately, we have recently had instances in which people incompetent in science at times took upon themselves the role of arbiters in disputes among scientists, and in so doing hampered their initiative and stood in the way of free, creative discussion of scientific topics." See *Plenum TsK KPSS* (March 1965), pp. 25–26, quoted in Thane Gustafson, *Reform in Soviet Politics: Lessons of Recent Policies on Land and Water* (Cambridge: Cambridge University Press, 1981), p. 31.

3. It should be noted that Soviet interest in rocketry extends back to the pioneering efforts of K. E. Tsiokovskiy (1857–1935). Korolev, however, was able

to drive the political leadership to see the possibilities of realizing the political and military potential of Soviet rocketry.

4. Depending, of course, on the political and military impact of the weapon and the cost. A million rubles on handguns or continuing tank research and production may not require Politburo approval, while the same sum spent on space weaponry would.

5. See Abraham S. Becker, "Sitting on Bayonets: The Soviet Defense Burden and the Slowdown of Soviet Defense Spending" (Santa Monica: Rand/UCLA Center for the Study of Soviet International Behavior, 1985), especially part 3.

6. It is probable that the Ministry of Foreign Affairs and the KGB have had an increasing role in the Politburo's decision-making for *defense* since 1973, when the Minister of Foreign Affairs (Gromyko), the Chairman of the KGB (Andropov), and the Minister of Defense (Grechko), were admitted to the Politburo. Part of the shift is presumably due to the participation of the Ministry of Foreign Affairs in the SALT negotiations, and it is ironic that Gromyko wanted the Soviet delegation to be headed by a military officer, a proposal Grechko refused to consider. See Arkady N. Shevchenko, *Breaking with Moscow* p. 202–203.

Military "pride of place" was further eroded with Ustinov's appointment as Minister of Defense in 1976. Placing an economic manager (which, after all, was Ustinov's background), rather than a military commander, in the post of minister of defense was probably part of an effort to impose greater economic efficiency on the Ministry of Defense and the Soviet defense effort. In Ustinov's first major statement after being appointed minister of defense, he expressed an idea that may have reflected the main theme of his tenure as minister. After noting that the armed forces had already received the most up-to-date weapons, Ustinov pointedly added that it was the personnel, not the weapons, that were responsible for high combat readiness. See D. F. Ustinov, "Partiyno-politiche-sauyu rabotu v armii i na flote—na uroven' trebovaniy XXV s'ezda KPSS," in Izbrannyye rechi i stat'i (Moscow: Politicheskoy literatury, 1979), p. 285. Brezhnev, in one his last major speeches before his death, returned to this same theme in October, 1982.

7. For example, Yakovlev's concern over building a vertical take-off and landing (VTOL) aircraft, and his requirement that other designers participate in the project in an apparent effort to spread the risk and responsibility.

An interesting nonmilitary example is the series of discussions that took place over the safety and locations of nuclear reactors. For a useful discussion of the evolution of Soviet views on this subject, focusing on the leading scientists involved (Dollezhal' and Kapitsa in particular), see Joan T. Debardeleben, "Esoteric Policy Debate," pp. 227–253. Kapitsa in particular took a public stance on the problems of fission reactors.

8. For examples of such involvement during the Great Patriotic War, see Jerry F. Hough, "The Historical Legacy in Soviet Weapons Development," in Valenta and Potter, eds., *Soviet Decisionmaking*, pp. 90–91. For an example

from the time of Khrushchev, see his discussion of placing missiles in silos in N. Khrushchev, *Khrushchev Remembers,* pp. 48–49.

9. The Politburo, it should be remembered, has increasingly been dominated by generalists, especially those with a background in regional Party work, while specialists have been concentrated in the Council of Ministers. See T. H. Rigby, "The Soviet Politburo: A Comparative Profile 1951–1971," *Soviet Studies* (July 1972), 24(1):3–23) and "The Soviet Government Since Khrushchev," *Politics,* (May 1977), 12(1):5–22.

10. It is tempting to suggest that an indicator of a military industrial complex is the production of "more-than-enough" weapons. The first problem with using such an approach is one of definition. The problem of how much is enough has challenged policy makers for years. Determining how much is too much compounds the problem. In addition, a military-industrial complex might exist which does not lead to excessive weapons production. Its efforts to bring pressure to bear might fail because of (for example) a strong executive capable of resisting its efforts. Such an event does not indicate that a military industrial complex does not exist, but that its power is constrained.

11. As it is, the Soviets are much slower at predeployment technical development, engineering, and testing of strategic weapons systems. The Department of Defense estimates that the technological phase of a Soviet weapon's development takes six years, twice the United States average of three years. The engineering and testing phase of a Soviet weapon is estimated at five years while it averages less than four years for United States weapons. See *Soviet Military Power,* 4th ed., (Washington: GPO, 1985), pp. 40–41.

12. Former Chief of the General Staff N. V. Ogarkov has been a leading exponent of this concern. See, for example, his *Istoriya uchit bditel'nosti* (Moscow: Voyenizdat, 1985) and *Vsegda v gotovnosti k zashchite otechestva* (Moscow: Voyenizdat, 1982).

13. It is probably confined within the Ministry of Defense to the General Staff's Operations Directorate.

Appendix B. The Defense Industries Ministries of the Soviet Union

1. It should be emphasized that these are production *estimates* provided by an organization with a vested interest, and that there is some disagreement between the DIA and the CIA over production. It seems that DIA estimates emphasize production capabilities, rather than observed production. Unfortunately, alternative estimates (for example, those of the CIA) are not available for many weapons systems. For the years 1977 to 1983, the CIA estimates that the Soviets produced "about" 15,500 tanks, "about" 5,000 fighter aircraft, "more than" 30 major surface combatants, and "some" 70 attack submarines. See *The Congressional Record,* August 10, 1984, pp. S10386–89, and *Allocation of Resources in the Soviet Union and China—1984,* p. 17.

2. The last three, while involved in defense industry, are not covered in detail in this work because of the dual-use nature of their products. Tanks and missiles have only one real function, while radio technology may have many.

3. *Soviet Acquisition of Militarily Significant Western Technology: An Update* (September 1985), p. 4. The Ministry of Petroleum Refining and Petrochemical Industry, the Ministry of Chemical Industry, and the Ministry of Electrical Equipment Industry are also able to submit requests through the VPK.

4. See, for example, the U.S. government report, *Soviet 'Acquisition of Militarily Significant Western Technology: An Update* (September 1985), pp. 4 and 31, in which the Ministry's responsibilities are described as mostly in the areas of armor and electro-optics.

5. Identification of the deputy ministers for each of these ministries is based mainly on the obituary and publication evidence and the CIA's quasi-annual *Directory of Soviet Officials: National Organizations.*

6. See the discussion in various texts on Soviet administrative organization. Also see U.S. Defense Intelligence Agency, *Ground Forces R&D Resources— USSR: Ministry of the Defense Industry (MOP)* DST-1830S-333-79 (30 November, 1979), p. 7.

7. U.S. Defense Intelligence Agency, *Military Product R&D Management— USSR (U)*, DST-1830S-529-81 (25 March, 1981), p. 22.

8. See his biography in *Izvestiya,* November 17, 1985, upon his appointment to head Gossnab, the State Supply Agency.

9. *Soviet Acquisition of Militarily Significant Western Technology: An Update* (September 1985), p. 32.

10. It is possible that G. M. Tabakov and/or N. D. Khokhlov held this position in the second half of the 1960s and in the early 1970s based on their positions in the obituary of Isayev and Yangel, but I have been unable to confirm this.

11. See the interview with Udarov, "Byt' Novatorami," *Krasnaya zvezda* (February 9, 1986), p. 1.

12. Mikhail Agursky, "The Research Institute of Machine-Building Technology," p. 2.

13. Victor Yevsikov, "Re-entry Technology and the Soviet Space Program (Some Personal Observations)," Falls Church, VA.: Delphic Associates, 1982.

14. Agursky, "The Research Institute of Machine-Building Technology."

15. Nikita Khrushchev, *Khrushchev Remembers*, p. 48.

16. Central Intelligence Agency, *Directory of Soviet Officials of National Organizations* (1984), *Soviet Acquisition of Militarily Significant Western Technology: An Update* (September 1985), p. 33; DIA, *The Soviet Weapon-Acquisition Process, with Special Emphasis on the Ground Forces*, DST-1830S-336-80 (September 12, 1980), p. 43.

17. For example, the author found the ministry's location on Gorky Street in Moscow by accident: it was identified in a brief biographical note about the architect who designed the building.

18. See, for example, *Soviet Military Power*, no. 3, p. 44.

19. "Soviet Acquisition of Militarily Significant Western Technology: An Update" (September 1985), p. 4.

20. *Izvestia*, Nov. 23, 1986, p. 1.

21. Raymond Garthoff, *Detente and Confrontation* (Washington, D.C.: Brookings Institution, 1985) p. 756–757.

22. See *The New York Times*, July 20, 1986, p. 1.

23. See Philip Hanson, *Soviet Industrial Espionage: Some New Information* (London: Royal Institute of International Affairs, 1987), p. 16.

24. U.S. Defense Intelligence Agency, *The Soviet Weapon-Acquisition Process, with Special Emphasis on Ground Forces*, DST-1830S-336-80 (December 12, 1980), p. 43; *Soviet Acquisition of Militarily Significant Western Technology: An Update* (September 1985), pp. 4, 31.

25. It is *possible* that this plant was the Kovrov Motorcycle Plant, directed from 1954 to 1960 by P. V. Finogenov (later deputy minister of defense industry [1965–1973], first deputy minister [1973–1979], and minister of Defense Industry [1979–]). This plant also appears to have produced guns (perhaps not coincidentally, in 1979, Bakhirev was coauthor of a book about the gun designer Degtyarev). It is possible to speculate that the relationship between these two men would be particularly close, with Bakhirev having worked under Finogenov for a number of years at the plant and Finogenov having worked under Bakhirev at the Ministry, or highly competitive for the same reasons.

26. DIA, *The Soviet Weapon-Acquisition Process,"* p. 43. See also *Soviet Military Power*, various years.

27. CIA *Directory of Soviet Officials: National Organizations*, 1985.

28. Biographical information from Kalmykov's obituary, *Pravda*, Mar. 23, 1974, and his biography appearing in the 1966 *Deputaty Verkhovnogo Sovyeta*.

29. Biographical information from *Bolshaya Sovyetskaya Entsiklopediya Yezhegodnik* (1981), and *Deputaty Verkhovnogo Sovyeta* (1984). The BSE states that Pleshakov served in the Army in 1944 and 1945, then was chief of a lab, then a department, and finally a director of an NII between 1945 and 1964. The *Deputaty* biography says Pleshakov served in the Army from 1942 to 1952, then was chief of a lab, a department, a sector, and then director of an NII. A biographical note prepared by the US Arms Control and Disarmament Agency described Pleshakov as a "specialist in aeronautical application and radio engineering."

30. The BSE gives the later figure, while the Deputaty gives 1965 as the year Pleshakov became first deputy minister.

31. *Pravda*, Dec. 5, 1985, p. 2.

32. See A. Fedoseyev, *Zapadnya*, 2d ed., and Henry Eric Firdman, "Decision-making in the Soviet Microelectronics Industry."

BIBLIOGRAPHY

English-Language

Agursky, Mikhail and Hannes Adomeit. "The Soviet Military Industrial Complex and Its Internal Mechanism." National Security Series No. 1/78. Kingston, Ontario: Centre for International Relations, Queen's University, 1978.

Agursky, Mikhail and Hannes Adomeit. "The Soviet Military Industrial Complex." *Survey* (Spring 1979), 24(2):106–124.

Agursky, Mikhail. "The Research Institute of Machine-Building Technology: A Part of the Soviet Military-Industrial Complex." Soviet Institutions Paper no. 8. Jerusalem: Soviet and East European Research Centre, 1975? (In Russian, with English summary.)

Allison, Graham T. and Morton H. Halperin. "Bureaucratic Politics: A Paradigm and Some Policy Implications." In Raymond Tanter and Richard H. Ullman, eds., *Theory and Practice in International Relations*, pp. 40–79. A supplement to *World Politics*. (Spring 1972), vol. 24.

Bibliography

Amman, Ronald and Julian Cooper, eds. *Industrial Innovation in the Soviet Union.* New Haven: Yale University Press, 1982.

Amman, Ronald and Julian Cooper, eds. *Technical Progress and Soviet Economic Development.* Oxford: Basil Blackwell, 1986.

Amman, Ronald, Julian Cooper, and R. W. Davies, eds., *The Technological Level of Soviet Industry.* New Haven: Yale University Press, 1977.

Aspaturian, Vernon V. "The Soviet Military-Industrial Complex: Does It Exist?" *Journal of International Affairs* (1972), 26(1):1–28.

Azrael, Jeremy R. *Managerial Power and Soviet Politics.* Cambridge, Mass.: Harvard University Press, 1966.

Barghoorn, Frederick C. *Politics in the USSR.* 2d ed. Boston: Little, Brown, 1972.

Barashkov, L. " 'Vikings' from the Outside." *Literaturnaya gazeta,* July 21, 1976, p. 11. [CDSP, 28(33):15]

Barnett, A. Doak. *Cadres, Bureaucracy, and Political Power in Communist China.* New York: Columbia University Press, 1967.

Beck, Carl. "Bureaucratic Conservatism and Innovation in Eastern Europe." *Comparative Political Studies* (July 1968), 1(2):275–294.

Beissinger, Mark R. The Politics of Convergence: The Diffusion of Western Management Ideas in the Soviet Union. Ph.D dissertation, Harvard University, 1982.

Belov, A. " 'Methods Nannies.' " *Literaturnaya gazeta.* July 13, 1977, p. 11. [CDSP, 29(34):13]

Berliner, Joseph. *The Innovation Decision in Soviet Industry.* Cambridge, Mass.: MIT Press, 1976.

Bjorkman, Thomas N. and Zamostny, Thomas J. "Soviet Politics and Strategy Toward the West: Three Cases." *World Politics* (January 1984), 36(2):189–214.

Bornstein, Morris and Daniel R. Fusfeld. *The Soviet Economy: A Book of Readings.* 4th ed. Homewood, Ill.: Richard D. Irwin, 1974.

Brown, A. H. "Problems of Interest Articulation and Group Influence in the Soviet Union." *Government and Opposition,* (Spring 1972), 7(2):229–243.

Budnik, Ye. I. "The Economic Ties Between Retail Trade and Industry: How Can They Be Improved." *Eko* (September–October 1975) no. 5, pp. 107–121. [Current Digest of the Soviet Press (hereafter CDSP), 28(4):9–11]

Bykov, V. "Business Contacts with People—How Difficult They Are." *Eko* (July–August 1978), no. 4, pp. 177–182. [CDSP, 31(21):13]

Caldwell, Dan. "Bureaucratic Foreign Policy-Making." *American Behavioral Scientist* (September/October 1977), 21(1):87–110.

Castles, Francil G. "Interest Articulation: A Totalitarian Paradox." *Survey* (Autumn 1969), no. 73, pp. 116–132.

Chaiko, Lev. *Helicopter Construction in the USSR.* Falls Church, Va.: Delphic Associates, 1985.

Checinski, Michael. "A Comparison of the Polish and Soviet Armaments Decisionmaking Systems." Rand Report R-2662-AF. January 1981.

Chekalin, Aleksandr. "Choice at the First Level." *Literaturnaya gazeta.* June 1, 1977, p. 11. [CDSP, 29(22):21]

Colton, Timothy J. "Civil-Military Relations in the Soviet Union: The Developmental Perspective." *Studies in Comparative Communism* (Autumn 1978), 11(3):213–224.

Cuff, Robert D. "An Organizational Perspective on the Military-Industrial Complex." *Business History Review* (Summer 1978) 52(2):250–267.

Cutler, Robert M. "The Formation of Soviet Foreign Policy: Organizational and Cognitive Perspectives." *World Politics* (April 1982) 34(3):418–430.

Dawisha, Karen. "Soviet Security and the Role of the Military: The 1968 Czechoslovak Crisis." *British Journal of Political Science,* 10:341–363.

Dawisha, Karen. "The Limits of the Bureaucratic Politics Model: Observations on the Soviet Case." *Studies in Comparative Communism* (Winter 1980), 13(4):300–331.

Deane, Michael J., Ilana Kass, and Andrew J. Porth, "The Soviet Command Structure in Transformation." *Strategic Review* (Spring 1984), 12(2):55–70.

Debardeleben, Joan T. "Esoteric Policy Debate: Nuclear Safety Issues in the Soviet Union and German Democratic Republic." *British Journal of Political Science* (April 1985), vol. 15, part 2, pp. 227–253.

Dunmore, Timothy. "Local Party Organs in Industrial Administration: The Case of the *Ob"edinenie* Reform." *Soviet Studies* (April 1980), 32(2):195–217.

Dunskaya, Irina. *Security Practices at Soviet Scientific Research Facilities.* Falls Church, Va.: Delphic Associates, 1983.

Ekonomicheskaya gazeta. "New Methods of Economic Management in Action." (January 1981), no. 1, p. 2. [DCSP, 33(2):6–7]

Ekonomicheskaya gazeta. "On Progress in Introducing the New Methods of Economic Management." (February 1981), no. 9 p. 22. [CDSP 33(11):15, 24]

Eko. "The Topic of Discussion Is 'Rules of the Game.' " (1975), no. 6, pp. 116–147. [CDSP 28(14):5–8]

Eko. "The Association in the System of Production Ties." (March–April 1976), no. 2, pp. 154–168. [CDSP 28(21):4–5]

Evangelista, Matthew A. "Why the Soviets Buy the Weapons They Do." *World Politics* (July 1984), 36(4):597–618.

Fedoseyev, Anatol. "Design in Soviet Military R&D: The Case of Radar Research in Vacuum Electronics." Papers on Soviet Science and Technology no. 8. Harvard University Russian Research Center, May 1983.

Firdman, Henry Eric. *Decision-making in the Soviet Microelectronics Industry: The Leningrad Design Bureau: A Case Study.* Falls Church, Va.: Delphic Associates, 1985.

Fortescue, Stephen. "Research Institute Party Organizations and the Right of Control." *Soviet Studies* (April 1983), 35(2):175–195.

Frankenstein, John. "People's Republic of China: Defense Industry, Diplomacy, and Trade." In J. E. Katz, ed. *Arms Production. . . ,* pp. 89–102.

Friedgut, Theodore H. "Interests and Groups in Soviet Policy-Making: the MTS Reforms." *Soviet Studies* (October 1976), 28(4):524–547.

Garthoff, Douglas F. "The Soviet Military and Arms Control." *Survival* (November–December 1977), 19(6):242–250.

Garthoff, Raymond L. "SALT and the Soviet Military." *Problems of Communism* (January–February, 1975), 24(1):21–37.

Gelman, Harry. The Brezhnev Politburo and the Decline of Detente. Ithaca: Cornell University Press, 1984.

Gitelman, Zvi. "Comment [on Janos article]." *Studies in Comparative Communism* (Spring 1979), 12(1):35–38.

Glagolev, Igor S. "The Soviet Decision-Making Process in Arms Control Negotiations." *Orbis* (winter 1978), 22(4):767–775.

Glassman, Jon D. "Soviet Foreign Policy Decisionmaking." In Andrew W. Cordier, ed., *Columbia Essays in International Affairs*, vol. 3, 1967. The Dean's Papers. New York: Columbia University Press, 1968.

Gorlin, Alice C. "The Power of Soviet Industrial Ministries in the 1980s." *Soviet Studies* (July 1985), 37(3):353–370.

Greenberg, Karl. *Central Materials Research Institute (TsNIIM) of the Soviet Ministry of Defense Industry*. Falls Church, Va.: Delphic Associates, 1986.

Groth, Alexander J. "USSR: Pluralist Monolith?" *British Journal of Political Science*, 9:445–464.

Halbert, Gerald A. "World Tank Production." *Armor*, (March–April 1981), pp. 42–47.

Hammer, Darrell P. *USSR: The Politics of Oligarchy*. Hinsdale, Ill.: Dryden Press, 1974.

Hanson, Philip. "Estimating Soviet Defence Expenditure." *Soviet Studies* (July 1978), 30(3):403–410.

Hanson, Philip. "The Novosibirsk Report: Comment." *Survey* (spring 1984), 28(1):83–87.

Harasymiw, Bohdan. "*Nomenklatura:* The Soviet Communist Party's Leadership Recruitment System." *Candaian Journal of Political Science* (December 1969), 2(4):493–512.

Hill, Ronald J. "Party-State Relations and Soviet Political Development." *British Journal of Political Science*, 10:149–165.

Holloway, David. "The Soviet Union." In Milton Leitenberg and Nicole Ball, eds. The Structure of the Defense Industry: An International Survey. New York: St. Martins, 1983.

Holloway, David. *The Soviet Union and the Arms Race*. New Haven: Yale University Press, 1983.

Holmes, Leslie. *The Policy Process in Communist States: Politics and Industrial Administration*. Beverly Hills: Sage, 1981.

Hough, Jerry. *The Soviet Prefects: Party Organizations in Industrial Decision Making*. Cambridge, Mass.: Harvard University Press, 1969.

Hough, Jerry F. " 'Interest Groups' and 'Pluralism' in the Soviet Union." *Soviet Union/Union Sovietique* (1981), vol. 8, part 1 pp. 103–109.

Hough, Jerry F. "The World as Viewed from Moscow." *International Journal* (spring 1982), 37(2):183–219.

Hough, Jerry F. and Merle Fainsod. *How the Soviet Union is Governed.* Cambridge, Mass.: Harvard University Press, 1979.

Jackson, William D. "The Soviets and Strategic Arms: Toward an Evaluation of the Record." *Political Science Quarterly* (summer 1979), 94(2):243–261.

Janos, Andrew C. "Interest Groups and the Structure of Power: Critique and Comparisons." *Studies in Comparative Communism* (spring 1979), 12(1):6–20.

Jenkins, Bill and Andrew Gray. "Bureaucratic Politics and Power: Developments in the Study of Bureaucracy." *Political Studies* (June 1983), 3(2):177–193.

Jones, Ellen. "Committee Decision-Making in the Soviet Union." *World Politics* (January 1984), 36(2):165–188.

Jonsson, Christer. "Soviet Foreign Policy and Domestic Politics: A Case Study." *Cooperation and Conflict* (1977) 12:129–148.

Katz, James Everett, ed. *Arms Production in Developing Countries: An Analysis of Decision-Making.* Lexington, Mass.: Lexington Books, 1984.

Kaera, R. "Executive is a Profession." *Literaturnaya gazeta.* February 23, 1977, p. 11. [CDSP, 29(10):13–14]

Kelley, Donald R. "Interest Groups in the USSR: The Impact of Political Sensitivity on Group Influence." *Journal of Politics* (August 1972), 34(3):860–888.

Kelley, Donald R. "Environmental Policy-Making in the USSR: The Role of Industrial and Environmental Interest Groups." *Soviet Studies* (October 1976), 28(4):570–589.

Kelley, Donald R. "Group and Specialist Influence in Soviet Politics: In Search of a Theory." In Richard B. Remnek, ed., *Social Scientists and Policy Making in the USSR*, pp. 108–137. New York: Praeger, 1977.

Khrushchev, Nikita. Strobe Talbott, ed. *Khrushchev Remembers.* Boston: Little, Brown, 1970.

Khrushchev, Nikita. Strobe Talbott, ed. *Khrushchev Remembers: The Last Testament.* Boston: Little, Brown, 1974.

Kolkowicz, Roman. "The Military and Soviet Foreign Policy." *Journal of Strategic Studies* (December 1981), 4(4):337–355.

Kostandov, L. A. "Timely Discussion." *Literaturnaya gazeta.* February 23, 1977, p. 11. [CDSP, 29:(10):12–13]

Kulagin, G. A. "My Partners, the Authorities, and the 'Rules of the Game.' " *Eko* (March–April 1975), no. 2, pp. 82–95. [CDSP, 28(14):1–5]

Kulagin, Georgy. "With Whom Are We to Fill Vacancies?" *Literaturnaya gazeta.* August 4, 1976, p. 10 [CDSP, 28(37):6].

Kushnirsky, Fyodor I. *Soviet Economic Planning, 1965–1980.* Boulder, Colo.: Westview Press, 1982.

Lane, David. *Politics and Society in the USSR.* 3d ed. New York: New York University Press, 1978.

Latham, Richard J. "People's Republic of China: The Restructuring of Defense-Industrial Policies." In J. E. Katz, ed., *Arms Production. . .* , pp. 103–122.

Latifi, O. "Promoted to a Post." *Pravda.* July 17, 1981, p. 2. [CDSP, 33(29):18–19]

Lebedinskiy, N. P., ed. *Guidelines on Methods Pertaining to the Compilation of the State Plan for Development of the USSR National Economy.* JPRS translation number 49344 (3 December 1969).

Lee, William T. "The 'Politico-Military-Industrial Complex' of the USSR." *Journal of International Affairs* (1972), 26(1):73–86.

Leggett, Robert E. and Rabin, Sheldon T. "A Note on the Meaning of the Soviet Defence Budget." *Soviet Studies* (October 1978), 30(4):557–566.

Levikov, Aleksandr. "How to Become a Minister." *Literaturnaya gazeta.* November 5, 1975, p. 11. [CDSP, 28(30):1–3]

Levikov, Aleksandr. "The Cheshkov Level." *Literaturnaya gazeta.* (December 17, 1975, p. 11 [CDSP, 28(30):3–5]

Levikov, Aleksandr. "New Job." *Literaturnaya gazeta.* January 28, 1976, p. 11. [CDSP, 28(30):5–6]

Levikov, Aleksandr. "Professionals of Management." *Literaturnaya gazeta.* February 12, 1976, p. 12. [CDSP, 28(30):6–7]

Lozansky, Edward D., ed. *Andrei Sakharov and Peace.* New York: Avon, 1985.

Marfels, Christian. "The Structure of the Military-Industrial Complex in the United States and Its Impact on Industrial Concentration." *Kyklos,* (1978), 31:409–423.

McDonnell, John C. "The Defense Industry." In David R. Jones, ed., annual volumes of *Soviet Armed Forces Review Annual* [SAFRA]. Gulf Breeze, Fla.: Academic International Press, 1978–1980.

McDonnell, John C. "The Soviet Defense Industry as a Pressure Group." In Michael McGwire, Ken Booth, and John McDonnell, eds., *Soviet Naval Policy: Objectives and Constraints.* New York: Praeger, 1975.

McDonnell, John C. "Book Reviews *The Military in Contemporary Soviet Politics: An Institutional Analysis.*" *Soviet Union/Union Sovietique* (1978), vol. 5, part 1, pp. 133–134.

Medvedev, Roy. *Khrushchev.* Brian Pearce, trans. Garden City, N.Y.: Anchor, 1984.

Medvedev, Zhores. *Andropov.* Middlesex, England: Penguin, 1984.

Medvedev, Zhores. *Gorbachev.* New York: Norton, 1986.

Meissner, Boris. "Soviet Foreign Policy and Afghanistan." *Aussen Politik.* English ed. (March 1980), 31:260–282.

Mills, Richard M. "The Soviet Leadership Problem." *World Politics* (July 1981), 33(4):590–613.

Moore, John H. "Agency Costs, Technological Change, and Soviet Central Planning." *Journal of Law and Economics* (October 1981), 24:189–215.

Morokhov, I. D. et al. "Third International Congress on Peaceful Uses of Underground Nuclear Explosions," *Soviet Atomic Energy* (trans. from *Atomnaya energiya*) (May 1973), 34(5):407–409.

Murphy, Paul J., ed. *The Soviet Air Forces.* Jefferson, N.C.: McFarland, 1984.

Nathan, James A. and James K. Oliver. "Bureaucratic Politics: Academic Windfalls and Intellectual Pitfalls." *Journal of Political and Military Sociology* (Spring 1978), 6:81–91.

Newhouse, John. *Cold Dawn: The Story of SALT.* New York: Holt, Rinehart, Winston, 1973.

Nossal, Kim Richard. "Allison Through the (Ottawa) Looking Glass: Bureaucratic Politics and Foreign Policy in a Parliamentary System." *Canadian Public Administration* (Winter 1979), 22(4):610–626.

Noulting, Louvan E. *The Planning of Research, Development, and Innovation in the USSR.* Foreign Economic Report no. 14. Washington: U.S. Department of Commerce, July 1978.

Nove, Alec. *The Soviet Economic System,* 2d ed. London: George Allen and Unwin, 1980.

Odom, William. "Comment [on Janos article]." *Studies in Comparative Communism* (spring 1979), 12(1):20–27.

Oliver, James H. "Citizen Demands and the Soviet Political System." *APSR* (1968), 63(2):465–475.

Orlov, Ia. L. "Heavy Industry and Consumer Goods: Organization and Planning." *Problems of Economics* 22(3):21–39.

Parfenov, V. "The Ministry Conducts a Search." *Pravda.* May 11 and May 13, 1978, p. 2. [CDSP, 30(19):10–11].

Parfenov, Vasily. "Overcoming the Force of Inertia." *Pravda.* August 10, 1981, p. 2. [CDSP, 33(32):5–6]

Parrott, Bruce. *Politics and Technology in the Soviet Union.* Cambridge, Mass.: MIT Press, 1983.

Peters, B. Guy. "The Problem of Bureaucratic Government." *The Journal of Politics* (1981), 43:56–82.

Petrov, Vladimir. "Formation of Soviet Foreign Policy." *Orbis* (fall 1973), 17(3):819–850.

Pick, Otto. "Practice and Theory in Soviet Arms Control Policy." *The World Today* (July–August 1982), 38(7):257–263.

Ploss, Sidney. "New Politics in Russia?" *Survey* (autumn 1973), 19(4):23–35.

Polikanov, Sergei. *Nuclear Physics in the Soviet Union: Current Status and Future Prospects.* Falls Church, Va.: Delphic Associates, 1984.

Popov, G. "Economic Management: Some Questions of Theory and Practice." *Kommunist* (December 1976), no. 18, pp. 70–81. [CDSP, 29(10):10–11]

Powell, David. "In Pursuit of Interest Groups in the USSR." *Soviet Union/Union Sovietique* (1979), vol. 6, part 1, pp. 99–125.

Pravda. "In the CPSU Central Committee and the USSR Council of Ministers." April 3, 1973, pp. 1–2. [CDSP, 25(14):1–4]

Pravda. "Personnel Certification." February 21, 1977, p. 1. [CDSP, 29(8):21–22]

Pravda. "In the CPSU Central Committee and the USSR Council of Ministers." July 29, 1979, pp. 1–2. [CDSP, 31, (30):1–6, 14]

Pravda. "Improve the Management Mechanism." December 16, 1981, p. 1. [CDSP, 33, (50):21–22]

Pravda. "Expanded Meeting of the Collegium of the Ministry of Railroads." December 14, 1982, p. 3. [CDSP, 34 (50):22–23]

Pravda. "Behind the Decisions of the 26th CPSU: A New Branch is Being Born." November 27, 1982, p. 2. [CDSP 34 (48):5–6, 13]

Pravdin, A. "Inside the CPSU Central Committee." *Survey* (autumn 1974), 20(4):94–104.

Puffer, Sheila M. "Inside a Soviet Management Institute." *California Management Review* (fall 1981), 24(1):90–96.

Radio Liberty Dispatch. "New Soviet Defense-Oriented Ministry Established." February 8, 1968.

Radio Liberty Research. "Personnel Changes in Leningrad Oblast." RL no. 287/83. July 29, 1983.

Rahr, Alexander G., compiler. *A Biographic Directory of 100 Leading Soviet Officials.* Munich: Radio Liberty, 1984.

Rigby, T. H. "Bureaucracy and Democracy in the USSR." *The Australian Quarterly* (March 1970), 42(1):5–14.

Rigby, T. H. "Hough on Political Participation in the Soviet Union." *Soviet Studies* (April 1976), 28(2):257–261.

Rigby, T. H. and Bohdan Harasymiw, eds. *Leadership Selection and Patron-Client Relations in the USSR and Yugoslavia.* London: George Allen & Unwin, 1983.

Razauskas, Romuladas. "The Kind of Director I Want." *Literaturnaya gazeta.* August 25, 1976, p. 10. [CDSP, 28(37):6–7]

Sadykiewicz, Michael. "Soviet Military Politics." *Survey* (winter 1982) 26(1):180–210.

Sakharov, Andrei D. Harrison Salisbury, ed. *Sakharov Speaks.* New York: Alfred A. Knopf, 1974.

Schapiro, Leonard. "The General Department of the CC of the CPSU." *Survey* (summer 1975), 21(3):53–65.

Schroeder, Gertrude E. "Soviet Economic 'Reform' Decrees: More Steps on the Treadmill." In Joint Economic Committee, Congress of the United States, *Soviet Economy in the 1980s: Problems and Prospects,* part 1. Washington GPO, 1983.

Schwartz, Joel J. and William R. Keech. "Group Influence and the Policy Process in the Soviet Union." *American Political Science Review* (1968), 62(3):840–851.

Sheren, Andrew. "Structure and Organization of Defense-Related Industries." In Joint Economic Committee, Congress of the United States, *Economic Performance and the Military Burden in the Soviet Union.* Washington: GPO, 1970.

Shevchenko, Arkady N. *Breaking with Moscow.* New York: Alfred A. Knopf, 1985.

Simes, Dimitri K. "The Soviet Invasion of Czechoslovakia and the Limits of Kremlinology." *Studies in Comparative Communism* (spring–summer 1975), 8(1–2):174–180.

Smith, Gerard. *Doubletalk: The Story of SALT I.* Lanham, Md.: University Press of America, 1984.

Solomon, Peter H., Jr. *Soviet Criminologists and Criminal Policy: Specialists in Policy-Making.* New York: Columbia University Press, 1978.

Solomon, Peter H., Jr. "Soviet Policy-Making in Comparative Perspective." *Soviet Union/Union Sovietique* (1981), 8(1):110–118.

Solomon, Susan Gross. *Pluralism in the Soviet Union: Essays in Honour of H. Gordon Skilling.* New York: St. Martin's Press, 1983.

Sotsialisticheskaya Industriya. "The Costs of Connivance." October 4, 1981, p. 2. [CDSP, 33(40):9–10]

Spielmann, Karl F. "Defense Industrialists in the USSR." *Problems of Communism* (September–October, 1976), pp. 52–69.

Steinhaus, Alexander. *The Beginnings of Soviet Military Electronics, 1948–1961: A Personal Account.* Falls Church, Va.: Delphic Associates, 1986.

Stevenson, Paul. "The Military-Industrial Complex: An Examination of the Nature of Corporate Capitalism in America." *Journal of Political and Military Sociology* (fall 1973), 1:247–259.

Stewart, Philip D. "Soviet Interest Groups and the Policy Process: The Repeal of Production Education." *World Politics* (October 1969), 22(1):29–50.

Talbott, Strobe. *Endgame: The Inside Story of SALT II.* New York: Harper and Row, 1979.

Talbott, Strobe. *Deadly Gambits: The Reagan Administration and the Stalemate in Nuclear Arms Control.* New York: Alfred A. Knopf, 1984.

Tarschys, Daniel. "The Soviet Political System." *European Journal of Political Research* (1977), 5:287–320.

Teague, Elizabeth. "The Foreign Departments of the Central Committee of the CPSU." *Radio Liberty Research Bulletin,* supplement (October 27, 1980).

Teague, Elizabeth. "The Soviet Defense Council—Modern Successor to the Wartime GKO." *Radio Liberty Research* (June 19, 1981), RL-246/81.

Terry, Sarah Meiklejohn. "The Case for a 'Group' Approach to Polish Politics: Comment [on Janos article] by Sarah Meiklejohn Terry." *Studies in Comparative Communism* (spring 1979), 12(1):28–34.

Turetsky, Mikhail. *The Introduction of Missile Systems into the Soviet Navy (1945–1962).* Falls Church, Va.: Delphic Associates, March 1983.

Turkevich, John. "How Science Policy is Formed." *Survey* (winter 1977–1978), 23(1):87–116.

Ulsamer, Edgar. "Moscow's Technology Parasites." *Air Force Magazine* (December 1984), pp. 52–60.

United States Department of Defense. Project Have Stork. *Organization, Activities, and Physical Resources of the USSR All-Union Ministry of Defense Industry (MOP),* PHS-153A-69-1 (September 1969).

United States Department of Defense. Defense Intelligence Agency. *Estimated Expenditures for Research and Development by the Soviet Ministry of Aviation Industry (MAP)*, DIA-450-2-6-71-INT (July 1971).

United States Department of Defense. Defense Intelligence Agency. "Intercontinental Strategic Forces Summary, USSR," DDB-2680-253-85 (August 1985).

United States Government. *Soviet Acquisition of Militarily Significant Technology: An Update.* September 1985.

United States Senate. Subcommittee on National Policy Machinery. *National Policy Machinery in the Soviet Union: Report of the Committee on Government Operations.* Washington: GPO, March 29, 1960.

Valenta, Jiri. "Soviet Decisionmaking and the Czechoslovakia Crisis of 1968." *Studies in Comparative Communism* (spring–summer, 1975), 8(1–2):147–173.

Valenta, Jiri. "The Bureaucratic Politics Paradigm and the Soviet Invasion of Czechoslovakia." *Political Science Quarterly* (spring 1979), 94(1):55–76.

Valenta, Jiri, and William Potter, eds. *Soviet Decisionmaking for National Security.* London: George Allen and Unwin, 1984.

Vertman, A. A., Ye. S. Kalinnikov et al. "The Advanced Training Institute Comes of Age." *Eko* (March–April 1977), no. 2, pp. 81–110. [CDSP, 29(15):6–7]

Volz, Arthur G. "Soviet Tank Industry." *Jane's Defense Review* (1983), 4(1):49–56.

Volz, Arthur G. "Standardization in the Warsaw Pact." *Armor* (March–April, 1979), pp. 22–26.

Voslensky, Michael. *Nomenklatura.* Eric Mosbacher, trans. Garden City, N.Y.: Doubleday, 1984.

Vtorushin, S. "The Division Was—Abolished." *Pravda.* June 6, 1970, p. 3. [CDSP, 32(23):17]

White, Stephen. "Communist Systems and the 'Iron Law of Pluralism.' " *British Journal of Political Science,* 8:101–117.

White, Stephen. "The Supreme Soviet and Budgetary Politics in the USSR." *British Journal of Political Science* (January 1982), 12(1):75–94.

Williams, Larry W. "Soviet Self-Propelled Artillery." *Armor* (September–October, 1978), pp. 18–20.

Williams, Larry W. and Joseph E. Backofen, Jr. "Origins of Soviet Tank Guns." *Armor* (March–April, 1978), pp. 48–51.

Woods, Stan. "Weapons Acquisition in the Soviet Union." *Aberdeen Studies in Defense Economics* (summer 1982), no. 24.

Yanov, Alexander. *Detente After Brezhnev: The Domestic Roots of Soviet Foreign Policy.* Berkeley: Institute of International Studies, University of California, 1977.

Yegorov, M. V. "Put the introduction of new methods on a planned basis," *Ekonomicheskaya gazeta* (November 1980), no. 45, p. 7. [CDSP, 32(46):7 +]

Yevsikov, Victor. *Re-entry Technology and the Soviet Space Program (Some*

Personal Observations). Delphic Associates Monograph Series on Soviet Union. Falls Church, Va.: Delphic Associates, December 1982.

Zaleski, Eugene. "R&D: Planning and Financing." *Survey* (spring 1977–1978), 23(2)16–38.

[Zaslavskaya, Tatyana]. "Doklad o Neobkhodimosti Bolee Uglublennogo Izucheniya v SSSR Sotsial'nogo Mekhanizma Razvitiya Ekonomiki." AS 5042, August 26, 1983. Translated in *Survey* (spring 1984), 28(1):88–108. With comment by Philip Hanson, "The Novosibirsk Report: Comment," pp. 82–87.

Russian-Language

Academy of Sciences of the Ukrainian SSR, 1919–1979. Kiev: Naukova Dumka, 1980.

Aleksandrov, A. P., Yu. M. Bulkin, . . . Ye. V. Kulov et al. "Fizicheskiy energeticheskiy pusk pervogo bloka Leningradskoy AES im. V. I. Lenin." *Atomnaya energiya* (August 1974), 37(2):99–107.

Alekseyev, Mikhail. "U noroga v zavtra." *Pravda.* December 31, 1979, p. 1.

Andrianov, V. N. "Sovershenstvovaniye khozrascheta." *Ekonomicheskaya Gazeta* (August 1970), no. 35, p. 6.

Antonov, O. K. "Chto vmesto 'vala'?" *Trud.* March 13, 1983, p. 2.

Antropov, P. Ya. "Perspektivy poiskov promyshlennykh mestorozhdeniy urana v depressionnykh zonakh zemnoy kory." *Geologicheskiy zhurnal* (1969), 29(5):75–82.

Antropov, P. Ya. "Perspektivy poiskov promyshlennykh mestorozhdeniy urana v depressionnykh zonakh zemnoy kory." *Izvestiya Armyanskoy SSR. Nauki o zemle* (1969), no. 6, pp. 37–43.

Antropov, P. Ya. "O nekotorykh geologicheskikh kontseptsiyakh zemli." *Geologicheskiy zhurnal* (1975), 35(3):139–143.

Antropov, P. Ya. *Toplivno-energeticheskiy potentsiyal zemli.* 2d ed. Moscow: Nauka, 1976.

Antropov, P. Ya., L. S. Yevseyeva, and G. P. Poluarshinov. "Mestorozhdeniya urana v osadochnykh porodakh depressiy." *Sovetskaya geologiya* (September 1977), no. 9, pp. 32–36.

Antropov, P. Ya. et al. "Ispol'zovaniye metodov lazernogo gazoanaliza dlya resheniya ryada geologicheskikh i promyslovykh zadach." *Sovetskaya geologiya* (1975), no. 10, pp. 92–98.

Arlazorov, Mikhail. *Doroga na kosmodrom.* Moscow: Politizdat, 1984.

"Artilleriyskaya Promyshlennost'." *Velikaya Otechestvennaya Voyna, 1941–1945: Entsiklopediya.* Moscow: Sovetskaya Entsiklopediya, 1985.

Bakhirev, V. "Vysokoye kachestvo," *Izvestiya,* 1st ed. (June 30, 1970), excerpts in *Izvestiya* (July 2, 1971), p. 3.

Bibliography

Bakhirev, V. V. and Kirillov, I. I. *Konstruktor V. A. Degtyarev.* Moscow: Voyenizdat, 1983.

Baklanov, O. D. et al, "Metodika rascheta transformatorov polnykh soprotivleniy na pryamougolnykh volnovodakh," *Pribory i sistemy* (1970), no. 14, pp. 15–22.

Baklanov, O. D. et al, "Transformator polnykh soprotivleniy na tsilindricheskom volnovode," *Pribory i sistemy* (1970), no. 14, pp. 11–15.

Barashev, P. "Dver', otkrytaya v nebo." *Pravda.* December 13, 1972, p. 6.

Baravka, V. "Sovyetuyas' s lyud'mi," *Ekonomicheskaya Gazeta* (June 1970), no. 23, p. 6.

Batrasov, V. I. *Rezervy rosta.* Gor'kii: Volgo-Vyatskoye, 1979.

Bekleshov, V. K. et al. *Organizatsiya i planirovaniye deyatel'nosti otraslevykh NII i KB v priborostroyenii.* Moscow: Mashinostroyeniye, 1986.

Bezsonov, N. "Izobreteno—100%, osvoyeno—(.?.%)." *Nauchno-tekhnicheskiye obshchestva SSSR* (1968), no. 9, p. 44.

Bogolyubov, K. M. et al, eds. *Spravochnik partiynogo rabotnika: vypusk dvadtsat' chetvertyy, chast' vtoraya.* Moscow: Politicheskaya Literatura, 1984.

Bolotin, D. N. *Sovetskoe strelkovoe oruzhiye.* Moscow: Voyenizdat, 1983.

Botvin, A. "Nravstvenno krasiv." *Pravda.* May 19, 1973, p. 4.

"Boyevaya Programma." *Pravda,* December 17, 1971.

Bruderev, G. "Sredstva unichtozheniya—potrebitel'skaya produktsiya." *Posev* (April 1983), no. 4, pp. 30–33.

Chalmayev, V. "Tankoviy konveyer Stalingrada." *Volga* (1975), no. 2, pp. 151–169.

Churin, A. I. and V. A. Klyachko. "Sovremennoye sostoyaniye problemy opresneniya vody." *Vestnik Akademii Nauka* (1965), no. 6, pp. 34–47.

Churin, A. I. et al, "Sovmeshcheniye krupnykh atomnykh elektrostantsiy s opresnitel'nymi ustanovkami." *Atomnaya energiya* (November 1968), 25(5):394–402.

Churin, Aleksandr and Viktor Smagin. " 'Zhivaya vlaga' Kazakhstana." *Sovetskaya latviya* (October 31, 1969), p. 3.

Davitnidze, I. L. *Kollegii ministerstv: pravovoye polozheniye i organizatsiya raboty.* Moscow: Yuridicheskaya Literature, 1972.

Dement'yev, P. V. "Ne tol'ka samolety." *Izvestiya.* May 22, 1971, p. 1.

Denisov, N. "Garantiya vysokogo kachestva." *Trud.* September 1, 1974, p. 2.

Derunov, P. F. "Sistema koeffitsientov opredeleniya urovnya organizatsii truda." *Narodnoye khozyaistvo kazakhstana* (1969), no. 1.

[Derunov, P. F.] *Ekonomicheskaya gazeta* (September 1969), no. 38, p. 29.

Derunov, P. F. "NOT i stanka." *Sotsialisticheskaya industriya.* June 6, 1972, p. 3.

Dzeniskevich, A. P. *Voyennaya pyatiletka rabochikh Leningrada, 1941–1945.* Leningrad: Lenizdat, 1972.

Fedoseyev, Anatol. *Zapadnya: chelovek i sotsialism.* 2d ed. Frankfurt: Posev, 1979.

Frolov, K. V., A. A. Parkhomenko, and M. K. Uskov. *Anatolii Arkad'evich Balgonravov.* Moscow: Nuaka, 1982.

Gay, D. *Nebesnoye prityazheniye.* Moscow: Moskovskii Rabochii, 1984.

Garbuz, Yu. "Proyekt No. 26." *Krasnaya zvezda.* January 19, 1986, p. 4.

Gayevoi, V. "Demokratiya i distsiplina." *Pravda.* February 11, 1980, p. 2.

Gerasimov, B. "Tvortsy boyevykh mashin." *Sotsiyalisticheskaya industriya* (May 17, 1970), p. 4.

Glushko, V. P. *Razvitiye raketostroyeniya i kosmonabtiki v SSSR.* Moscow: Mashinostroeniye, 1981.

Golovchenko, O. P. et al. "O nekotorykh voprosakh payki splava ZhS6K so stal'yu EI703." *Svarochnoye Proizvodstvo* (1969), no. 11, p. 33.

Goremykin, P. N. "Nekotoryye vazhnyye zadachi mashinostroyeniya v 1967 g." *Vestnik Mashinostroyeniya* (1967), no. 3, pp. 3–6.

Goremykin, P. N. "Resheniya Sentyabr'skogo (1965g.) Plenuma TsK KPSS i voprosy razvitiya mashinostroyeniya." *Vestnik mashinostroyeniya* (1965), no. 12, pp. 3–6.

Goremykin, P. N. "Vydayushchiis'a organizator promyshlennosti." *Voprosi istorii* (1968), no. 10, 114–116.

Grabin, V. "Usovershenstvovannaya divizionnaya." *Tekhnika i vooruzheniye* (August 1969), pp. 16–17.

Grabin, V. "Vklad v pobedu." *Tekhnika i vooruzheniye* (May 1970), p. 7.

Grinberg, M. A., Voytekhov, A. G., Suchkov, V. N. "Osnovyye napravleniya tekhnicheskogo progressa v oblasti proizvodstva khimicheskikh tovarov narodnogo potreblenniya." *Khimicheskaaya Promyshlennost'* (1969), no. 8, p. 6–8.

Gubarev, V. *Konstruktor: Neskol'ko stranits iz zhizni Mikhaila Kuz'micha Yangela.* Moscow: Izdatelstvo Politicheskoi Literatury, 1977.

Gusev, O. S. "Ekran glasnosti." *Pravda.* February 29, 1972.

Gusev, O. "Rezul'tat venchayet delo." *Pravda.* December 7, 1978, p. 3.

Iz istorii Sovetskoi kosmonavtiku. Moscow: Nauka, 1984.

Kalabin, V. B., Babenko, V. A., and Buravtsev, A. V. "Girostabiliziruyushchaya ustanovka dlya kinos"emok s dvizhushchegosya avtomobilya." *Tekhnika kino i televideniya* (1973), no. 5, pp. 55–56.

Kalinin, N. G., ed. *Organizatsiya upravleniya v sisteme ministerstva.* Moscow: Izdatel'stvo Moskovska Universiteta, 1974.

Kamenitser S. Ye. and Rusinov, F. M., eds. *Organizatsiya, planirovaniye, upravleniye deyatel'nost'yu promyshlennykh predpriyatii.* Moscow: Vysshaya Shkola, 1984.

Karlik, Ye. M. *Ekonomika mashinostroyeniya.* Leningrad: Mashinostroyeniye, 1977.

Karnozov, L. "Konstruktor artilleriyskogo vooruzheniya." *Tekhnika i vooruzheniye* (January 1970), p. 18.

Kazas, V. I., Yu. V. Konyshev, and A. G. Laktionov. "Potochnyy samoletnyy pribor dlya izmereniya razmerov i kontsentratsii krupnykh kapel' v oblakakh." *Akademiya Nank SSSR. Izvestiya, Fizik Atmosfery i Okeana* (1965), 1(11):1212–1215.

Keldysh, M. V., ed. *Tvorcheskoe naslediye Akademika Sergeya Pavlovicha Koroleva.* Moscow: Nauka, 1980.

Khvedeliani, Ya. "Inzhener, ego rol' i mesto." *Zarya vostok.* June 2, 1970, p. 3.

Khvedeliani, Ya. "Avtoritet—mysl' i delo." *Komsomol'skaya pravda.* November 27, 1970, p. 1.

Khvedeliani, Ya. R. "Sovremennaya kontrol'no-izmeritel'naya tekhnika na mashinostroyitel'nykh predpriyatiyakh Gruzii." *Izmeritel'naya tekhnika* (1971), no. 2, pp. 99–102.

Khvedeliani, Ya. R. "Chem 'pronyat" letuna?" *Pravda.* February 11, 1973, p. 2.

Khvedeliani, Ya. and N. Redyukhin. "Rezervy makhodit kazhdyy." *Trud.* May 29, 1973, p. 2.

" 'Kirovets' nabirayet silu." *Trud.* January 29, 1969, p. 2.

Kir'yan, M. M., ed. *Voenno-tekhnicheskii progress i Vooruzhennyye Sily SSSR.* Moscow: Voyenizdat, 1982.

Kochetkov, Aleksandr. "Tankograd." *Moskva* (1975), no. 5, pp. 136–143.

Komissarov, B. "Ekonomicheskaya politika partii na sovremennom etape." *Kommunist vooruzhenykh sil* (1971), no. 10, pp. 10–17.

Komissarov, B. and L. Nikiforov. "Tsentral'naya narodnokhozyaystvennaya zadacha." *Politicheskoye samoobrazovaniye* (December 1965), no. 12, pp. 3–11.

Konyshev, Yu. V. "Ne chuzhaya zabota." *Pravda.* June 16, 1981, p. 4.

Konyshev, Yu. V. and Lationov, A. G. "Sameletnyy Fotoelektricheskii Izmeritel' Oblachnykh Kapel'." *Akademiya Nuk SSSR. Izvestiya, Fizik Atmosfery i Okeana* (1966), 2(7):766–769.

Kosyrev, Ye. "Razvitiye strelkovogo oruzhiya." *Tekhnika i vooruzheniye* (January 1971), pp. 8–11.

Kotin, Zh. "Tanki—voyna umov." *Tekhnika—molodezhi.* (June 1970), pp. 24–26.

Kotov, F. "Desyataya pyatiletka—pyatiletka kachestva i effektovnosti v interesakh blagosostoyaniya naroda." *EKO* (1976), no. 1, pp. 4–15.

Kotov, F. "Platsdarmy sozdayuts'a segodnya." *Sotsiyalisticheskaya industriya.* February 20, 1974, p. 2.

Kotov, F. "Programma dolgovremennogo sotrudnichestva." *EKO.* (1972), no. 5, pp. 91–95.

Kotov, F. "Reglamentatsiya truda—deistvennoe sredstvo razvitiya sotsiyalisticheskogo sorevnovaniya." *Sotsiayalisticheskii trud.* (1972), no. 4, pp. 74–77.

Kotov, F. Ya. and V. D. Dudkin. "Programma dolgovremennogo sotrudnichestva." *Eko* (1972), no. 5, pp. 91–95.

Kotov, F. Ya. "Trudovaya estafeta pyatiletok." *Eko* (1976), no. 1, pp. 12–15.

Kruglov, M. "Sistemy upravleniya kachestvom produktsii." *Tekhnika i vooruzheniye* (June 1976), p. 7.

Kudrevatykh, Leonid. "Konstruktor V. G. Grabin." *Moskva* (1969), no. 6, 168–174.

Kurin, N. "Po resheniyu GKO." *Tekhnika i vooruzheniye* (June 1975), pp. 10–11.

Kuz'mina, L. *Generalnyy Konstruktor Pavel Sukhoi.* (Minsk: Belarus', 1985.

Levshin, B. V. *Sovetskaya nauka v. gody Velikoi Otechestvennoi Voiny.* Moscow: Nauka, 1983.

Lyubchenko, A. "Na plechi zavoda." *Leningradskaya Pravda.* July 13, 1967, p. 2.

Lyubchenko, A. "Khozyayeva zavoda." *Leningradskaya pravda.* January 9, 1968, p. 2.

[Lyubchenko, A. A.] "Rech' tov. A. A. Lyubchenko." *Trud.* March 1, 1968, p. 3.

Lyubchenko, A. "Kirovskii—strane." *Leningradskaya Pravda.* January 8, 1972, p. 3.

Lyulka, A. "Idti neprotorennoi tropoi." *Krasnaya Zvezda.* August 30, 1983, p. 2.

Makedon, Yu. A., ed. *Organizatsiya proyektirovaniya v sudostroyenii.* Leningrad: Sudostroyeniye, 1979.

Maksimovskii, V. "I nuzhno, i nygodno." *Izvestiya.* March 4, 1971, p. 3.

Malofeyev, P. "Zavodskoy institut: budni i poiski." *Izvestiya.* March 26, 1965, p. 3.

Maslyukov, Yu. D. "Vnedreniye yedinoy sistemy tekhnologicheskoy tekhnologicheskoy podgotovki proizvodstva." *Stabdardty i kachestva* (May 1978), no. 5, pp. 15–16.

Milanov, V. "Raketnii zalp s 'kompressora.' " *Komsomolskaya pravda.* March 28, 1969, p. 1.

Miroshnikov, A. V., ed. *Ekonomika organizatsiya i planorivaniye grazhdanskoi aviatsii.* Moscow: Transport, 1983.

Mishin, V. P. *Vvedeniye v mashinnoye proyektirovaniye letatel'nykh apparatov.* Moscow: Mashinostroyeniye, 1978.

Mishin, V. P. *Osnovy proyektirovaniya letatel'nykh apparatov (transportnyye sistemy).* Moscow: Mashinostroyeniye, 1985.

Moskovskii Gosudarstvennyy Universitet im. M. V. Lomonosova. *Pravovoye polozheniye ministerstv SSSR.* Moscow: Yuridicheskaya Literatura, 1971.

Nezhlukto, V. Ya. "Nauchno-tekhnicheskii Sovet Ministerstva." *Izvestiya,* August 21, 1966, p. 2.

Nezhlukto, V. Ya. "Osnovnyye rezul'taty ispytaniy pervoy otechestvennoy gazoturbinnoy ustanovki GTU-20) dlya morskikh sudov." *Sudostroyeniye* (July 1965), no. 7, pp. 22–36.

Nezhlukto, V. Ya. "Opyt dovodki i rezul'taty zavodskikh ispytaniy gazoturbinnykh dvigateley ustanovki (GTU-20 LKZ," *Energomashinostroyeniye* (October 1965), no. 10, pp. 1–5.

Nikolayev, V. "Tanki: ikh nastoyashcheye i budushcheye." *Tekhnika i vooruzheniye* (September 1975), pp. 14–16.

Nikoforenko, A. "Kachestvo cherez standarty." *Tekhnika i vooruzheniye* (September 1975), pp. 4–6.

Nosovskii, N. E. "Artilleriiskaya promyshlennost' v Velikoi Otechestvennoi Voine." *Istoricheskiye zapiski*. No. 87. Moscow: Nauka, 1971.

Odinets, M. "Zdravstvuy, zhizn!" *Pravda*. August 11, 1977, p. 6.

Orlov, V. "V zerkale lyudskoy molvy." *Pravda*. September 1, 1980, p. 7.

"Period perevooruzheniya." *Tekhnika i vooruzheniye* (June 1974), pp. 18–19.

Petrov, F. "Tak kovalos' orzhiye." *Tekhnika i vooruzheniye* (October 1965), pp. 12–19.

Petrov, F. "V poiskakh konstruktivnogo sovershenstva." *Tekhnika i vooruzheniye* (November 1968), pp. 2–4.

Petrov, O. "Zaglyadyvaya v zaftra." (interview with F. Ya. Kotov) *Sovetskii sport*. June 9, 1974, p. 1.

Petukhov, R. M., and L. S. Postnova. *Ekonomika sudostroitel'noy promyshlennosti*. Leningrad: Sudostroyeniye, 1984.

"Po planu perevooruzheniya." *Tekhnika i vooruzheniye* (May 1974), p. 18.

Popov, G. Kh. and Krasnopoyas, Yu. I., eds. *Organizatsiya upravleniya obshchestvennym proizvodstvom*. Moscow: Moskovskyy Universitet, 1984.

"Proizvodstvo artilleriyskogo vooruzheniya, 1941–1945." *Tekhnika i vooruzheniye* (December 1974), pp. 12–13.

Rebrov, M. "Ostayus' veren mechte." *Krasnaya zvezda*. January 25, 1986, p. 3.

Reznik, Yakov. *Sotboreniye broni*. Moscow: Voyenizdat, 1983.

Rodionov, P. A. et al. *Partiinaya rabota v usloviyakh proizvodstvennykh ob"edineniy*. Moscow: Politicheskaya Literatura, 1984.

Romanov, A. "Nauka i rakety." *Sotsiyalisticheskaya industriya* (December 28, 1974), p. 3.

Rybalka, V. V. and Shishov, V. V., ed. *Kryl'ya rodiny*. Moscow: DOSAAF, 1984.

Sabinin, Ye. "Vremya Khozyaistvennika." *Sotsialisticheskaya industriya*. (July 22, 1970), p. 3.

Sabinin, Ye. "Vospitaniye distsipliny truda." *Ekonomicheskaya gazeta* (October 1973), no. 41, p. 6.

Saksonov, I. "Razrabotka konstruktorskoy dokumentatsii." *Tekhnika i vooruzheniye* (March 1970), p. 27.

Sarkisian, S. A. and Minayev, Ye. S. *Ekonomicheskaya otsenka letatel'nykh Apparatov*. Moscow: Mashinostroeniye, 1972.

Sarkisian, S. A. and Starik, D. E. *Ekonomika aviatsionnoi promyshlennosti*. Moscow: Vysshaya Shkola, 1980.

Sarkisian, S. A. and D. E. Satik. *Ekonomika aviatsionnoi promyshlennosti*. 2d ed. Moscow: Vysshaya Shkola, 1985.

Sergeyev, Yu. "Samoye massovoye oruzhiye." *Tekhnika i vooruzheniye* (December 1970), p. 27.

Shishkov, N. "Kryl'ya rodiny." *Sotsialisticheskaya industriya* (August 21, 1983), p. 1.

Shkurko, Ye. "Mashinostroiteli prinimayut mery dlya udovletvoreniya trebovanii myasnoi promyshlennosti." *Myasnaya industriya SSSR* (May 1966), pp. 26–27.

Shmelev, Igor'. *Tanki v boyu*. Moscow: Molodaya Gvardiya, 1984.

Silayev I. S. and Darovskikh, I. I. "Osnovnyye printsipy sistemy KANARSPI i ikh organizatsionno-tekhnicheskaya realizatsiya," *Standarty i kachestvo* (1974), no. 2, pp. 16–19.

Sivets, V. "Nasha zabota o mastere." *Sotsialisticheskaya Industriya.* February 18, 1970, p. 2.

Sivets, V. N. "Sistema obespecheniya vysokogo kachestva, uvelicheniya resursa i povysheniya nadezhnosti." *Standarty i kachestvo.* (1973), np. 4, pp. 42–45.

Smirtyukov, M. S. *Sovetskiy gosudarstvennyy apparat upravleniya.* Moscow: Politizdat, 1984.

Sovetskaya voyennaya entsiklopediya. 8 vols. Moscow: Voyenizdat, 1976–1980.

Soyich, O. V. "Molodoi spetsialist." *Pravda Ukrainy.* March 7, 1965, p. 3.

Soyich O. "Dolgoletiye mashin." *Izvestiya.* April 14, 1965, p. 3.

Soyich, O. V. "Dolgoletiye mashin." *Standardizatsiya.* (1965), no. 6, pp. 41–42.

Spirin, S. and A. Titov. "Sotsiyalisticheskoe planirovaniye—i oborona strany." *Kommunist vooruzhennykh sil* (1971), no. 4, pp. 40–47.

Stepanchenko, V. O. "Vsyudu, gdye rabotayet chelovek." *Trud.* October 1, 1968, p. 2.

Stepanchenko, V. O. "Sila sorevnovaniya." *Ekonomicheskaya gazeta* (January 1969), no. 2, p. 5.

Stepanchenko, V. O. "O samom nasushchnom." *Ekonomicheskaya gazeta* (April 1971), no. 16–17, p. 28.

Stepanchenko, V. O. "Dorogoi poiska i uspekha." *Ekonomicheskaya gazeta* (1971), no. 4, p. 12.

Stepanchenko, V. O. "V sodruzhestve s naukoi." *Ekonomicheskaya gazeta* (November 1971), no. 45, p. 6.

Stepanchenko, V. O. "V Tsentre Vnimaniya—Tekhnicheskii Progress." *Kommunist Ukrainy* (August 1973), no. 8, pp. 72–79.

Stepanchenko, V. "Politiku Partii Odobryayem." *Pravda.* May 5, 1974, p. 1.

Stepanchenko, V. "Vozglavlyayit Kommunisty." *Pravda.* December 24, 1974, p. 1.

Strazhena, Irina. *Tyul'pany s kosmodroma.* Moscow: Molodaya Gvardiya, 1978.

Studenikin, P. "Artilleristy—oruzheiniki—fronty." (interview with M. Olebsky) *Sovetskoe voyennoye obozheniye* (1983), no. 11, 19–21.

Stukolov, P. M., G. M. Lapshin, and K. I. Yakuta. *Ekonomika elektronnoi promyshlennosti.* Moscow: Izdatel'stvo "Vysshaya Shkola," 1983.

Subbotin, M. "Gorizonty vliyaniya." *Izvestiya.* October 10, 1968, p. 2.

Subbotin, M. "Material'nyye fondy i byudzhet sem'i." *Izvetiya.* January 16, 1972, p. 3.

Suchkov, V. N. "Opredeleniye poter' toka v proizvodstve khlora i shchelochi diafragmennym metodom." *Khimicheskaaya promyshlennost'* (1969), no. 2, p. 49 + .

Sulaberidze, Dzh. "My—dimitrovtsy." *Zarya vostoka.* March 22, 1980, p. 2.

Taksir, K. I. *Upravleniye promyshlennost'yu SSSR,* 3d ed. Moscow: Vysshaya Shkola, 1985.

Tereb, A. "Dzerzhintsy." *Krasnaya zvezda.* December 11, 1982, p. 2.

Tiktin, S. "SSSR i kosmos—bez lupy i komp'yutera." *Posev* (1982), no. 10, pp. 46–50.

Tolubko, V. *Nedelin: pervyy glavkom strategicheskikh.* Moscow: Molodaya Gvardiya, 1979.

Torochkov, V. Yu., V. B. Kalabin, and V. S. Usov. "Stabilizatsiya opticheskoi osi aerofotos'emochnoi kamery pri pomoshchi zhidkostnogo klina." In *Izvestiya bysshikh uchebnykh zavedenii: geodeziya i aerofotos'emka* (1973), no. 4, pp. 125–128.

Trud. "Bol'shaya otdacha malykh mashin." (interview with Derunov). March 12, 1971, p. 2.

Trud. "Rech Tov. Yu. V. Kuznetsova." March 26, 1977, p. 4.

Tyamshanskiy, N. D. *Ekonomika i organizatsiya nauchno-issledovatel'skikh rabot v mashinostroyenii.* Leningrad: Mashinostroitelniye, 1967.

Tyulin, G., N. Yuryshev, and M. Komissarchik. "Ogon' vedut gvardeyskiye minomety." *Tekhnika i vooruzheniye* (September 1981), pp. 26–27.

Tyushkevich, S. A. *Sovetskiye Vooruzhennyye Sily: istoriya stroitel'stva.* Moscow: Voyenizdat, 1978.

Udarov, G. "Byt' novatorami." *Krasnaya zvezda.* February 19, 1986, p. 1.

Vanag, G. "Upravleniye kachestvom." *Trud.* January 6, 1979, p. 2.

Vannikov, B. L. "Oboronnaya promyshlennost' SSSR nakanune voiny." *Voprosi Istorii* (1968), no. 10, pp. 116–123.

Verbitskiy et al. *Armii stran Varshavskogo Dogovora: spravochnik.* Moscow: Voyenizdat, 1985.

Veretnik, L. D., N. S. Lychagin, and R. M. Sukhomlinov. "Svarnoy proshen' iz silumina dlya teplovoznogo dizelya D70." *Avtomaticheskaya svarka* (1967), no. 4, pp. 43–45.

Veretnik, L. D., N. S. Lychagin, A. Ye. Asnis, and A. I. Nazarenko. "Tekhnologichnost' i vibratsionnaya prochnost' svarnykh soyedineniy bloka dizelya Teplovoza." *Avtomaticheskaya Svarka* (1967), no. 7, pp. 53–55.

Vlasov, B. V. and G. B. Kats, eds. *Organizatsiya, planirovaniye, i upravleniye predpriyatiyem massogo mashinostroyeniya* (Moscow: Vysshaya Shkola, 1985).

Voronin, L. A., F. B. Zlotnikov, and P. G. Grodinskiy. "Krasnogorskiy mekhanicheskiy zavod rabotayet ponovomu." *Optiko-mekhanicheskaya promyshlennost'* (November 1967), pp. 73–80. [Also translated as "The Krasnogorsk Mechanical Works Operate in a New Fashion," *Soviet Journal of Optical Technology* (November 1967), 34(6):754–759.]

Voronin, L. A., A. M. Stesel', and Afontsev, A. P. "Povysheniye nadezhnosti kinofotoapparatury blagodarya osnashcheniyu konveyernoy sborki sovremennymy elektronnymy kontrol'nymy i trenirovochnymy ustroystvami." *Optiko-mekhanicheskaya promyshlennost'* (June 1968), pp. 51–57. [Also translated as "Improvement of Reliability of Still and Movie Equipment by Using Modern Electronic Quality Control and Testing Devices on the Assembly Line," *Soviet Journal of Optical Technology* (June 1968), 35(3):405–410]

Voyennyy Entsiklopedicheskii Slovar'. Moscow: Voyenizdat, 1983.

Yevtukuhov, L. "Dykhanie goryachei broni." *Krasnaya zvezda*. February 20, 1979, p. 4.

Zakharov, M. V. *50 let Vooruzhennykh Sil SSSR*. Moscow: Voyenizdat, 1968.

Zal'tsman, N. and G. Edel'gauz. "Vspominaya uroki tankograda." *Kommunist* (1984), no. 16, pp. 76–87.

Zaychenko, G. "Nashim mal'chishkam v nasledstvo—zavod." *Komsomol-'skaya Pravda*. January 22, 1967, p. 1.

Zaychenko, G. "Otsam na smeny." *Klub: khudozhestvennaya samodeyatel-'nost* (1967), no. 19, pp. 35–36.

Zaychenko, G. V. "Chelyabinskiy traktornyy." *Mashinostroitel'* (1967), no. 6, pp. 11–14.

Zaychenko, G. "Chelyabinskii traktornyy . . ." *Sel'skaya Zhizn*. June 2, 1968, p. 2.

Zaychenko, G. V. "Uchit'sya iskusstvu upravleniya." *Ekonomicheskaya gazeta* (September 1972), no. 39, p. 14.

Zhikharevich I. G. et al. *Sovershenstvovabiye organizatsii i upravleniya proizvodstvom v tsvetnoi metallurgii*. Moscow: Metallurgiya, 1984.

Zhukov, A. M., G. S. Noskova, and V. N. Suchkov. "Nekotoryye voprosy upakovki khimicheskikh tovarov narodnogo potrebleniya." *Khimicheskaaya Promyshlennost'* (1969), no. 8, pp. 62+.

Zubovskiy, G. I., V. B. Kalabin, V. V. Makartsev, G. K. Klimenko, "Kinoapparatura na vystavke 'Fotokina-72.' " *Tekhnika kino i televideniya* (1973), no. 4, pp. 72–80.

Zverev, S. "Dlya kolkhoznykh niv." *Sotsiyalisticheskaya industriya*. October 1, 1970, p. 2.

Zverev, S. "Nasha pomoshch' seln." *Sovetskaya latviya*. August 28, 1970, p. 2.

Zverev, S. "Vozmozhnosti otrasli." *Izvestiya*. July 7, 1971.

INDEX